IMAGES
of America

COOLIDGE

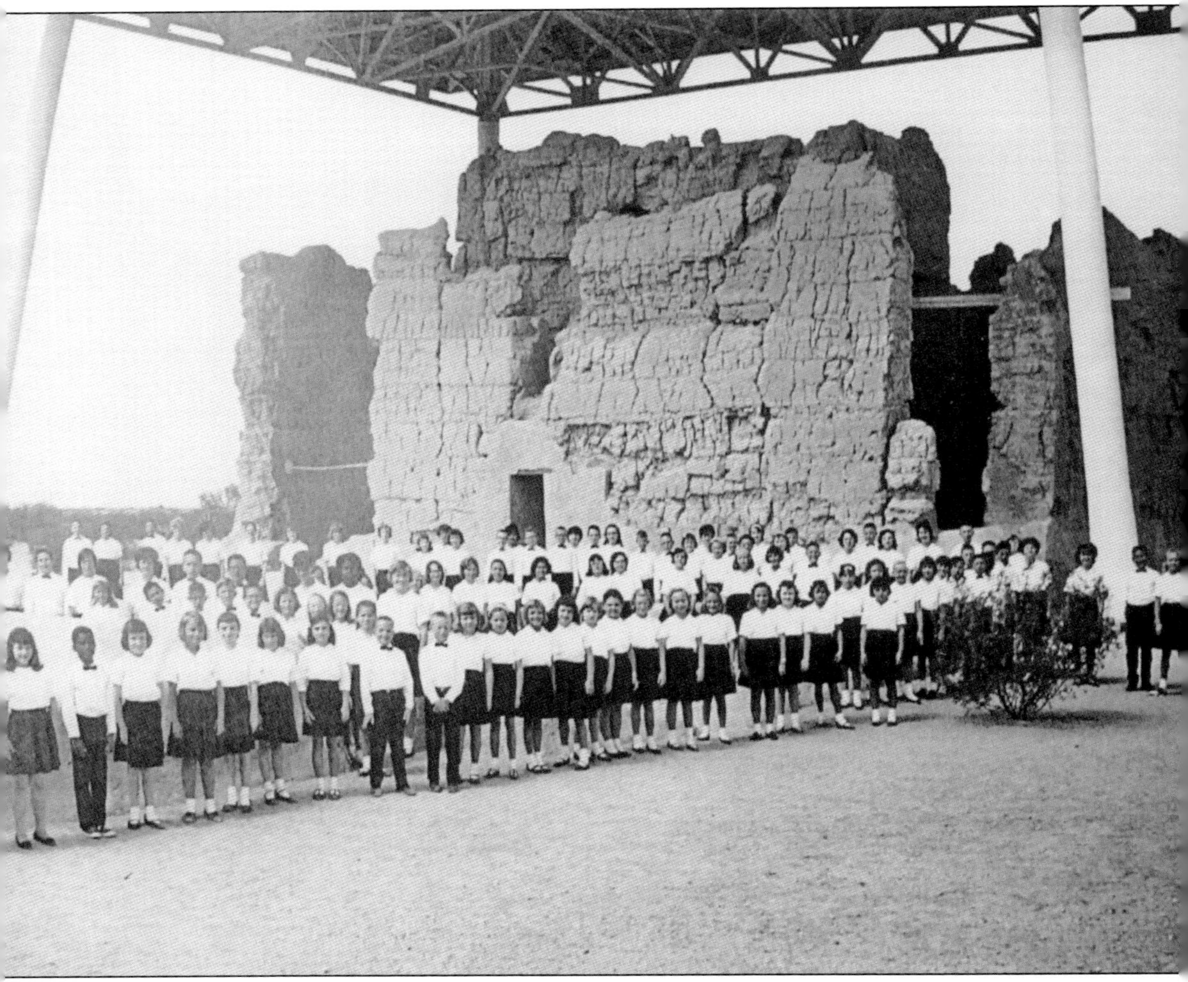

The Coolidge Children's Choir at the Casa Grande Ruins National Monument, the iconic landmark of Coolidge, was conducted by Charles M. Binford and included 113 boys and girls aged 8 through 14. During the years it existed after being founded in 1963, the musical group had the reputation of being one of the largest nonaffiliated choirs in the United States, which was quite an achievement for a town of 5,000 residents. (CHM.)

On the Cover: Taken by an unknown photographer in 1928, the first service station in Coolidge was established in 1925 by Carl H. Douglas of nearby Florence. The station was on the corner of Main Street and Coolidge Avenue and sold Shell gasoline as well as tires and other products. Limited automobile-repair service was also provided until Layman's Garage opened in 1927. Douglas operated service stations in nearby Florence, Eloy, and Casa Grande was well. (CHM.)

IMAGES
of America

COOLIDGE

Ralph A. Swain

ARCADIA
PUBLISHING

ISBN 978-1-4671-3385-2

Published by Arcadia Publishing
Charleston, South Carolina

Printed in the United States of America

Library of Congress Control Number: 2015933930

For all general information, please contact Arcadia Publishing:
Telephone 843-853-2070
Fax 843-853-0044
E-mail sales@arcadiapublishing.com
For customer service and orders:
Toll-Free 1-888-313-2665

Visit us on the Internet at www.arcadiapublishing.com

To Joseph Reed Chesley, whose love and dedication to the preservation of Coolidge's history has been an inspiration to us all

Contents

Acknowledgments

The author greatly appreciates the contributions from the following individuals, all of whom helped make this book possible: Joseph R. Chesley, to whom this work is dedicated and who always made himself available at a minute's notice; Janice Calvert and Richard Schaar for their moral support and valuable contacts; Gene Carter, a Coolidge pioneer; Jim Garrett Jr.; Rod Gipson; Taylor Hansen; Jacque Hendrie-Henry; Mike Henry; Tommy Henry; Dianna Herrera for sharing her family photographs; John Hill; Nathan Ingrao; Alma Jones and Wayne Wuertz for their historical notes; John Meadows and Nancy Meadows-Heikes; Phyllis Mikles for sharing her newspaper clippings and historical notes; Brenda McHugh Mitchell; Donna Ovitt; Elsie Laughlin Reeves; Irma Garcia Salazar for sharing five generations of Garcia family photographs; Bobby Skousen and Sherry Ulmer for sharing their stories; and Paul C. Unger.

The invaluable assistance of the following persons who had access to archival images is much appreciated: Diane Garcia, park ranger at the Casa Grande Ruins National Monument; Berlin Loa, director of the Museum of Casa Grande/Casa Grande Valley Historical Society; Lynn Parsons, executive director of the Coolidge Chamber of Commerce; and H. Christine Reid of the Pinal County Historical Society, Inc.

In addition to the images provided by the many Coolidge residents, other photographs appear courtesy of the Arizona State Library, Archives and Public Records, History and Archives Division, Phoenix (ASL); the Coolidge Chamber of Commerce (CCC); the Coolidge Historical Museum (CHM); the Library of Congress (LOC); the Museum of Casa Grande/Casa Grande Valley Historical Society (MCG/CGVHS); the National Park Service (NPS); and the Pinal County Historical Museum (PCHM). The images of the Coolidge Dam dedication in chapter two were provided by the Pinal County Historical Museum and were taken by Pacific and Atlantic Photos, Inc., 25 Park Place, New York City, NY, for the Arizona Sheriff's Association.

Introduction

The year 1924 was crucial for the future townsite of Coolidge. The Southern Pacific Railroad laid down its new main line through the mesquite desert on its way to Phoenix and west to California. In June, Congress approved the construction of the Coolidge Dam across the Gila River some 90 miles northeast of the future townsite. Those two events convinced Phoenix businessman Richard J. Jones to purchase 80 acres and plat the town the following year.

According to Alma Jones, she and her husband were sitting with Clement and Clara Seagoe on a Sunday in early 1925 at their ranch south of the townsite wondering what to call the new town. Jonesburg and Jonesville were mentioned, but Richard suggested Coolidge in honor of the president who signed the bill authorizing the building of the dam across the Gila. That dam would bring precious irrigation water to some 100,000 acres of potential farmland surrounding the Gila River Basin.

That August, the W.E. Nutt family travelling to California in a pickup truck topped with a homemade camper stopped to have a picnic in the vicinity of what would become Coolidge Avenue. Jones asked them if they would like to settle in Coolidge. Nutt, his wife, Dora, and daughter, Jesse, accepted and became the future town's first official residents. The wooden camper became their makeshift home and the next month served as a real estate office for the Phoenix outfit Nutt worked for. The following year, Dora became the first postmistress for Coolidge.

A big event was held in Phoenix on October 15, 1926, to celebrate the completion of the Southern Pacific mainline there, and Jones wasted no time putting the fledgling town of Coolidge on the map. He and a handful of residents placed four floats in the parade with the Coolidge Queen and her two attendants sitting up high on one of the floats. According to Richard's wife, Alma, "It put Coolidge on the map," and people began inquiring about the new little town in the desert. At that time, only a dirt highway passed through Coolidge between Casa Grande and Florence. It would not be long before everything changed.

Before the Coolidge Dam was completed in 1928, the little community was being described in Phoenix papers as the fastest-growing town in Arizona. Rightly so, because in three year's time Coolidge boasted a cotton gin, an oil company, several garages, an ice plant, a hotel, several grocery stores, a hospital, school, post office, restaurant, community church, and women's club to list just a few of the businesses that sprang to life.

The year 1929 was one of firsts, with the opening of the Arizona Southwest Bank, Hines Drug Company, Mandell and Bloch dry goods, Pinal Feed and Seed Company, and Pay 'n' Takit grocery store. The American Legion and the Lion's Club were also organized in 1929.

In 1930, the new Tucson-Phoenix Highway, today's State Route 87, made its way from Picacho straight north into town where travelers gassed up their cars at one of several service stations and stayed overnight at the auto camp on south Arizona Boulevard or in the more comfortable digs at the San Carlos Hotel. That year, the Masonic temple was erected, the county built a new school, and the *Examiner* began printing its newspaper in Coolidge, and the E.C. Grasty Implement Company opened in March with a grand-opening street dance.

From its beginning just five years earlier, when Coolidge had a population of three thanks to the Nutt family, steady growth saw the town swell to 1,000 by 1930 and then triple by 1940. By 1960, the town's population doubled from the 1940 number and then maintained its roughly 7,000 residents through the 1980s. Even with the opening of Interstate 10 from Picacho to Phoenix in 1966 after a long and bitterly fought battle over its location, the population continued to grow mostly due to the residential housing boom of the 1990s. Nevertheless, with Coolidge's present population just under 12,000, local businesses dried up in the city's core as traffic through town, once the only route between Tucson and Phoenix, diverted around Coolidge via Interstate10.

Some longtime residents claim previous city fathers and some influential local businessmen fought to keep national stores away from Coolidge much to the detriment of the town's economic viability. Today, Coolidge tends to lean toward being a bedroom community with many residents employed at the numerous state-operated and privately run prisons a few miles distant, as well as the Central Arizona College campus midway between Casa Grande and Coolidge to the west. Yet the town has become the home of a handful of industries with substantial national and international markets. Recent expansion of the career-tech facilities at the Central Arizona Valley Institute of Technology (CAVIT) and the beginnings of an ambitious project to convert a former elementary school into a community-based "makers space" for arts and innovation called the Artisan Village of Coolidge are just two examples of a deliberate move toward economic recovery.

Coolidge's location between greater Phoenix and Tucson makes the locale attractive to both old-timers and newcomers who seek respite from the noise and congestion of those metropolitan areas to the north and south. As of late, progressive-minded city officials, forward-thinking longtime residents, and the small but growing influx of newcomers with new ideas are demonstrating a revitalizing attitude that is embracing this small town with a rich and colorful past.

One

Before the Beginning

The importance of the Gila River and its tributaries cannot be overemphasized. Close to 90,000 square miles of drainage area were affected until fairly recently by what is considered the most important river system in the Southwest. Into this area came evidence of human settlement by a complex community of people who were master builders and irrigation-canal developers. Known in general terms as Hohokam, these ancestral peoples of the Sonoran Desert are referred to by their Native American descendants as Huhugam, which translates into "all used up." Clusters of these early communities date back several thousand years, but the establishment of permanent settlements began by 300 CE. Spanish missionaries in 1694 were the first European Americans to encounter the remains of this vast system of adobe structures and irrigation canals. In the vicinity of present-day Coolidge, the three-story Casa Grande was constructed from the local caliche clay and mixed with the waters of the life-sustaining river, yet the actual purpose of the massive structure remains a mystery, as does the sudden disappearance of these desert communities.

The communities maintained an intricate and sophisticated system of canals that diverted precious water from the Gila, Salt, and San Pedro Rivers' drainage basins. Just as sophisticated was the coordination necessary between the communities, each of which were clustered around ancient ball courts or platform mounds. These hunters and gatherers grew corn, squash, cotton, and agave and supplemented their diet with meat from rabbits and pack rats. Harvesting the fruit of the saguaro was an important dietary supplement as well as other fruits of the desert plants. Fish from the river was also on their menu, and the middle Gila River supplied a welcome diet of freshwater clams.

Members of the present-day Tohono and Akimel O'odham, as well as the Gila River Pima-Maricopa Indian Communities, consider themselves descendants of the Huhugam, although, admittedly, no definitive connection has been made.

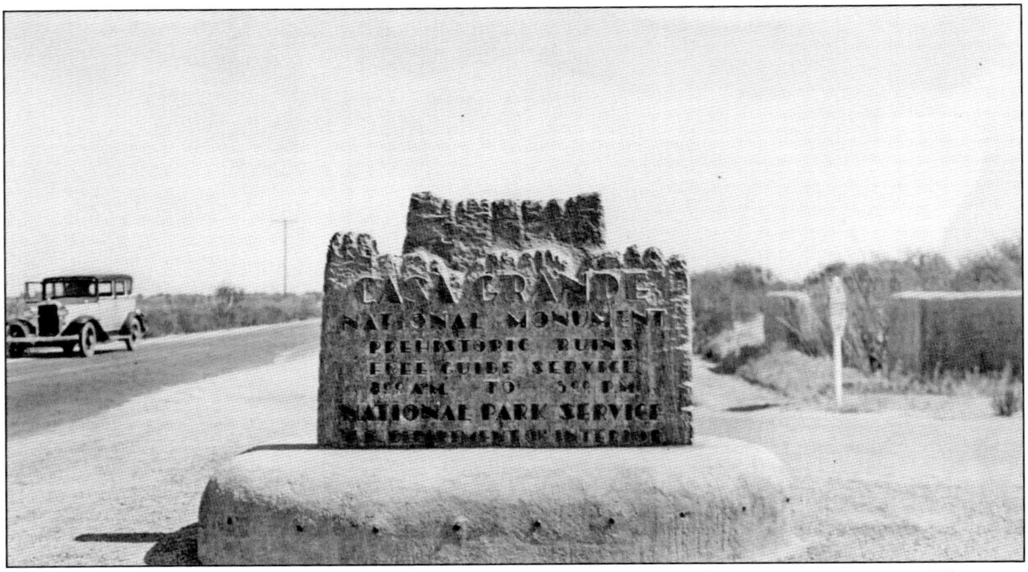

This 1935 photograph shows the entrance sign to the Casa Grande Ruins Monument. The sign is made of copper sheeting and now sits in front of the Casa Grande Ruins Visitors Center. An average of 70,000 visitors tour the national monument yearly. On June 22, 1892, Pres. William Henry Harrison set aside the ruins as the first federal land reserve. (ASL No. 02-1133.)

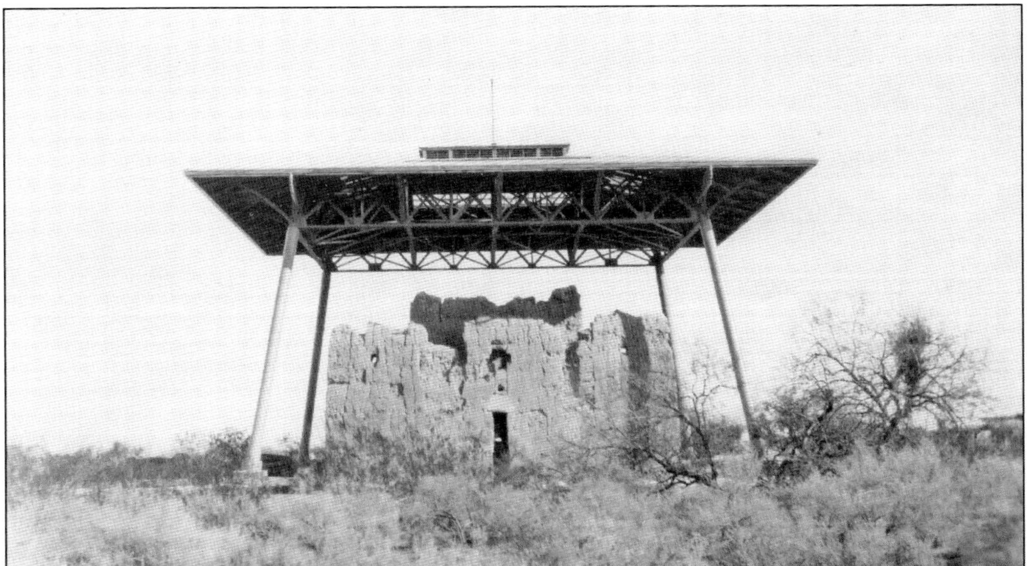

By an act of Congress, the construction of the first cover over the great house at the Casa Grande Ruins was an iron roof with wooden supports. It was completed on September 10, 1903, at a cost of $1,900. A new protective steel roof (pictured) was completed on December 12, 1932, at a cost of $27,742. (NPS.)

In 1901, Frank "Boss" Pinkley was appointed the first custodian to the Casa Grande Ruins at the age of 20 after moving to the area the year before to help his parents operate the Blackwater Trading Post. He served as superintendent until his death on February 14, 1940. His death came unexpectedly and suddenly minutes after he gave the welcoming speech to the first superintendents' conference at the ruins. (NPS.)

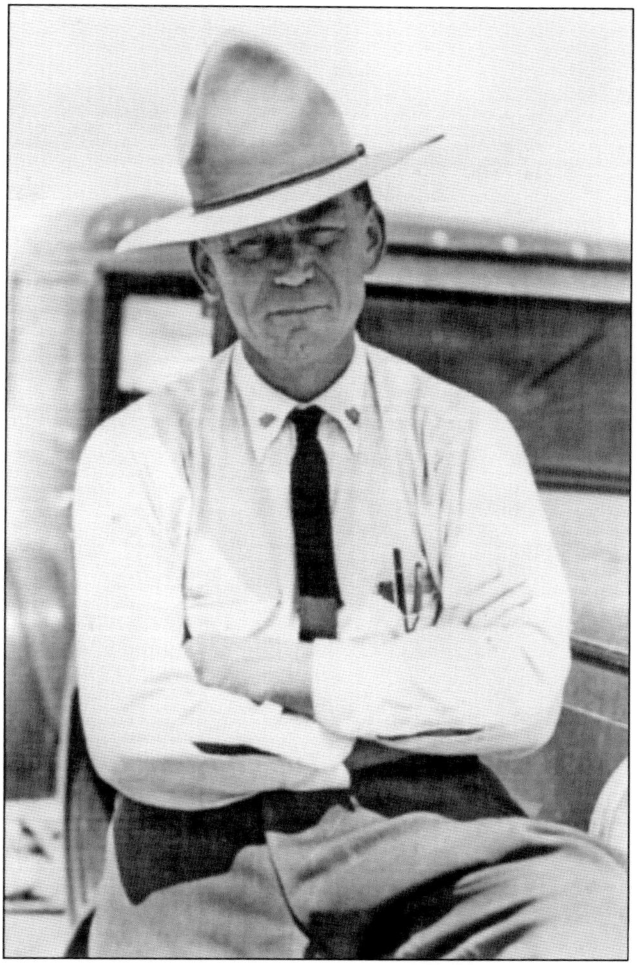

Supt. Frank Pinkley takes visitors to the Casa Grande Ruins National Monument on an onsite tour of the grounds in 1907. Excavation of the site was already under way by archeologists. On July 22, 1938, Pinkley and a colleague established the Southwest Monuments Association (later named the Southwest Parks and Monuments Association) supporting education and preservation of 18 monuments across Arizona and New Mexico. (NPS.)

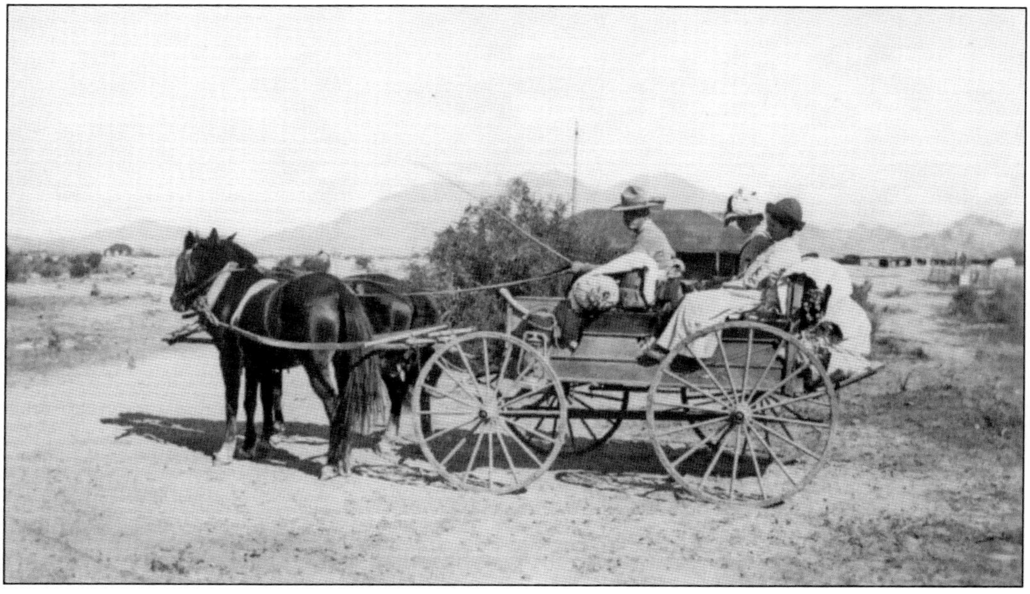

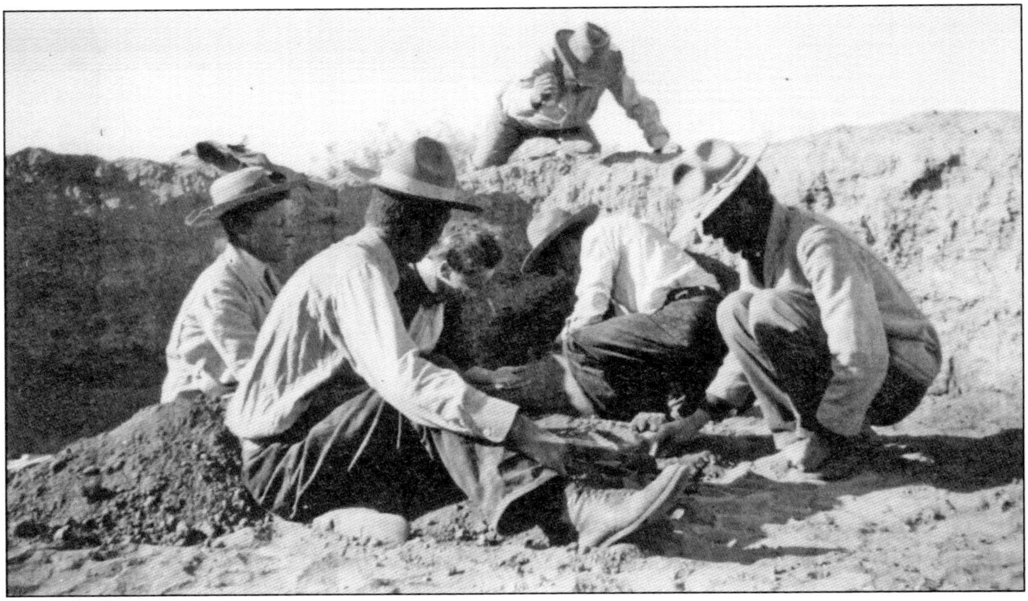

Years before the Casa Grande Ruins was designated a national monument on August 3, 1918, archeologists were excavating the site around the great house. Excavation continues on a limited basis today, and the park has requested Congress add additional acreage to the park boundaries. Archeologist Jimmie Schultz, in the foreground, supervises the excavation in this 1908 photograph. (NPS.)

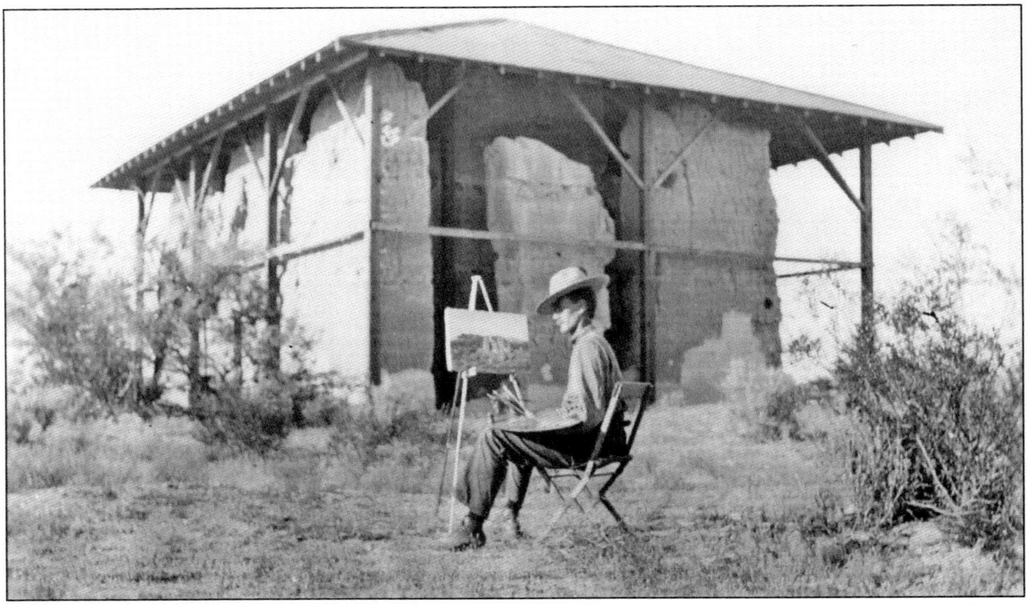

Supt. Frank Pinkley took this photograph of an unidentified artist at the ruins in the 1920s. The construction of the first protective roof over the great house at the Casa Grande Ruins was approved by Congress on June 28, 1902. The cost of the structure made of wood and steel was $1,900, and it was completed on September 10, 1903. (NPS.)

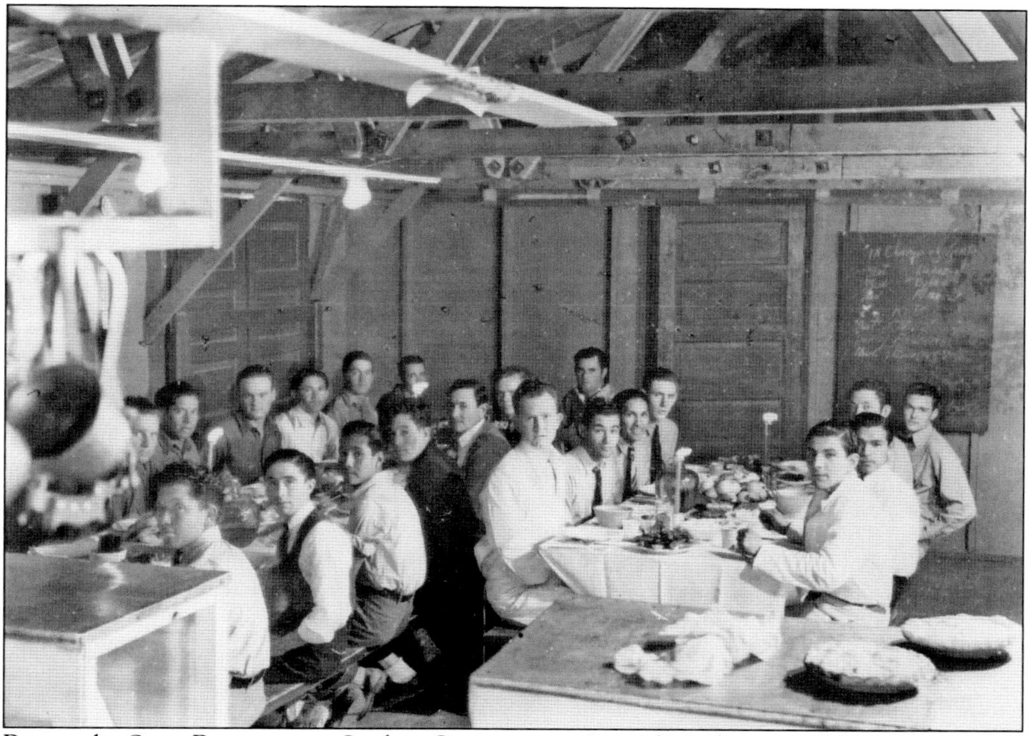

During the Great Depression, a Civilian Conservation Corps (CCC) camp was established at the Casa Grande Ruins Monument to construct adobe buildings for the support staff. Pictured here is Christmas dinner in 1938 at the ruins for those who participated in Pres. Franklin Roosevelt's New Deal program for putting young men back to work. (NPS.)

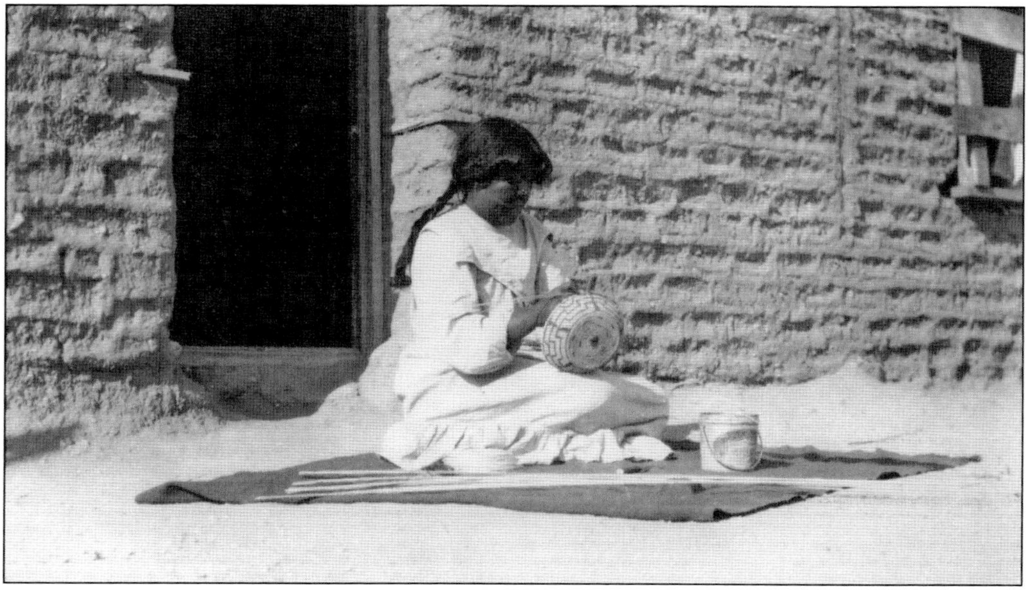

A Pima woman only identified as Alice weaves a basket in the same manner that her ancestors did many generations ago. The photograph is believed to have been taken by Supt. Frank Pinkley in the 1920s. Pinkley maintained a cordial relationship with the Native Americans and documented much of their activities on film. (NPS.)

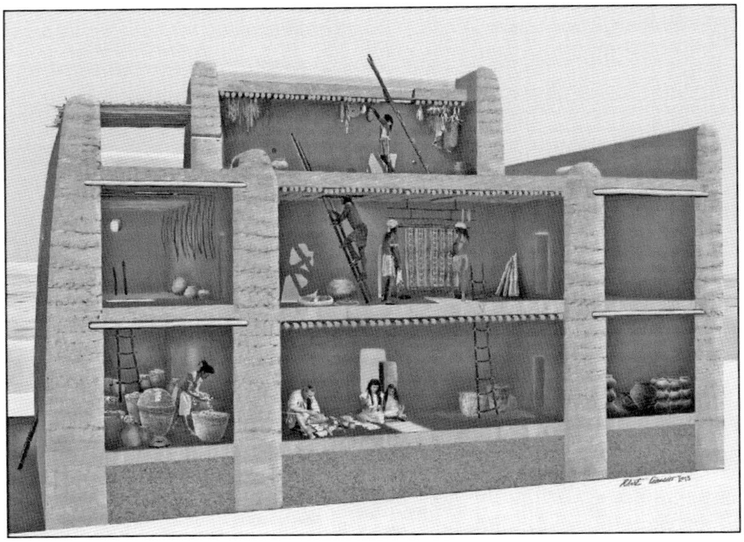

This previously unpublished image shows the cross section of the great house at the Casa Grande Ruins painted in 2013 by artist Robert Ciacco. Since the actual use of the structure is only an interpretation by the artist from information gathered by archeologists, the three-story building no doubt served a very important function to the ancient native community. (NPS.)

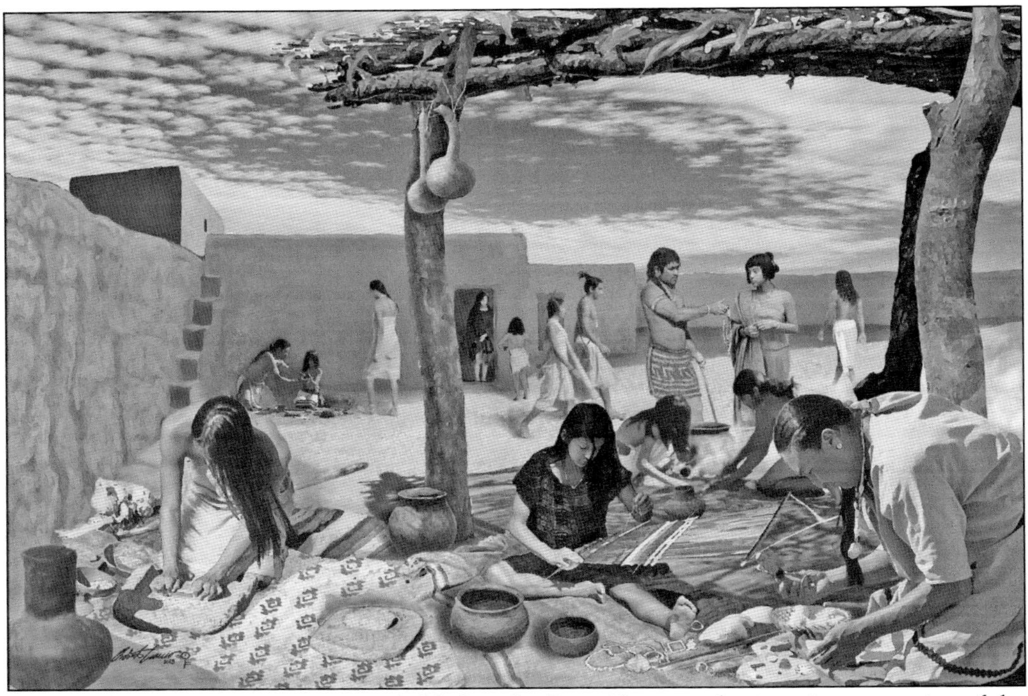

Artist Robert Ciacco's painting is titled *Life in the Great House*, and it is an interpretation of the communal activities that took place before the first Spanish explorers arrived in this area. Some archeologists theorize steps carved out of the clay walls were the common way of reaching the different levels. Other archeologists believe ladders made of sticks as depicted in the painting at the top of the page was the method used. (NPS.)

Two

A Dam Site Better

The Casa Grande Valley since prehistory has been subject to extreme drought and heat as well as monsoons and flash floods. Archeologists cannot agree whether the ancient native inhabitants disappeared due to extreme drought, devastating flash floods, or both.

For over 1,000 years, the ancestral people of the Sonoran Desert maintained an intricate network of ditches to divert water from the Gila River for their crops. This ancient civilization dwindled into nonexistence during the first half of the 13th century, but the remains of their rudimentary canals and the more elaborate mud shelters constructed out of the tough caliche soil survive. The successors to the ancestral people, the Pima and Papago, continued the practice of diverting Gila River water for their crops.

In 1862, the Homestead Act awarded white settlers 160 acres of free land if they would live on it, farm it, and develop it. Access to water was key to keeping the land fertile, and more canals were constructed along with continued utilization of some of the ancient ditches built by the ancestral Sonoran Desert people. During this time, 50 miles of canals were constructed to irrigate 7,000 acres in the vicinity of nearby Florence, but yearly flash floods washed away the flimsy ditches and destroyed the crops in its path.

Beginning in 1880, various attempts on a larger scale were made to capture the water from the Gila starting with the Florence Canal Company, which included the Picacho Reservoir, later the Casa Grande Valley Company, and finally the San Carlos Canal and Irrigation Company. Being systematically robbed of more and more water, the self-sufficient Pimas, who were always friendly to the settlers, began to see their crops suffer from lack of water.

Despite efforts to harness the Gila, political intrigue among powerful interests in Phoenix prevailed and resulted instead in the construction and completion of the Roosevelt Dam across the Salt River in 1911. It would be almost two decades before the Coolidge Dam would be completed on the Gila to irrigate 100,000 acres of Indian and non-Indian land in Pinal County.

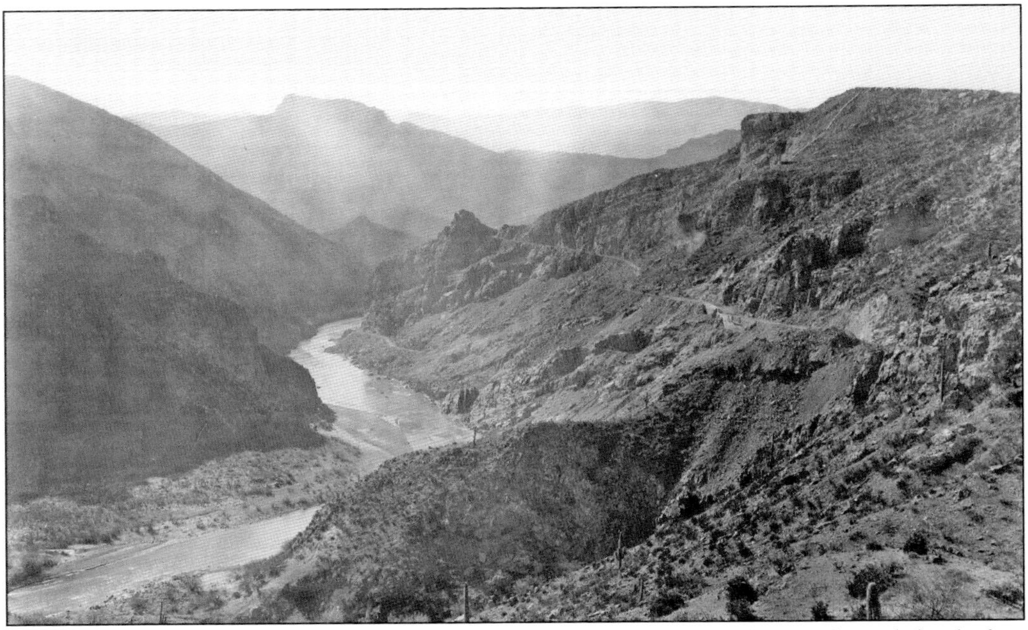

The San Carlos Box Canyon is on the Gila River, 80 miles northeast of Coolidge before commencement of the construction of Coolidge Dam. This photograph was taken on January 17, 1927, looking downstream toward the southwest. Although just a trickle during the dry season, the Gila turned into a raging torrent during the monsoons, wiping out farms and settlements as far as Florence, Arizona. (PCHM.)

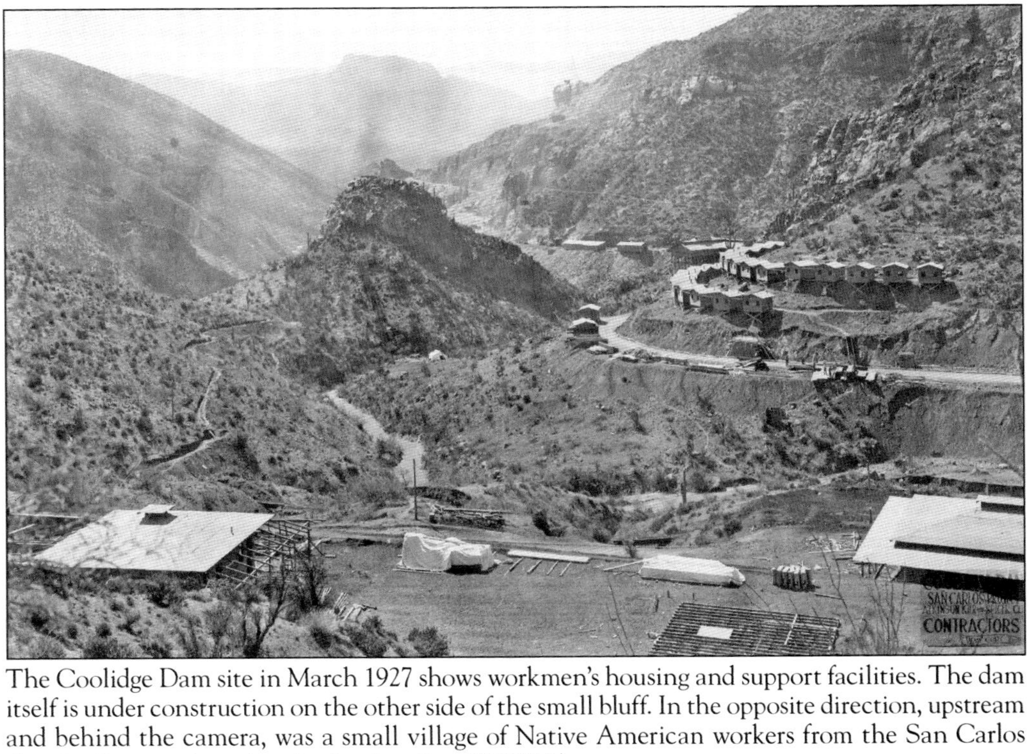

The Coolidge Dam site in March 1927 shows workmen's housing and support facilities. The dam itself is under construction on the other side of the small bluff. In the opposite direction, upstream and behind the camera, was a small village of Native American workers from the San Carlos Apache Reservation wherein the dam lies. (PCHM.)

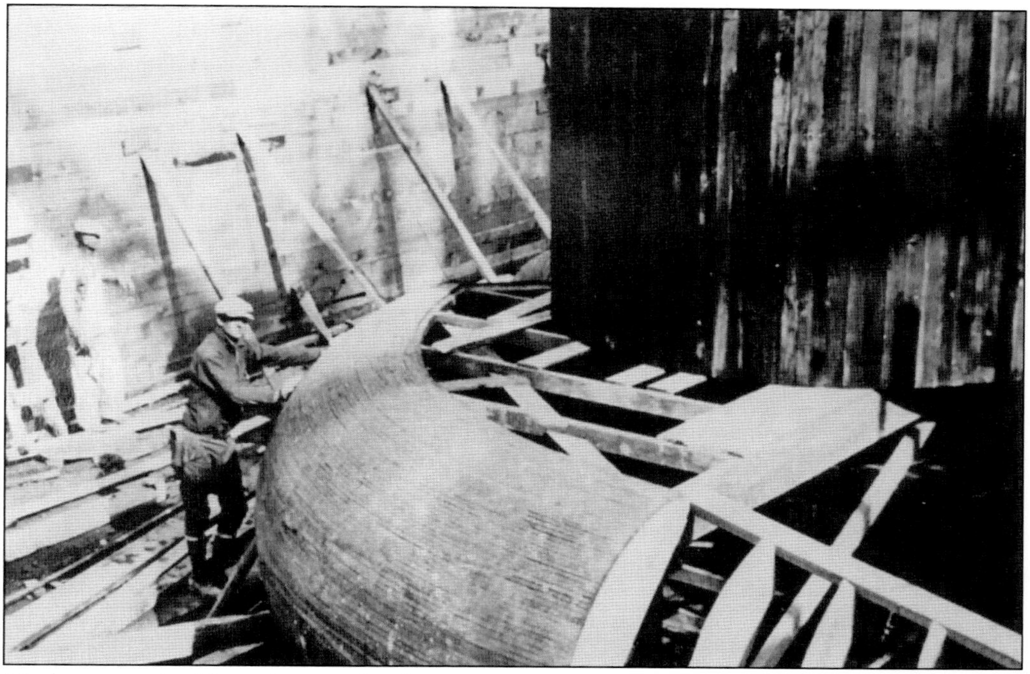

Workmen are building the wooden forms prior to pouring concrete to house one of the two hydroelectric generators. When at capacity, the generators would produce 10,000 kilowatts of electricity, which would send power to the Casa Grande Valley to operate irrigation pumps as well as power to the local area of the dam site. (CHM.)

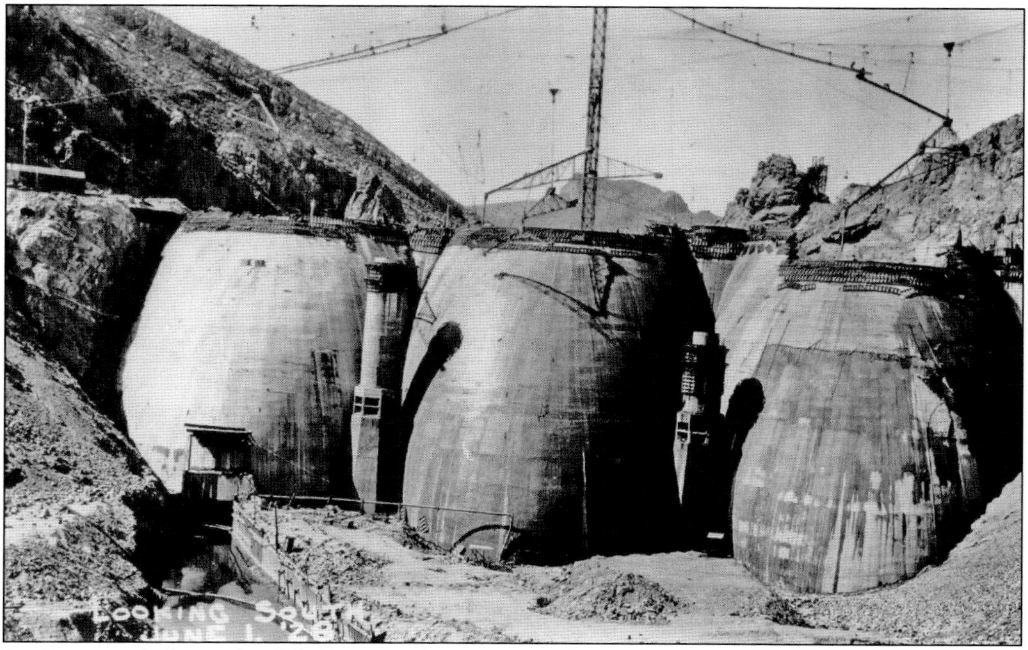

Looking south down the Gila River on June 1, 1928, the nearly completed concrete domes of the Coolidge Dam are set deep into the river bedrock and anchored on both rock walls of the canyon. Their shape was designed to withstand the tremendous pressure from the water that would fill behind it and were said to be earthquake-proof. (PCHM.)

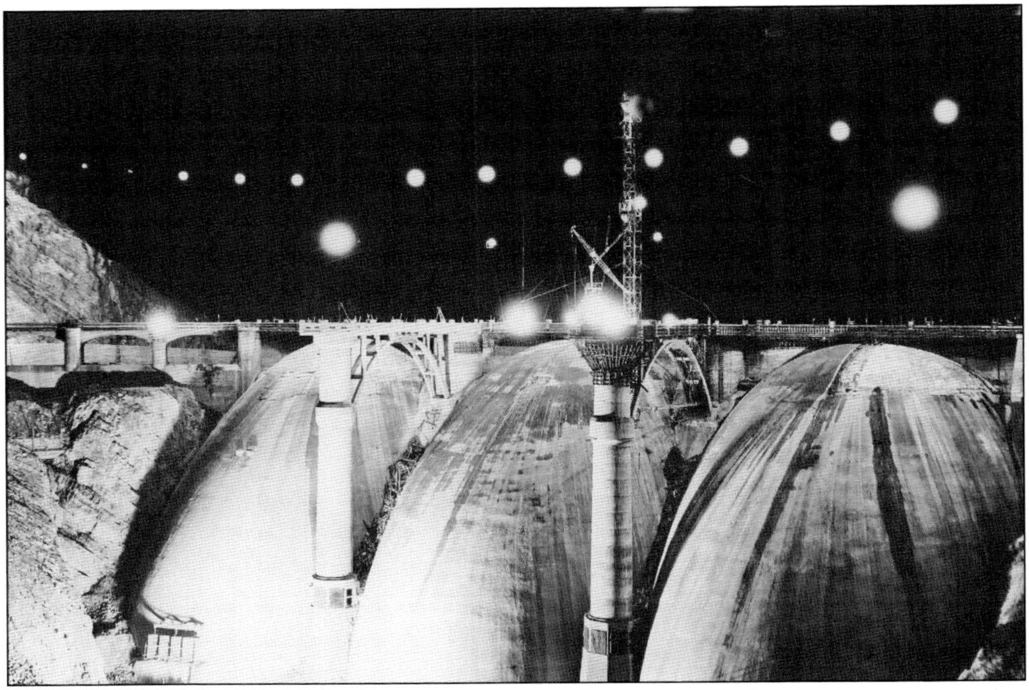

Work on the dam continued day and night, beginning in December 1926 and ending on November 16, 1928, when the Gila River bypass around the dam was closed. Every day, 1,500 cubic yards of concrete could be poured, made from gravel collected half a mile downstream. A bonfire burning waste timber just prior to completion of the dam causes the glow of light in the lower left. (PCHM.)

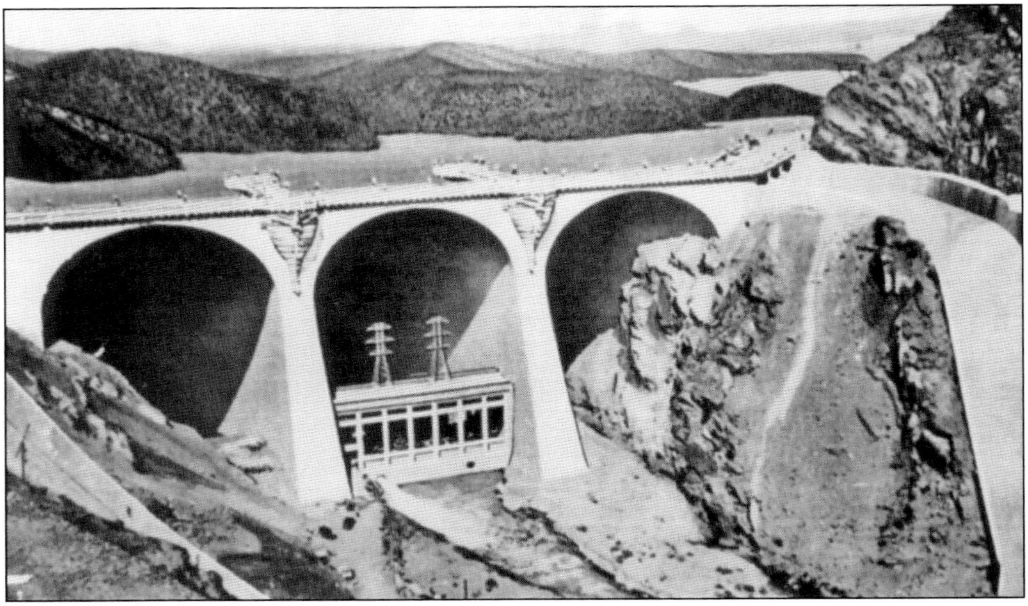

By 1930, the completed dam created a lake 25 miles long and three miles wide, holding 1.2 million acre feet of water. Some 500 Apaches were relocated as well as the San Carlos Indian Agency, which would have been below 100 feet of water. Indian graves were covered with a large concrete slab rather than removing the remains from the burial site. (CHM.)

On March 4, 1930, the Coolidge Dam was dedicated with former president Calvin Coolidge and his wife, Grace, in attendance. After smoking the peace pipe with Pima and Apache Indian representatives, a first for the traditionally warring tribes, Coolidge climbed to the speaker's rostrum and dedicated the dam by smashing a bottle of Gila River water on the structure. Thousands of spectators attended the event, and seated at the banquet table are Will Rogers (bottom left), Coolidge (in hat), and Grace (to the right of Coolidge). (PCHS.)

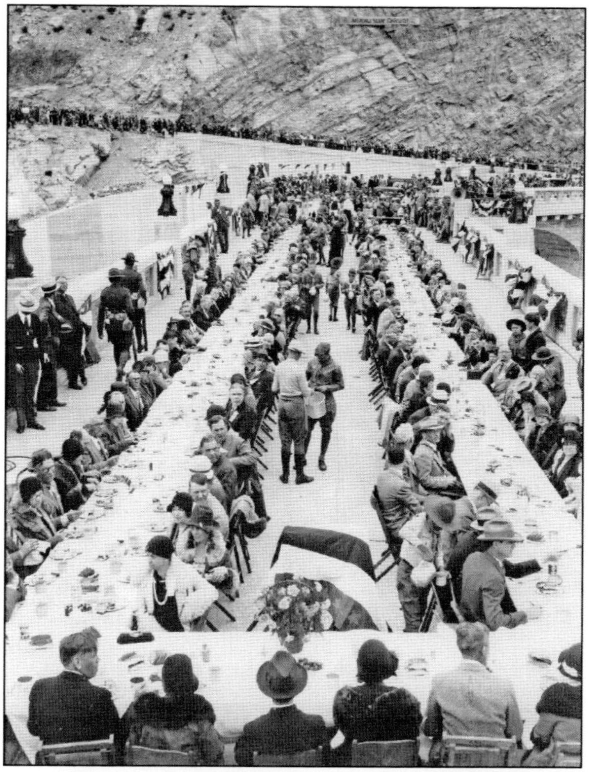

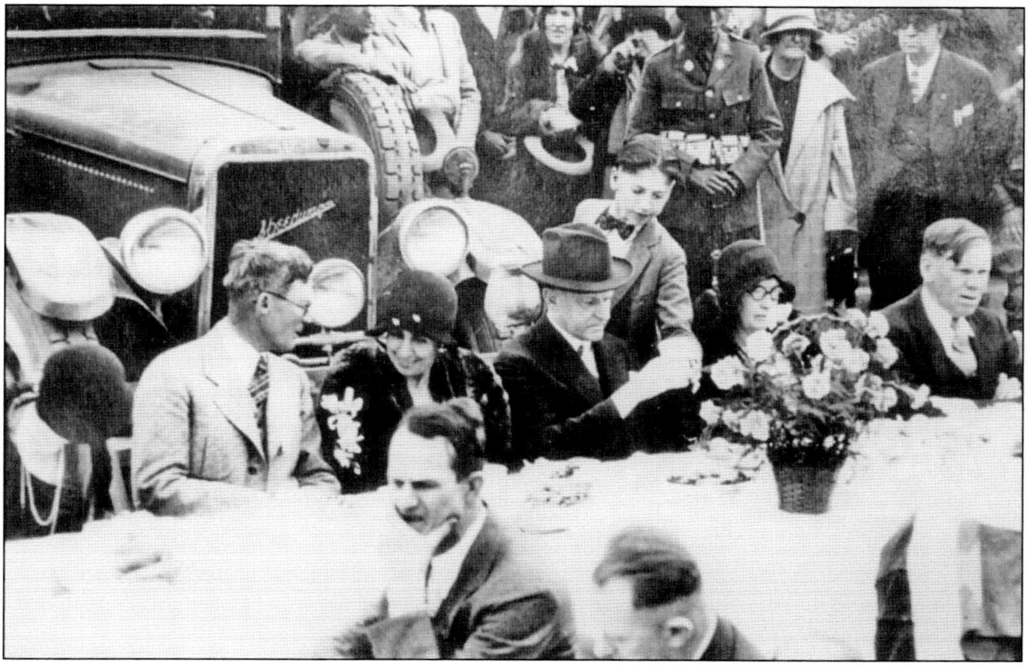

Coolidge is being served a glass of ice water during the banquet on top of the dam. To the left, his wife, Grace, visits with Arizona governor John C. Phillips, while humorist Will Rogers frowns on the far right. Coolidge's Secret Service car is parked behind him. Coolidge's personal Secret Service agent, Edmund Starling, was a close friend and confidant of the president. (CHM.)

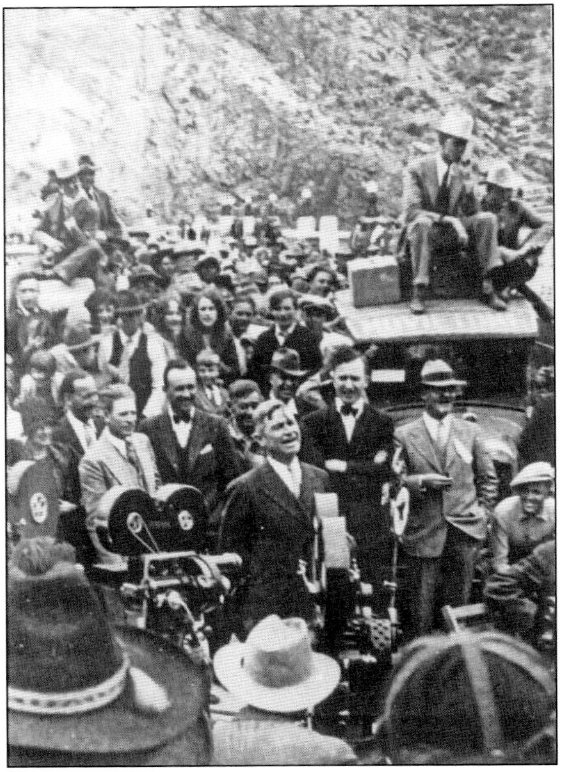

Although he was not listed in the official dedication program, the gregarious satirist Will Rogers, never suffering a loss for words, addressed the Fox Movietone newsreel cameras during the dedication. Looking across the reservoir, named San Carlos Lake, covered with a thick scum of green algae, Rogers said, "If this was my lake, I'd mow it." (CHM.)

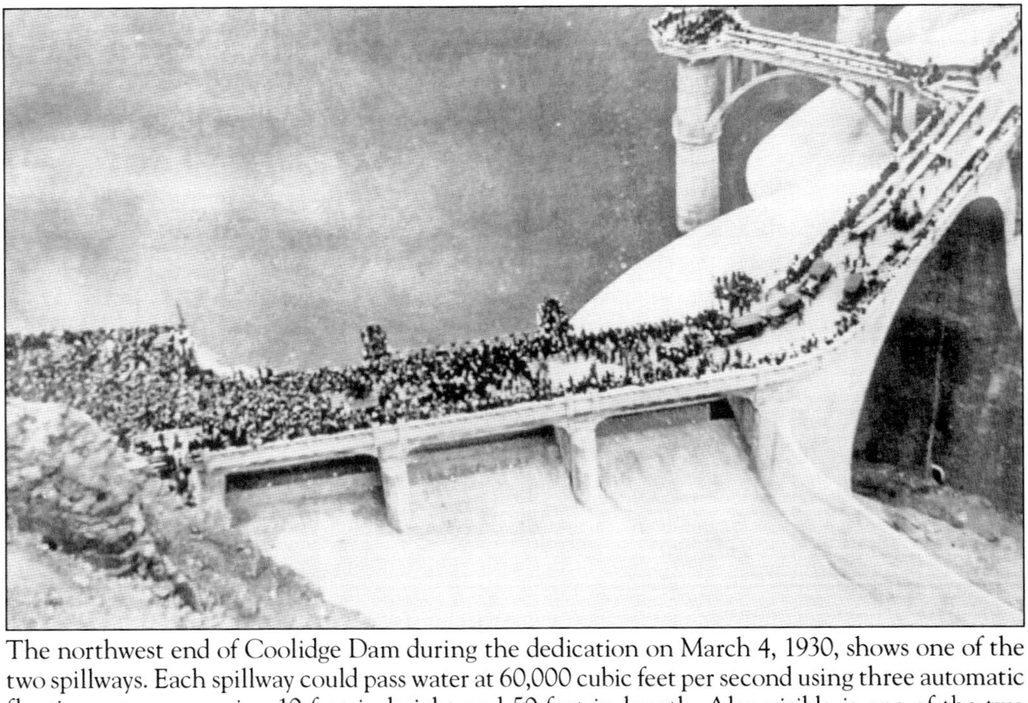

The northwest end of Coolidge Dam during the dedication on March 4, 1930, shows one of the two spillways. Each spillway could pass water at 60,000 cubic feet per second using three automatic floating gates measuring 10 feet in height and 50 feet in length. Also visible is one of the two outlet towers that could discharge water at 1,000 cubic feet per second into one of two power generating turbines for hydroelectric power. (CHM.)

Three

Our Community Roots

The names of city streets, county roads, parks, mountains, and neighborhoods of Coolidge and its environs reflect its rich heritage of diverse cultures and ethnicities. Spanish, Mexican, and Native American names highlight the influence of cultures that preceded the arrival of Anglo Europeans to the Southwest. Cabeza de Vaca, Coronado, Kino, and de Anza were early explorers of the desert Southwest. The two divisions of O'odham native people, Tohono (formerly Papago) and Akimel (formerly Pima), who today populate this region, provide a cultural heritage that is still celebrated in their artwork, music, and horsemanship (rodeos).

As Coolidge began to prosper economically due to the vast farmland and valuable water resources, the early ancestral tradition of cotton growing developed into a modern agricultural industry that created a prosperous farming community. Agriculture demanded industries that provided the necessary tools and machinery to sustain the bountiful harvests. Prior to the invention of cotton-picking machinery, farmers depended upon the labor of migrant workers. Anglo, Mexican American, and African American farmworkers were the lifeblood of the farming community around Coolidge. Their important contributions to the economic success of many of the farms and businesses that exist today cannot be overemphasized. The ranks of the farmworkers swelled the population of Pinal County, and businesses were established in Coolidge to provide food, clothing, shelter, and other necessities that were in demand.

Generations of pioneer families established businesses in Coolidge to meet the needs of a city on the move. At times, especially during the several annual celebration events as well as Saturdays, downtown Coolidge bustled with shoppers and visitors. Main Street, Coolidge, and Central Avenues were lined with cars, and the sidewalks were filled four and five deep with pedestrians.

Over the decades, Coolidge has experienced economic high points and low points. The Great Recession that began in 2007–2008 hit the community hard, and Coolidge did not escape the rash of home foreclosures that much of the country experienced. But, Coolidgeans are a tough and determined people who look to the future with optimism and hope. As of this writing, there are many positive signs for a return to more prosperous times.

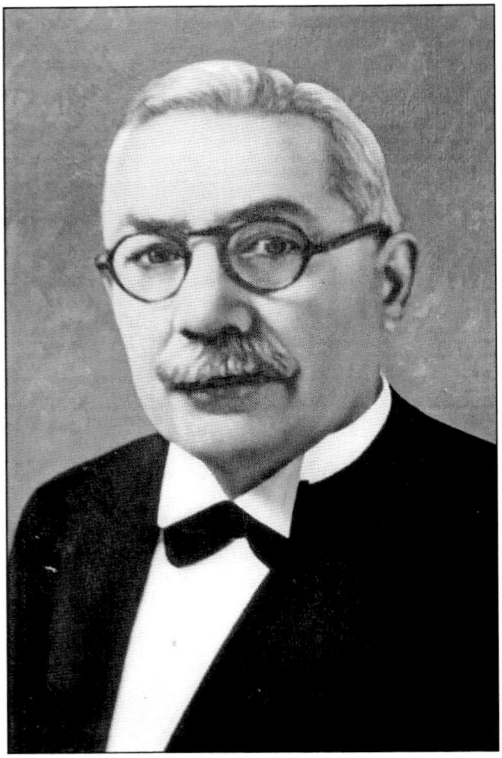

Richard J. Jones was the founder and community leader of Coolidge. His modest investment in 80 acres of mesquite-covered desert close to the Gila River and the Casa Grande Ruins paid off when Coolidge became known as the fastest-growing town in Arizona a few years after he platted the land in 1925 for a new townsite. (CHM.)

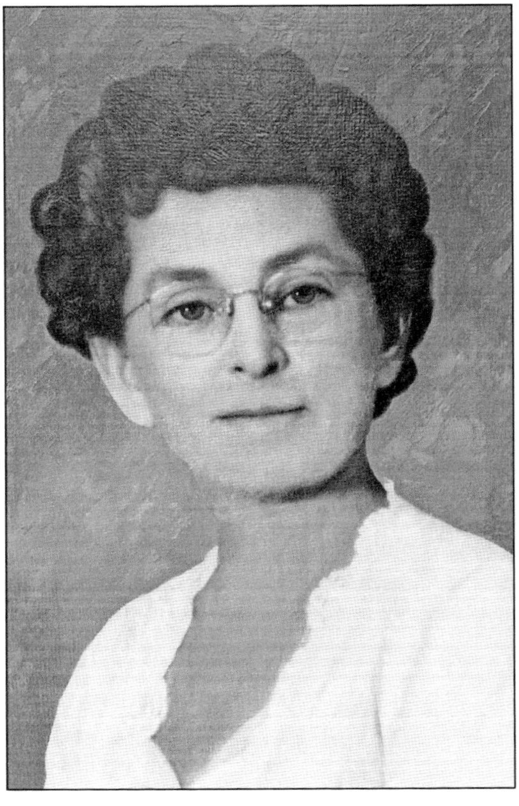

Alma Jones supported her husband's successful efforts to grow the little town of Coolidge. Richard died on May 17, 1941, but Alma lived for 40 more years and died at the age of 96 in San Diego, California. She kept daily records during the first decade of growth for the city and was instrumental in establishing many social activities, including the founding of the Coolidge Women's Club. (CHM.)

Asa "Ace" Gardner was sworn in on November 28, 1928, as Coolidge's first deputy. A crack shot with his .45-caliber, single-action revolver, Ace used a railroad boxcar as a jail before the city approved building him one in the new courthouse. The city fathers agreed to spend the money after the railroad inadvertently hauled the boxcar jail all the way to Phoenix before realizing it contained some of Coolidge's inmates. (CHM.)

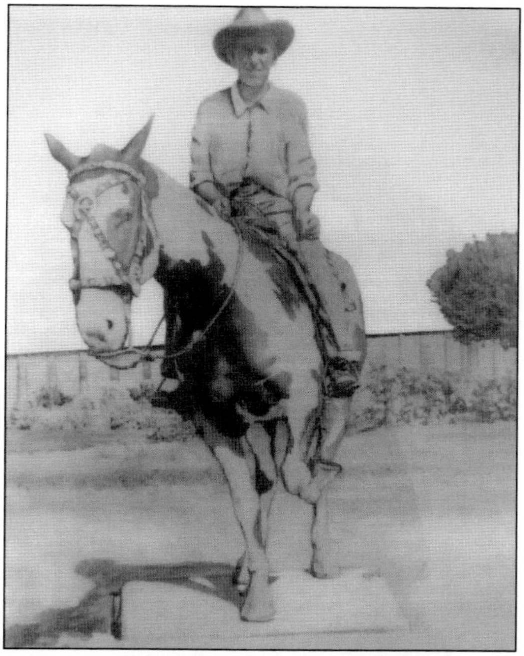

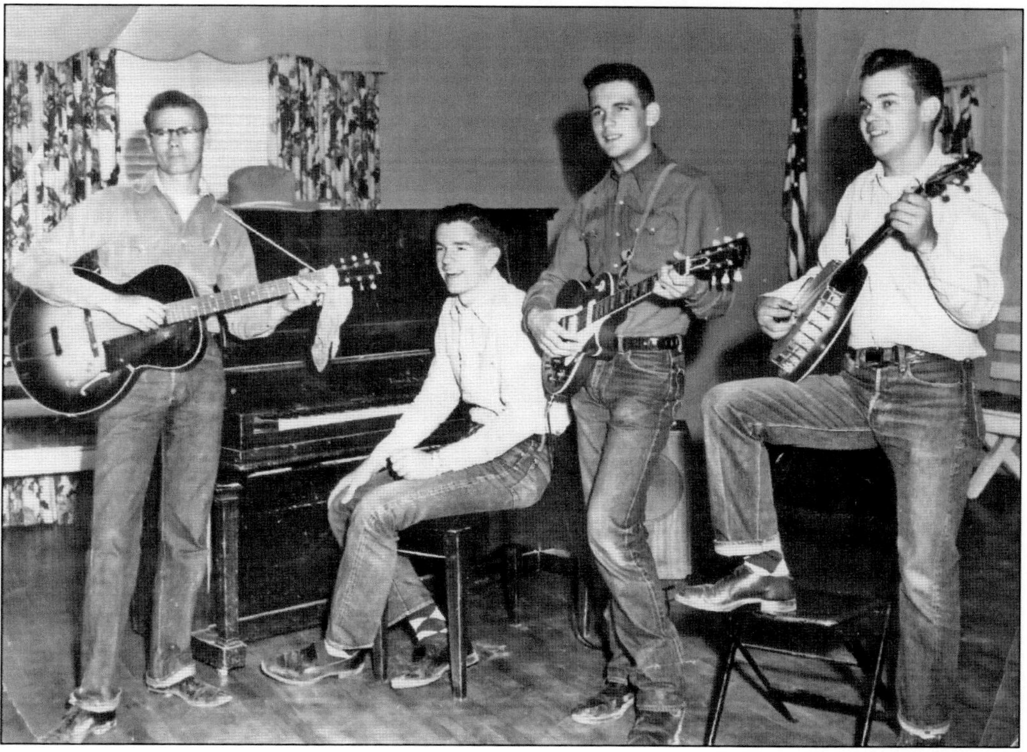

Coolidge was the hometown of a number of young musicians who went on to become well known and successful music artists. From left to right are Ed Myers, Jimmy Delbridge, Duane Eddy, and John Delbridge practicing at the Coolidge Women's Club in the early 1950s. Eddy became a famous rock 'n' roll guitarist, and Jimmy Delbridge, now known as Jimmy Dell, became a rockabilly and gospel artist who still tours in the United States and abroad. (John E. Hill.)

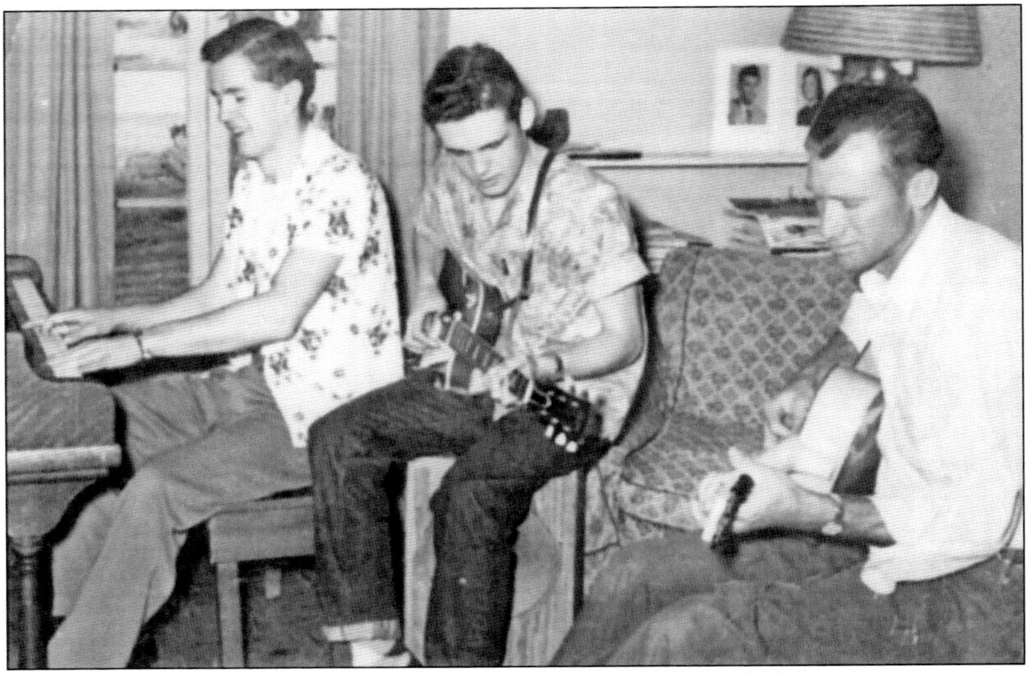

Jimmy "Dell" Delbridge (left), Duane Eddy (center), and E.B. "Lightning" McGee hold a jam session in a Coolidge home in this 1954 photograph taken by Claude Henry. Eddy's characteristic twangy guitar caught the attention of California surfing bands, as well as that of the nation's youth. In the late 1950s and early 1960s, songs such as "Rebel Rouser," "Theme from Peter Gunn," and "Because They're Young" made the top of the pop charts. (Mike Henry.)

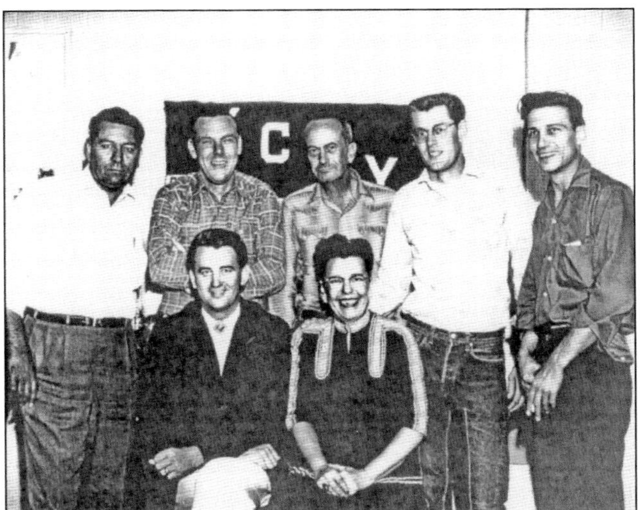

The staff of Coolidge's KCKY radio station included disc jockey and future country singer Waylon Jennings (standing, on the right). Also on the KCKY staff was Lee Hazlewood, who moved on to Los Angeles and became a well-known music producer, singer, and songwriter. Hazlewood produced a string of hits for Duane Eddy in the 1950s and Nancy Sinatra and Dean Martin in the 1960s. His own solo output and style has been described as an essential contribution of musical sound that is sometimes called "cowboy psychedelia." (John E. Hill.)

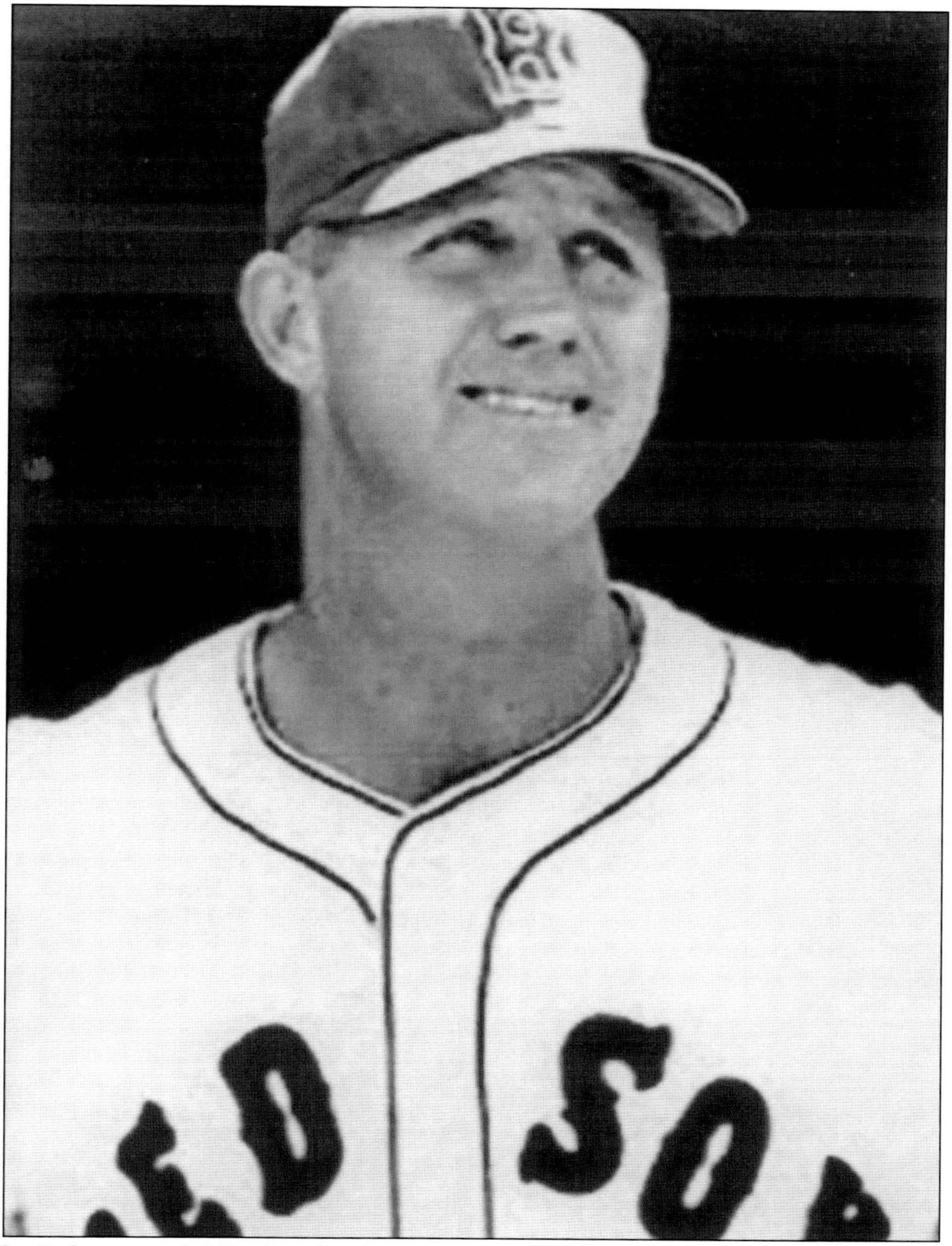

Joe Dobson attended Kenilworth School and Coolidge High School and was an accomplished pitcher for the baseball team. He went on to a 14-year career with the Cleveland Indians, the Boston Red Sox, and the Chicago White Sox. In 1948, he became an All-Star. Dobson won 106 games for the Red Sox and was inducted posthumously in the Red Sox Hall of Fame in 2012. At age nine, he lost his thumb and left index finger after an accident playing with a dynamite cap. His deformed hand did not hinder his ability to play baseball as an outstanding pitcher. (CHM.)

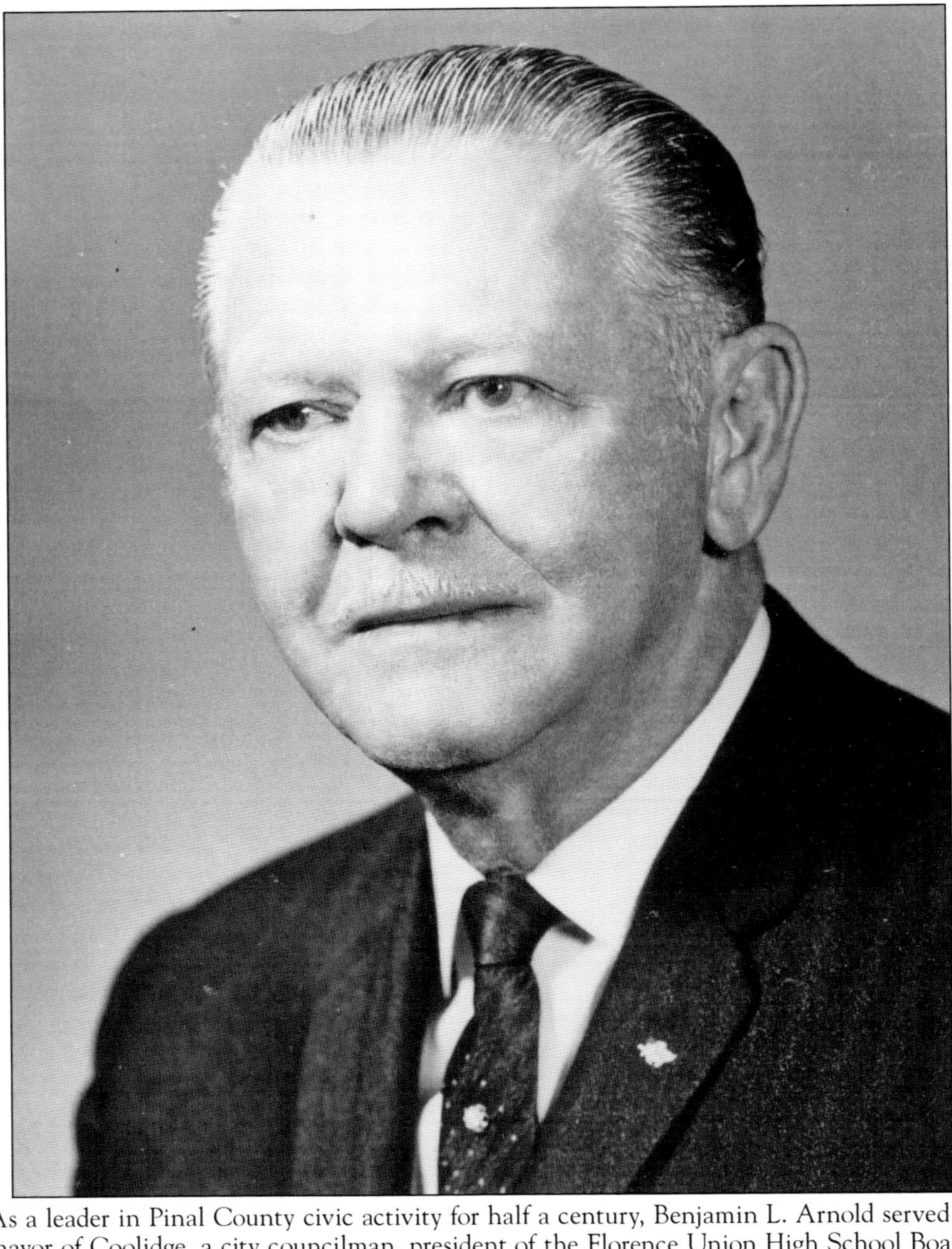

As a leader in Pinal County civic activity for half a century, Benjamin L. Arnold served as mayor of Coolidge, a city councilman, president of the Florence Union High School Board, and a distributor of Standard Oil products in Coolidge. He also served 12 years in the Arizona State Senate. As a young man he worked on the Florence-Kelvin, Florence-Casa Grande, and Ray-Superior Highways. During World War I, he served in naval aviation and with a flying-boat squadron in Pensacola, Florida. Returning to Arizona after the war, he operated a service station in Florence and married Sarah Whitlow, a former school girlfriend, on August 5, 1920. When the Rio Grande Oil wholesale bulk plant was moved from Florence to Coolidge in 1928, Arnold went with it. In the state senate he became known as one of its most knowledgeable and hardworking members. Arnold worked tirelessly to improve the universities, the state prison, the children's colony south of Coolidge, and other state institutions. (CCC.)

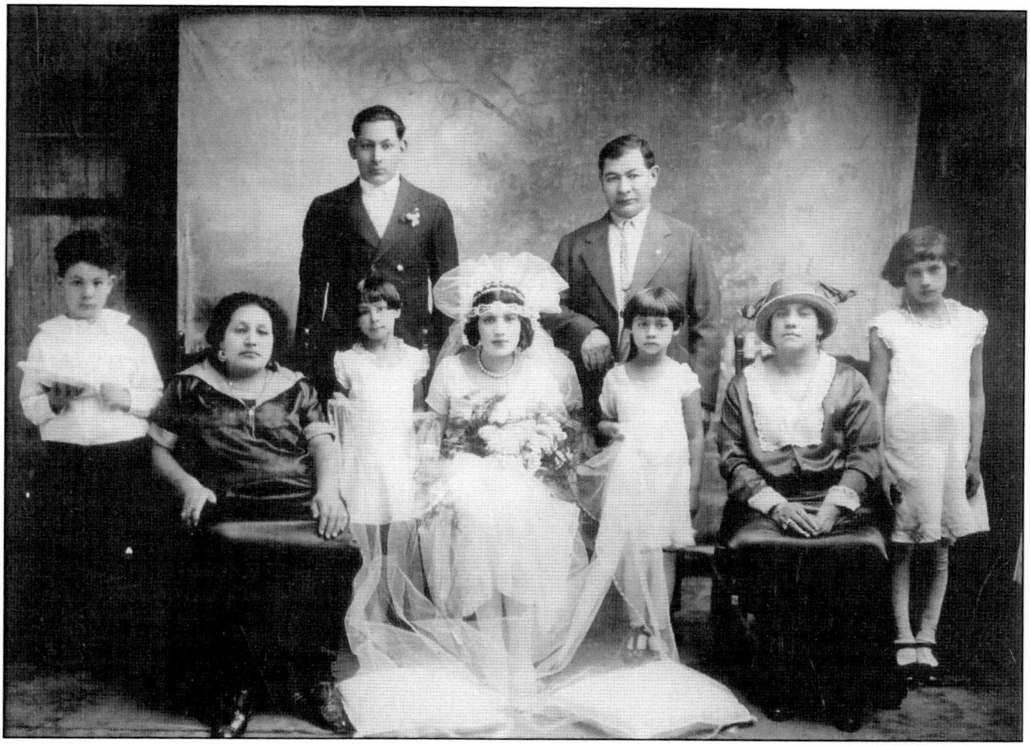

The Mexican American heritage of early Coolidge is portrayed in a formal photograph of the Jesus (standing, back right) Garcia family that took up residence at the corner of Main Street and Lincoln Avenue on July 24, 1930. The property was purchased for $800 from Richard J. Jones. Jimmy (standing, back left) opened a bar called Jim's Place and became a successful businessman who also served on the city council. (Irma Garcia Salazar.)

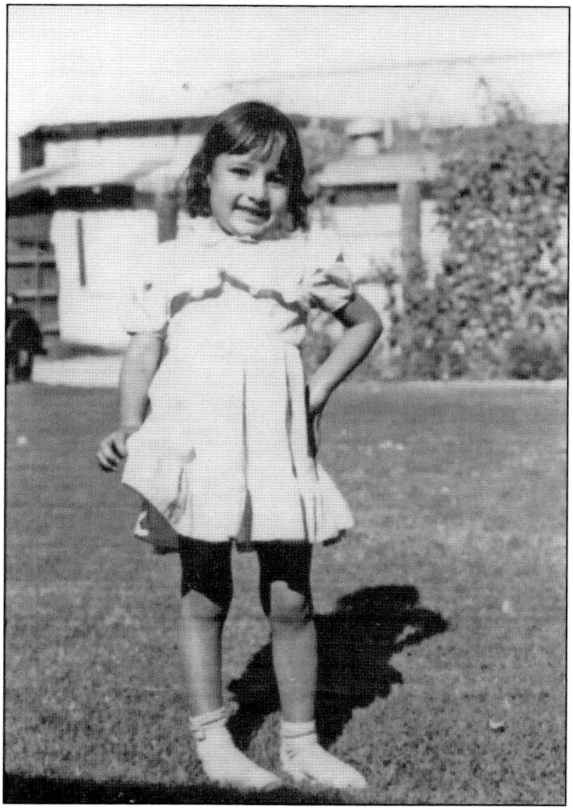

Three-year-old Irma Garcia stands behind her grandmother's house at Main Street and Lincoln Avenue in 1947. The Garcia family owned numerous businesses downtown that covered two city blocks. Her father, Miguel, in his spare time was a pitcher for the Sioux City Boosters baseball team. (Irma Garcia Salazar.)

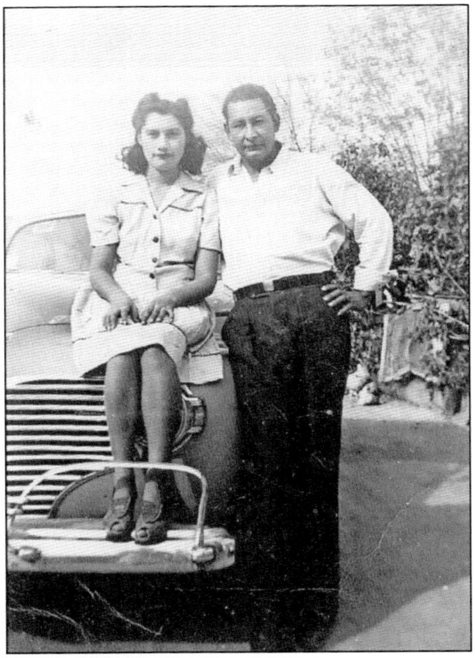

Miguel "Lito" Diaz Garcia and Olivia Ybarra, pictured here in 1942, were married on December 4, 1943. Miguel moved to Coolidge in 1945 and worked in the copper mines in Sonora and San Miguel, Arizona. For a brief time, he and his brother operated a trucking company. (Irma Garcia Salazar.)

Miguel "Lito" Garcia (right), pictured here with two unidentified fellow miners, operated drilling machinery in the underground magma mine at San Miguel located near Oracle, Arizona. Work in the mines was strenuous, and the miners had little protection from inhaling dust created by the drilling. (Irma Garcia Salazar.)

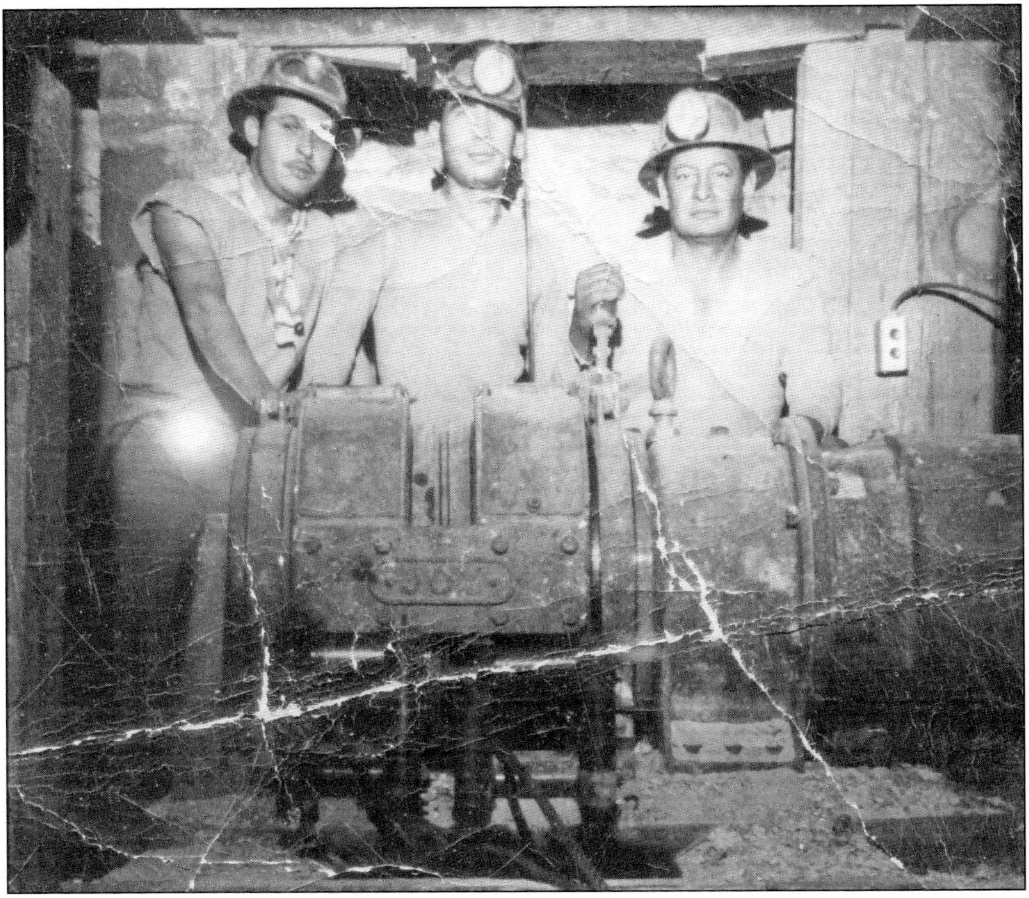

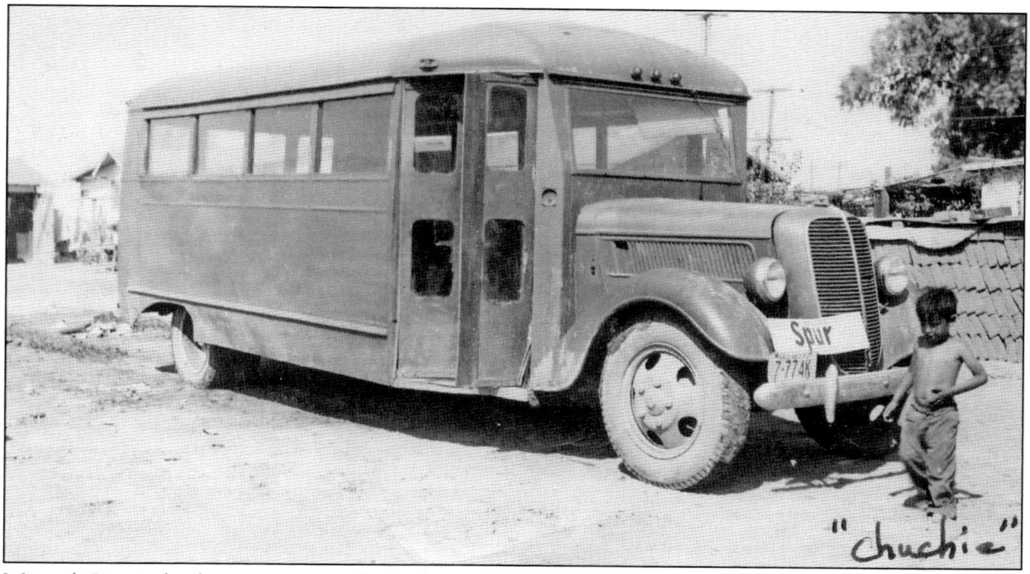

Miguel Garcia had a contract with the bracero program that was established during World War II to bring Mexican workers into the United States to supplement the labor force. Miguel owned and drove a bus to transport the braceros to their work sites. Behind Irma's little brother Jessie "Chuchie" Garcia are stacked adobe bricks used to build the worker's barracks that were located on Lincoln Avenue in Coolidge. (Irma Garcia Salazar.)

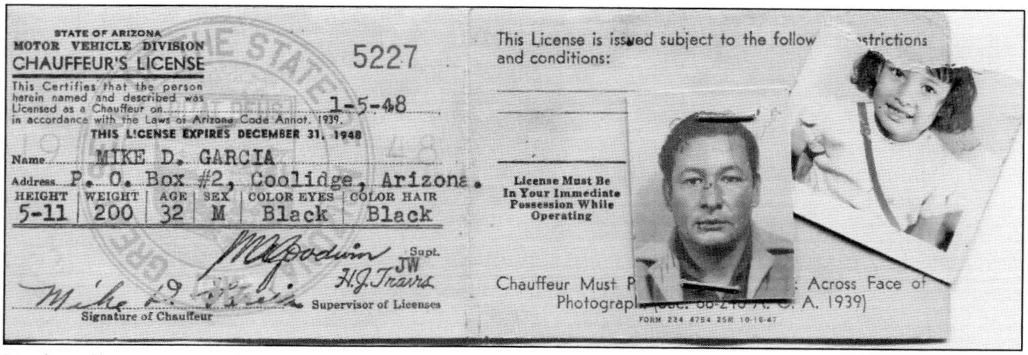
STATE OF ARIZONA
MOTOR VEHICLE DIVISION
CHAUFFEUR'S LICENSE
5227
This Certifies that the person herein named and described was Licensed as a Chauffeur on 1-5-48 in accordance with the Laws of Arizona Code Annot. 1939.
THIS LICENSE EXPIRES DECEMBER 31, 1948
Name MIKE D. GARCIA
Address P. O. Box #2, Coolidge, Arizona.

HEIGHT	WEIGHT	AGE	SEX	COLOR EYES	COLOR HAIR
5-11	200	32	M	Black	Black

Supt.
Signature of Chauffeur
Supervisor of Licenses

This License is issued subject to the follow[...] restrictions and conditions:

License Must Be In Your Immediate Possession While Operating

Chauffeur Must P[...] Across Face of Photograph [...] A. 1939)

To legally operate the bus and transport braceros, Miguel needed a chauffeur's license. According to his daughter Irma, her dad carried her photograph with his license wherever he travelled. The bracero program was begun in 1942 and discontinued permanently in 1964. (Irma Garcia Salazar.)

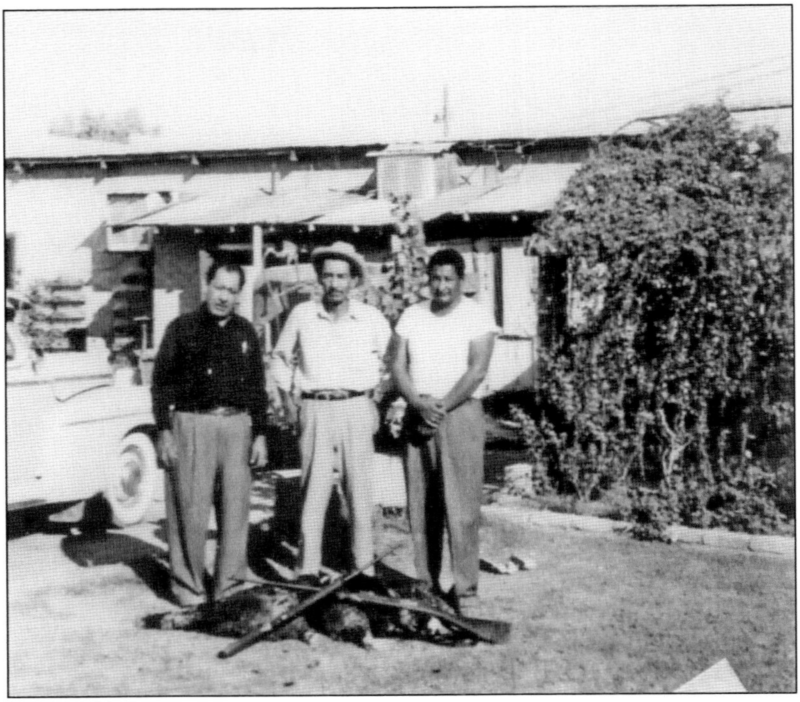

This November 1950 photograph is labeled "Turkey shoot at the Skousen Ranch." At the Garcia home on Main Street and Lincoln Avenue are, from left to right, Irma Garcia Salazar's uncles Jimmy and Francisco "Chico" Garcia, and father Miguel. The wild turkeys were plentiful that year just before the Thanksgiving holiday. (Irma Garcia Salazar.)

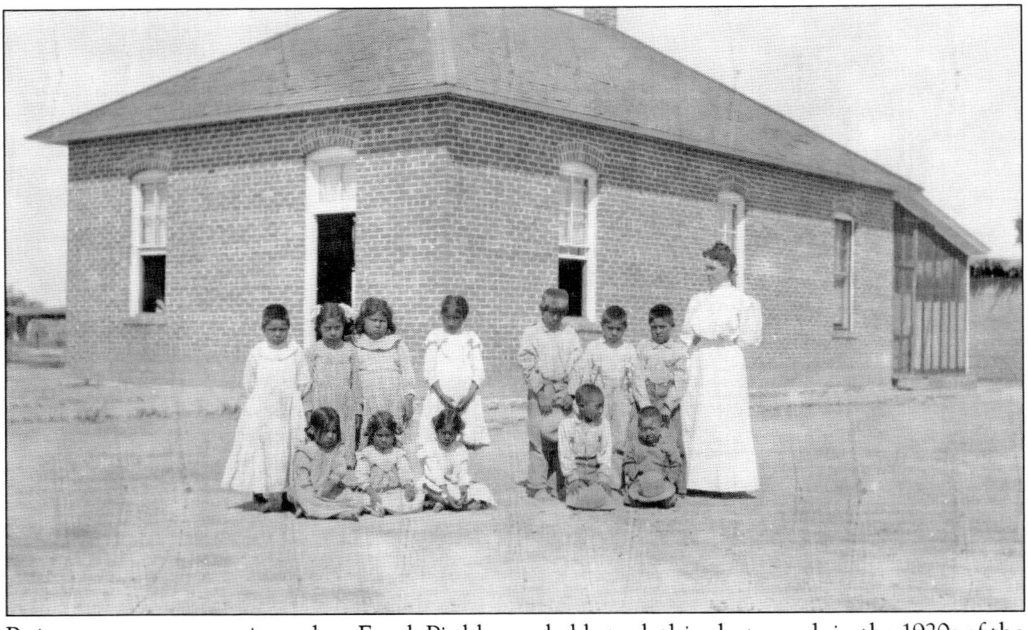

Ruins monument superintendent Frank Pinkley probably took this photograph in the 1920s of the Pima Indian School at Blackwater just north of Coolidge. Born in 1943, Dianna Herrera, a frequent visitor to Coolidge, lives in District Four (San Tan) of the Gila River Indian Community and remembers that many of her classmates only spoke the O'odham language. (Dianna Herrera.)

The Gila River Indian Community is located adjacent to the northern city limits of Coolidge and continues north to the southern edge of Chandler. Casa Grande Ruins National Monument superintendent Frank Pinkley took this photograph of a Pima family at Sacaton in the 1920s. (NPS.)

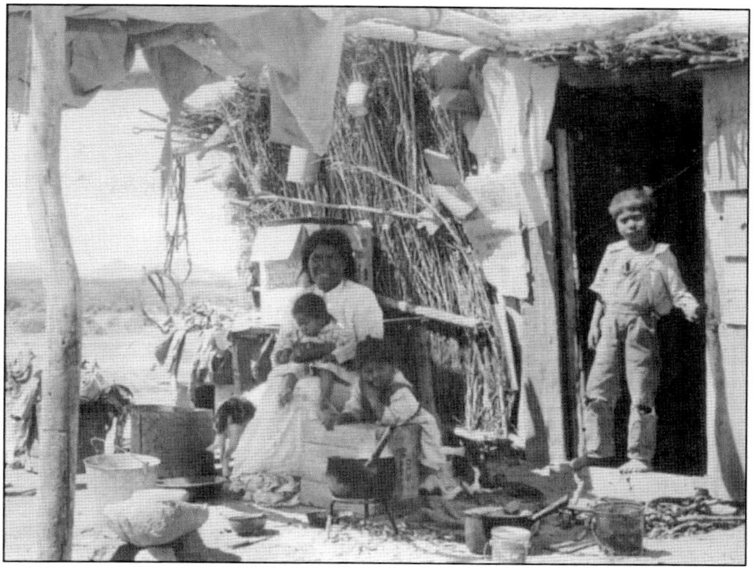

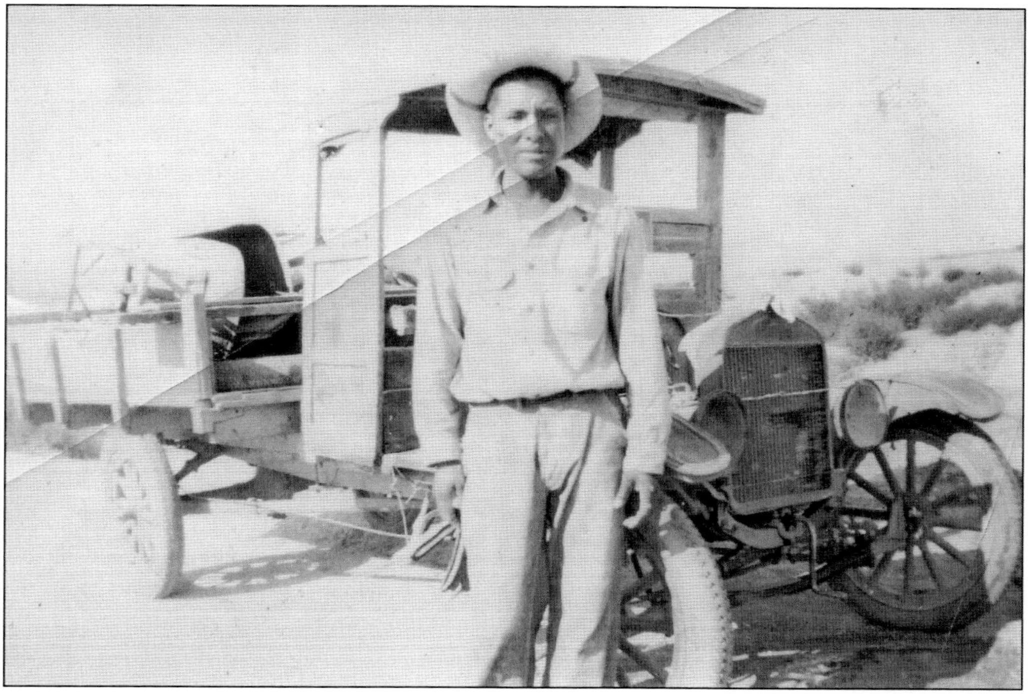

Dianna Herrera's father, Adam Porter, was a Presbyterian minister in Sacaton, and she remembers that all her activities centered around the church. He drove a school bus for the five southernmost districts of the Gila River Indian Community. Dianna said one day her nonnative teacher complained to her father about his children speaking the Pima language, and he responded, "I taught them their native tongue, it's your job to teach them English." (Dianna Herrera.)

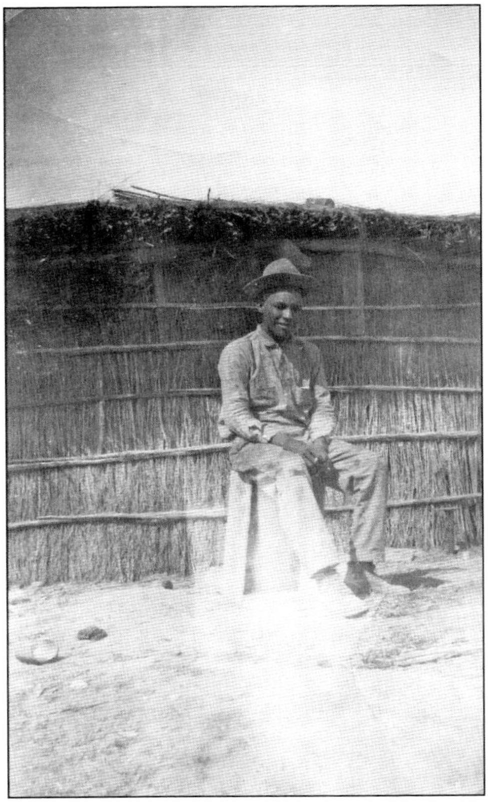

Dianna Herrera's father, Adam Porter, sits in front of her grandmother's house in Stotonic (Pima for "many ants") in District Four of the Gila River Indian Community. Traditional construction materials for the homes at the time were arrow weed supported by poles of mesquite. The roofs were covered with adobe made from native caliche clay mixed with water. (Dianna Herrera.)

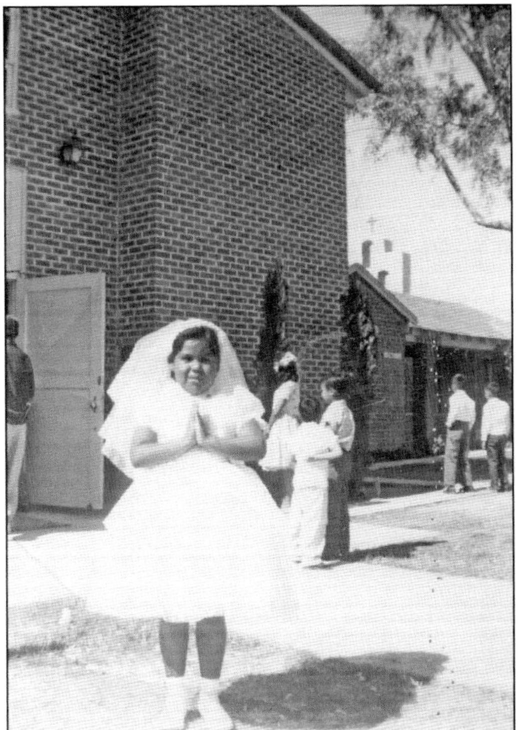

Dianna Herrera's cousin Priscilla Flores is pictured here at her first Communion in front of St. James Catholic Church in Coolidge. The church is still active and located at 401 West Wilson Avenue. Dianna's father was Pima Indian, and her mother was Mexican. She graduated from Coolidge High School in 1963 and became a licensed practical nurse working in the Bay Area of California, in nursing homes in Scottsdale, Arizona, and at nearby Florence Hospital for 23 years. (Dianna Herrera.)

The war years of the 1940s affected towns large and small around the United States. A board was established in Coolidge to administer the guidelines for war rationing. From left to right are Paul Hanna, Fred Jamieson, three unidentified, Bill Elliot, Bill McConnell (standing), Harold Wrenn, Jack Garrett Sr., unidentified, Arthur J. Faul, and Lucille Ware. (CHM.)

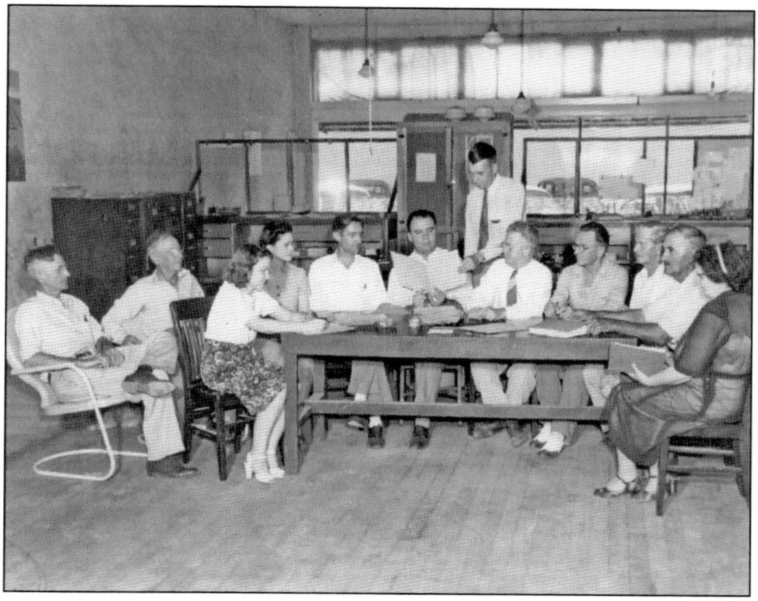

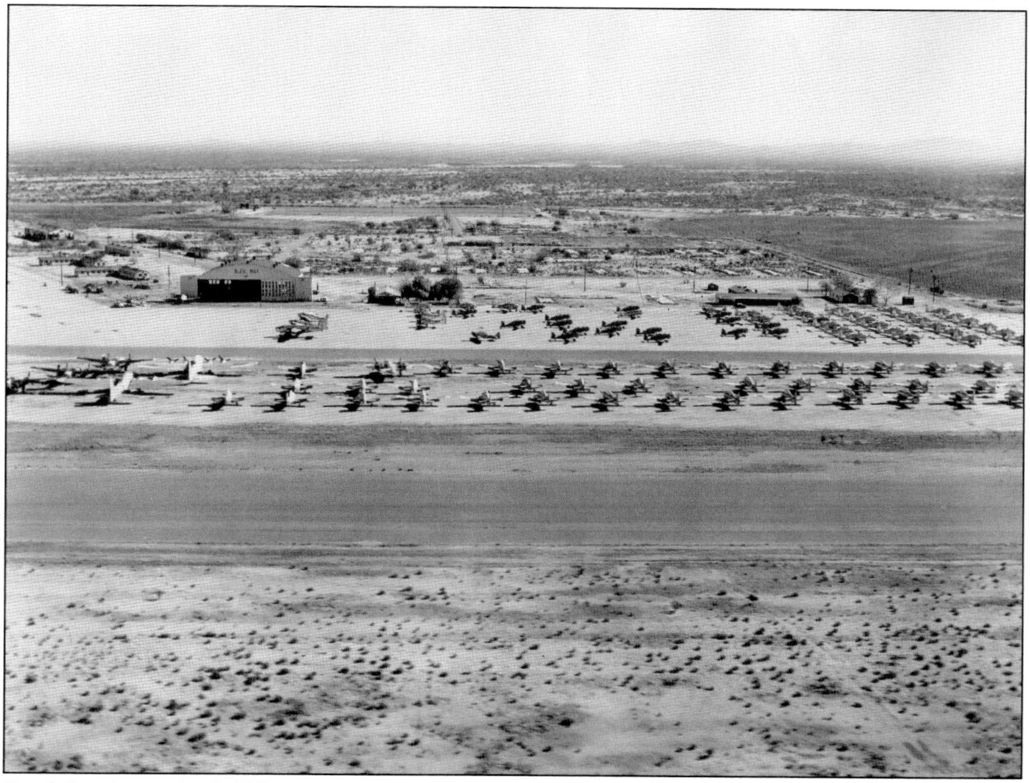

Coolidge Army Airfield began in 1941 on 1,277 acres as an Army Air Corps flight-training school. Two of the three original runways are still in operation today as the Coolidge Municipal Airport after it was transferred from Pinal County ownership to the City of Coolidge in March 1959. During World War II, the airfield was used for refueling and maintenance for Army, Navy, and Marine Corps planes en route to other bases. The large hangar in this June 21, 1945, photograph has been restored for use today. (CHM.)

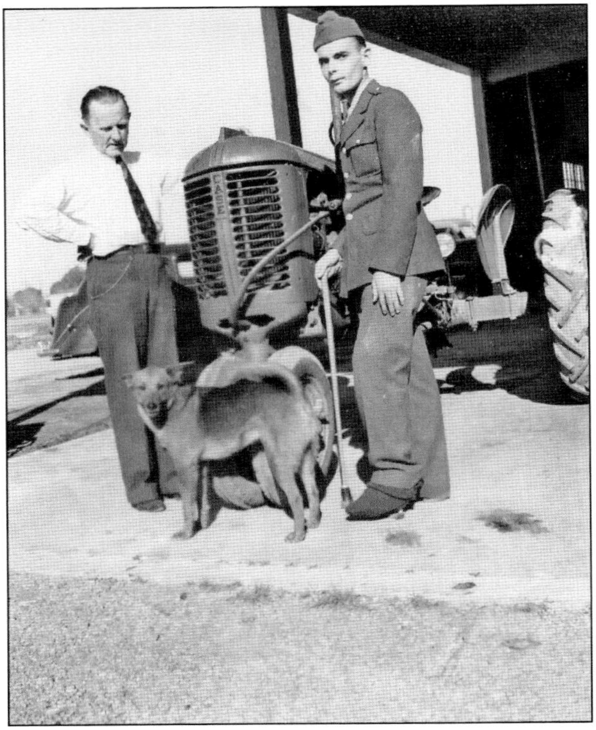

Jack Garrett Sr. (left) and his dog Brownie visit with his son, who was wounded while serving in the European theater. In August 1943, while recuperating in an Army evacuation hospital in Sicily, Jack Jr. witnessed from a few beds away one of the infamous Gen. George Patton slapping incidents of a soldier suffering from battle fatigue, recognized today as PTSD. Jack Sr. operated the Case Farm Store and later an Oldsmobile car dealership. Garrett Motors is still in business today selling Chevrolets and operated by his grandson Jim. (Jim Garrett Jr.)

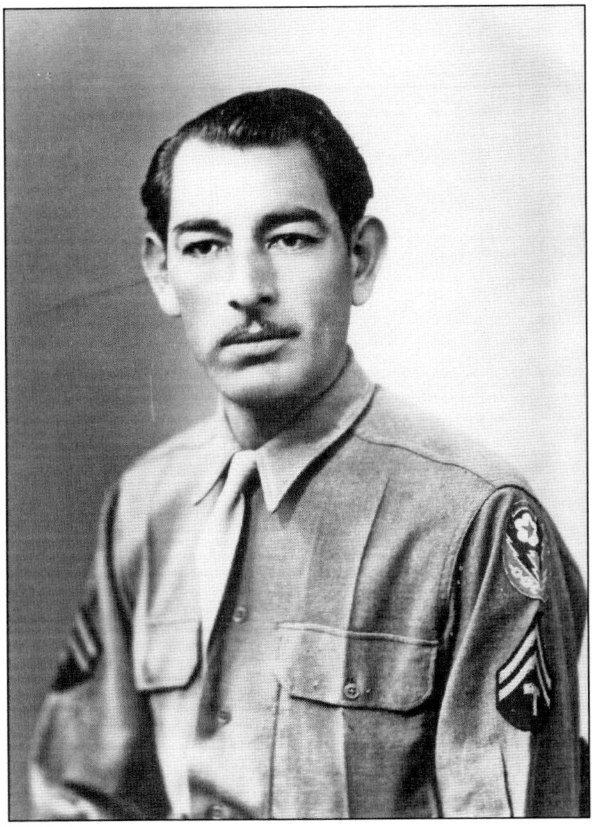

Irma Garcia Salazar's brother Francisco "Chico" Garcia served in the US Army during the war and, upon receiving his discharge, returned to Coolidge and worked in the family bar, Jim's Place, on Coolidge Avenue. He later worked for the Arizona State Highway Department until 1974. Both he and his brother donated their time and money to the St. James Catholic Church. (Irma Garcia Salazar.)

Naomi Kalko opened a grocery store in the mid-1930s in downtown Coolidge but closed it in 1942 when she joined the Women's Army Corps (WAC). Then Pam Meadows opened the Coolidge Flower Shop at 333 South Main Street. Today that flower shop is still in business and operated by her son John Meadows and Pam's granddaughter Nancy Meadows-Heikes. (John W. Meadows.)

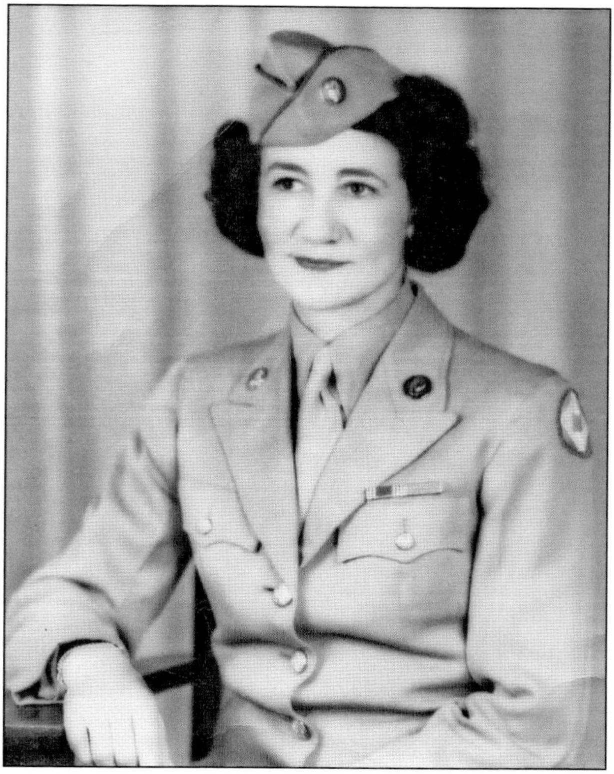

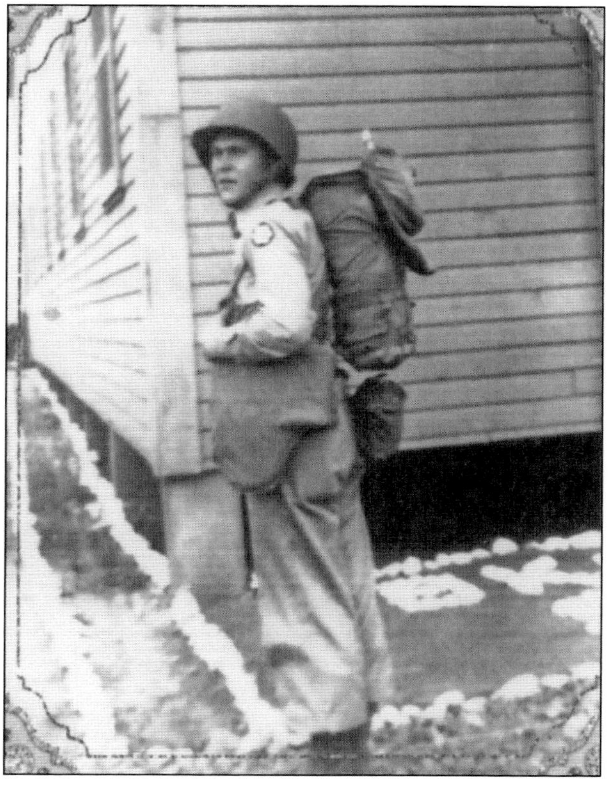

Joseph Reed Chesley moved with his family from the Safford area to Coolidge in January 1930 when he was six years old. He lived on Kennedy Avenue until he joined the Army in 1943 and underwent medical training at Fort White in Abilene, Texas. Upon his return home on Christmas Eve 1945, he tried to start an ice cream business. In 1946, he reenlisted in the Army Air Corps and served in cryptography until retiring in 1964. (Joseph Reed Chesley.)

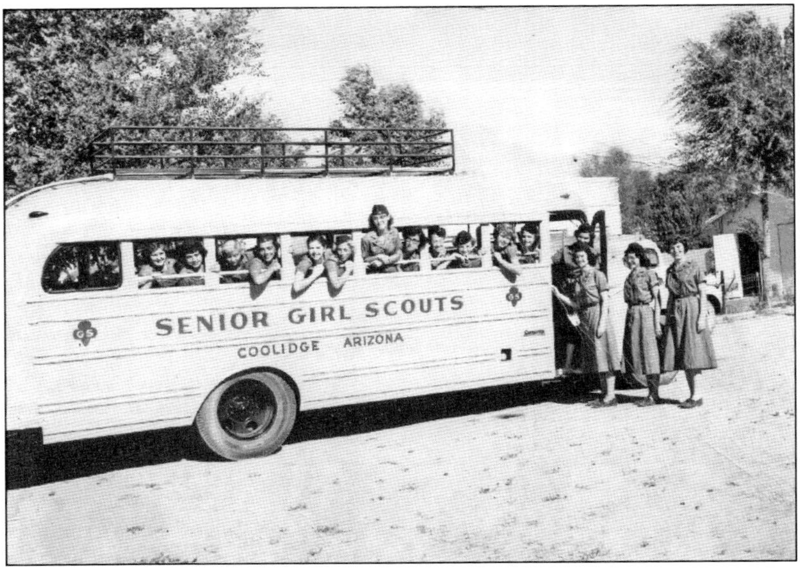

Coolidge senior Girl Scouts board their bus in 1953 for one of their many outings. Following four years of fundraising, the Girl Scouts used the money to take a 19-day trip touring the United States and Canada. (CHM.)

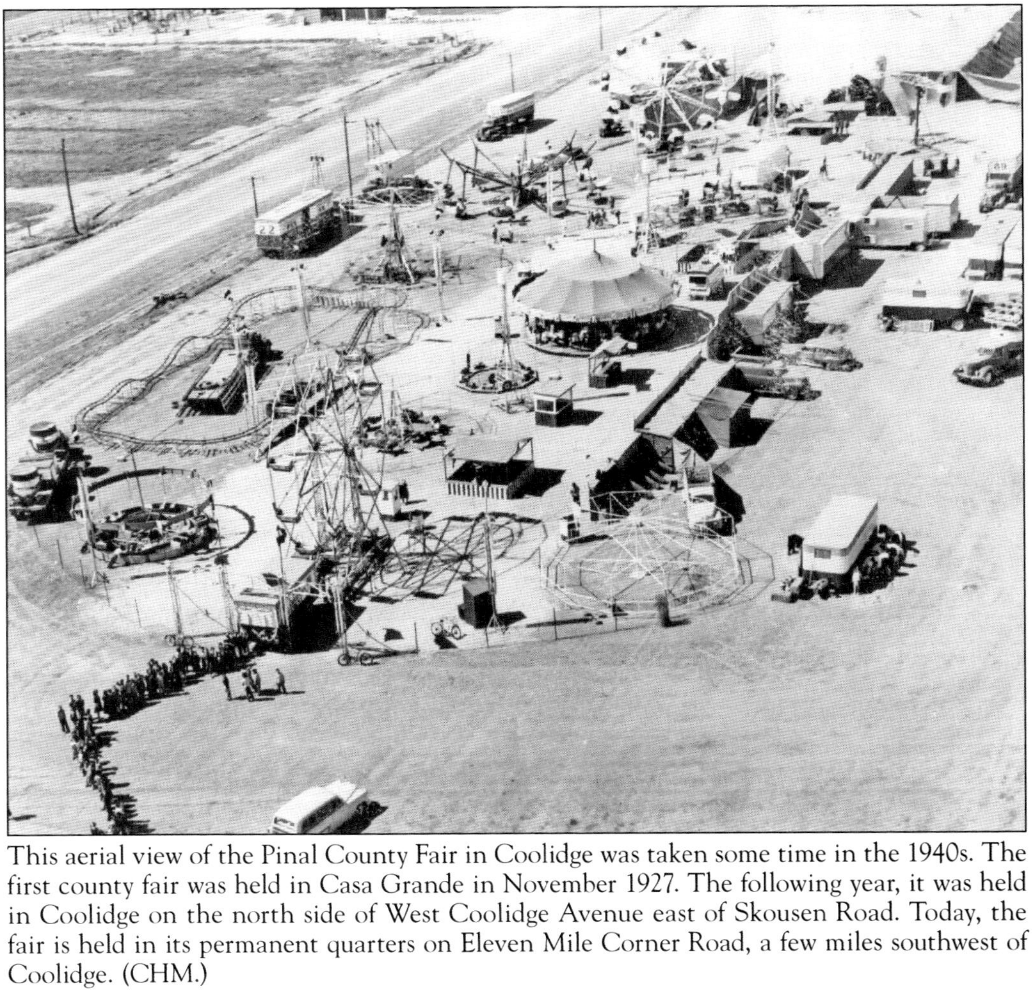

This aerial view of the Pinal County Fair in Coolidge was taken some time in the 1940s. The first county fair was held in Casa Grande in November 1927. The following year, it was held in Coolidge on the north side of West Coolidge Avenue east of Skousen Road. Today, the fair is held in its permanent quarters on Eleven Mile Corner Road, a few miles southwest of Coolidge. (CHM.)

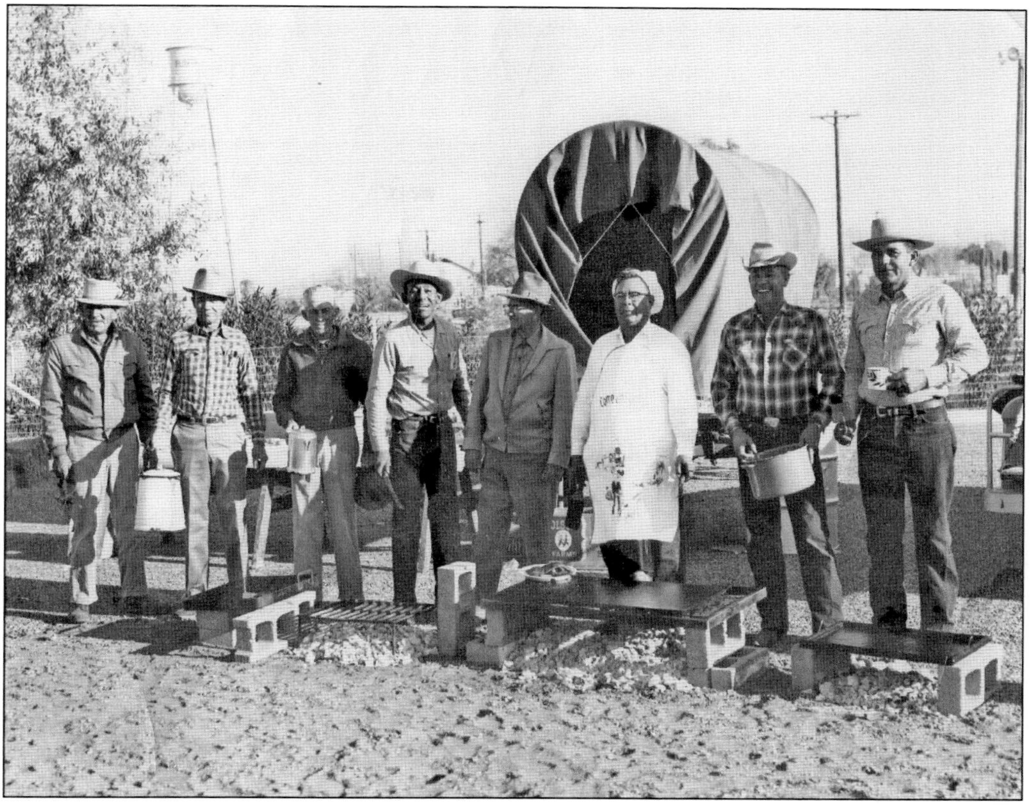

The crew of the state highway department in Florence held a Christmas party in the mid-1950s. From left to right are Frank Garcia (carpenter), Leo Morgan (truck driver), Odell Thornton (patch man), Jacob Aguilar (assistant foreman), Charles Smith (foreman), Gabe Salazar (truck driver), Louis Van Haren (mechanic), and Raul Padilla (high-lift operator). Salazar supervised the kitchen at the state prison and worked at a local café before joining the highway department. (Irma Garcia Salazar.)

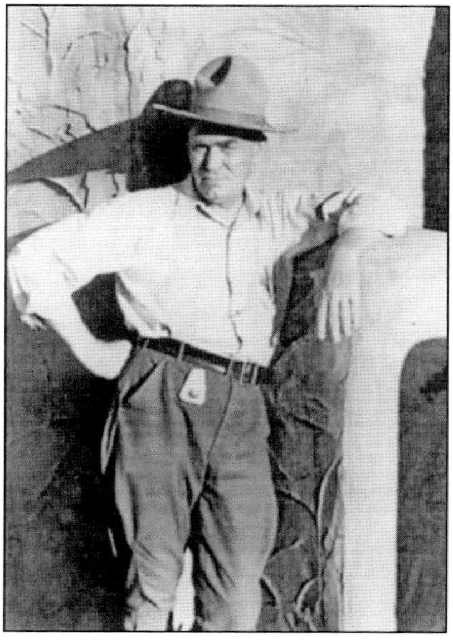

Frank "Boss" Pinkley is described as a true legend of the National Park Service. At the age of 19, he moved from Missouri to Arizona when doctor's tests indicated the possibility of tuberculosis. That first year, 1900, he helped his parents run the Blackwater Trading Post near Coolidge and the following year began serving as custodian of the Casa Grande Ruins Reserve. He died suddenly on Valentine's Day 1940 of a massive heart attack during a national monuments' custodians conference being held at the ruins. (NPS.)

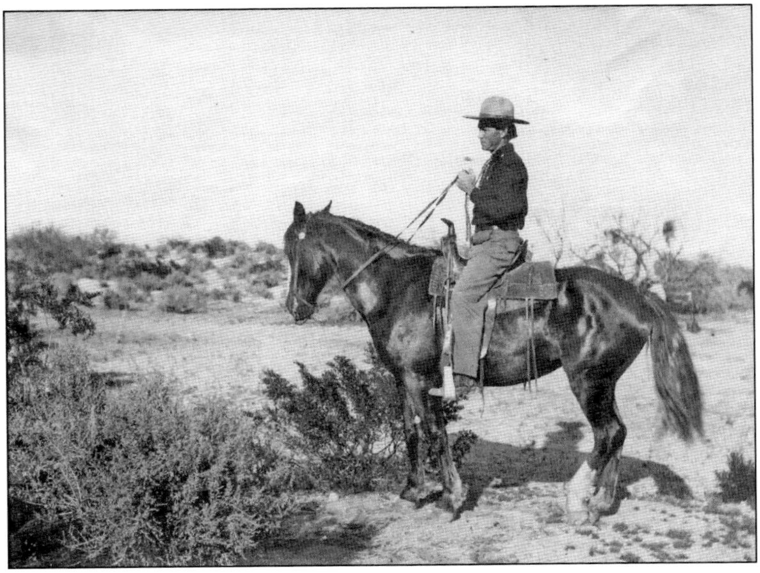

This 1908 photograph purportedly features Supt. Frank Pinkley astride his horse on the grounds of the Casa Grande Ruins. Pinkley was instrumental in establishing the Southwest Monument Association in 1938, which included a dozen designated national monuments in Arizona and New Mexico. (NPS.)

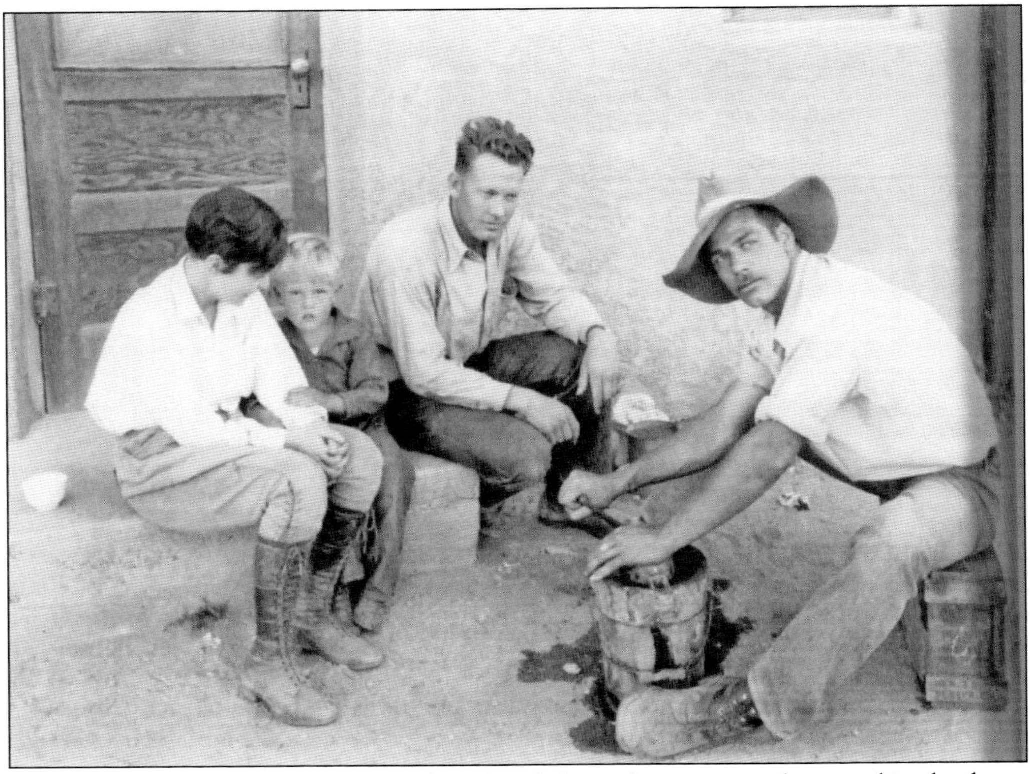

A popular pastime in Coolidge was making hand-churned ice cream to keep cool in the desert heat. Milton Snow took this photograph of archaeologist Julian Hayden (right) in 1939 taking a break from excavation work at the Casa Grande Ruins. Snow was a Farm Security Administration (FSA) photographer who was documenting life during the Great Depression in the Southwest. (Museum of Northern Arizona Photo Archives #MS35-10-18.)

Four

Cotton is King

From the time that Coolidge Dam began storing Gila River water for irrigating the 100,000 acres of land in Pinal County in 1930 to the introduction of the cotton-picking machine to the Coolidge area in the early 1950s, as many as 10,000 cotton pickers migrated to this area during harvest season. Native American pickers from the nearby reservations, Mexican American workers from California, Texas, and New Mexico, and African American migrants from Texas, Oklahoma, Arkansas, Louisiana, and Alabama all came to chop cotton. The small, mostly black, community of Randolph arose a few miles south of Coolidge on State Route 87 as a result of the families from the East who came to pick cotton.

For those who picked the lint from the opened bolls, the going rate in the early 1950s was $3 per 100 pounds. Many cotton pickers comprised an entire family unit, including the children. A hardworking, experienced family could pick 500 to 700 pounds a day, each dragging a long canvas sack by a shoulder strap. In those days, $15 to $20 a day was considered good pay for a thrifty family.

Clyle "Bobby" Skousen's dad moved his family from Sun Lakes, Arizona, where, as a tenant farmer, cotton was being grown for the Goodyear Tire and Rubber Company to use for tire cords. When Goodyear discontinued tenant farming, Coolidge became the Skousen's new home. He says most of the 900 acres that was purchased was covered with mesquite, but thankfully the landlord had it cleared. The Skousens hired mostly African American workers from Oklahoma initially to pick the cotton, but when the mechanical cotton-picking machine started appearing on farms around Coolidge, the need for local and migrant pickers diminished.

Although cotton is the king of crops in Pinal County, many other commodities were grown for market. Corn, melons, citrus fruits, grapes, gourds, and sugar beets were among the diverse products grown. For a while in the 1960s and 1970s, sugar beet production was a primary crop, second to cotton, and the large round tubers were processed at a sugar mill operated by Spreckels Sugar Company, which has long since closed.

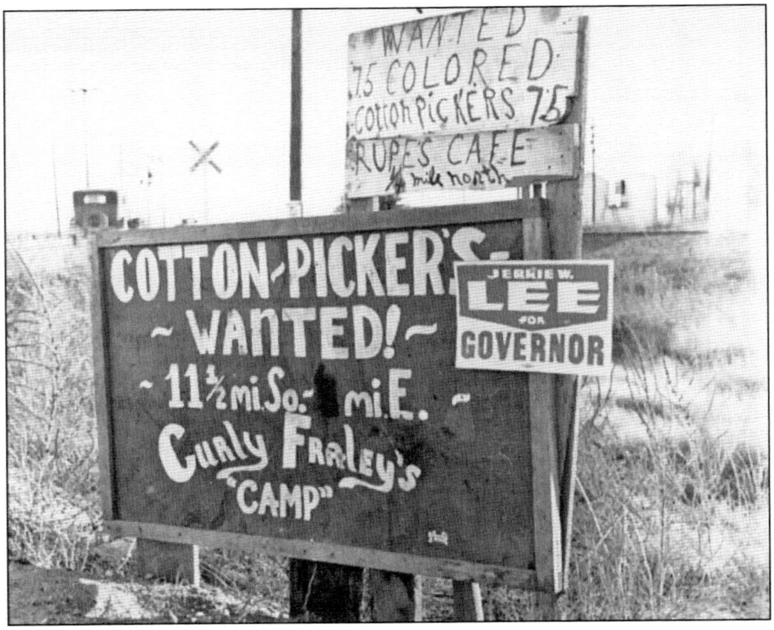

A sign south of Coolidge near Eloy beckons cotton pickers during harvest season. The hand-painted sign on top instructs African American pickers to sign up at Rupe's Café for 75 open slots at an area farm. Some farmers believed black pickers to be the best and fastest cotton pickers for the money. (National Archives.)

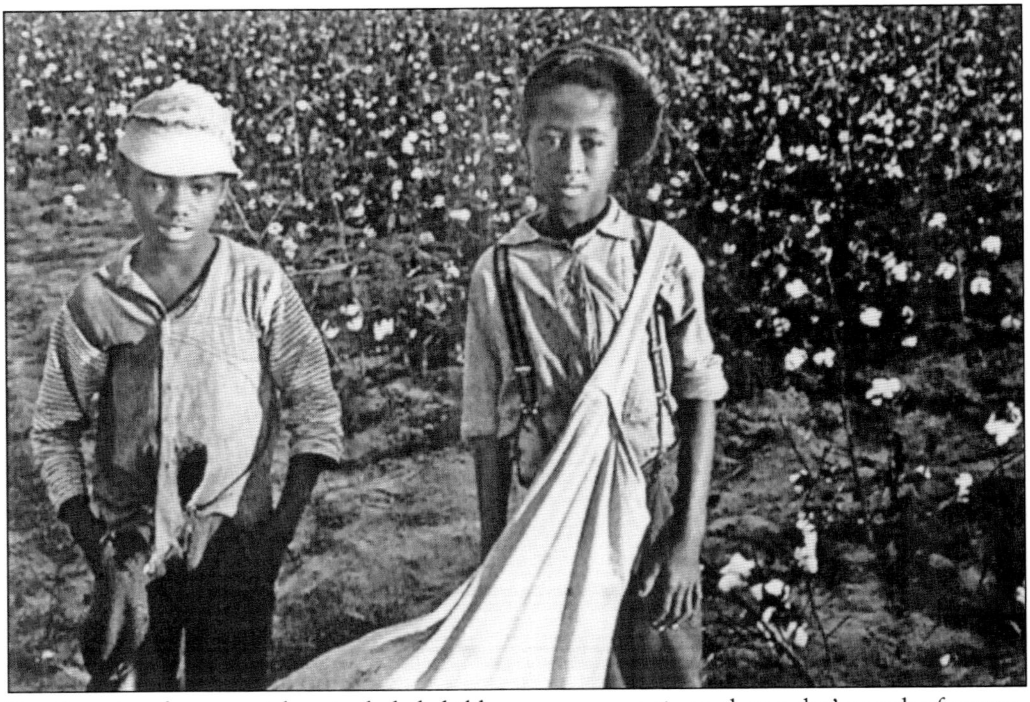

Family units of cotton pickers included children as young as six to chop a day's worth of cotton. The long canvas sacks were dragged down the furrows while the lint was quickly torn from each boll. A full bag could weigh upwards of 100 pounds. The sacks were dragged to a field scale hanging under a tripod just before the contents were dumped into a large screened-in wagon. (MCG/CGHS.)

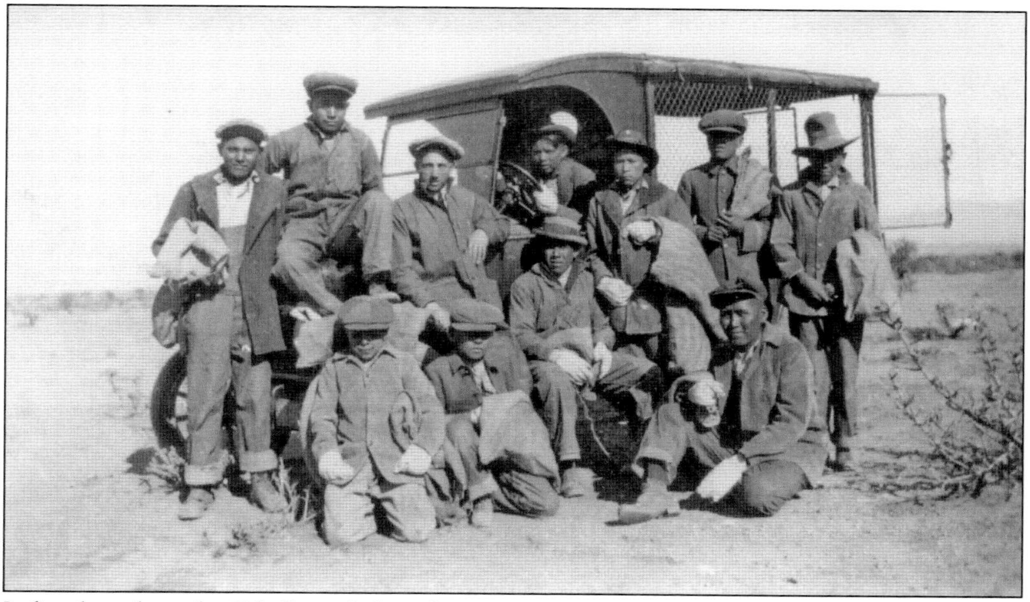

Indian boys from the Gila River Indian Community are pictured here dressed for cotton picking. Cotton sacks and gloves were mandatory gear, and the sharp spines of the cotton boll could slice fingers if gloves were not worn. The pickers were paid on Saturdays, when many of them would head to Coolidge to do their weekly shopping and seek out entertainment. (CHM.)

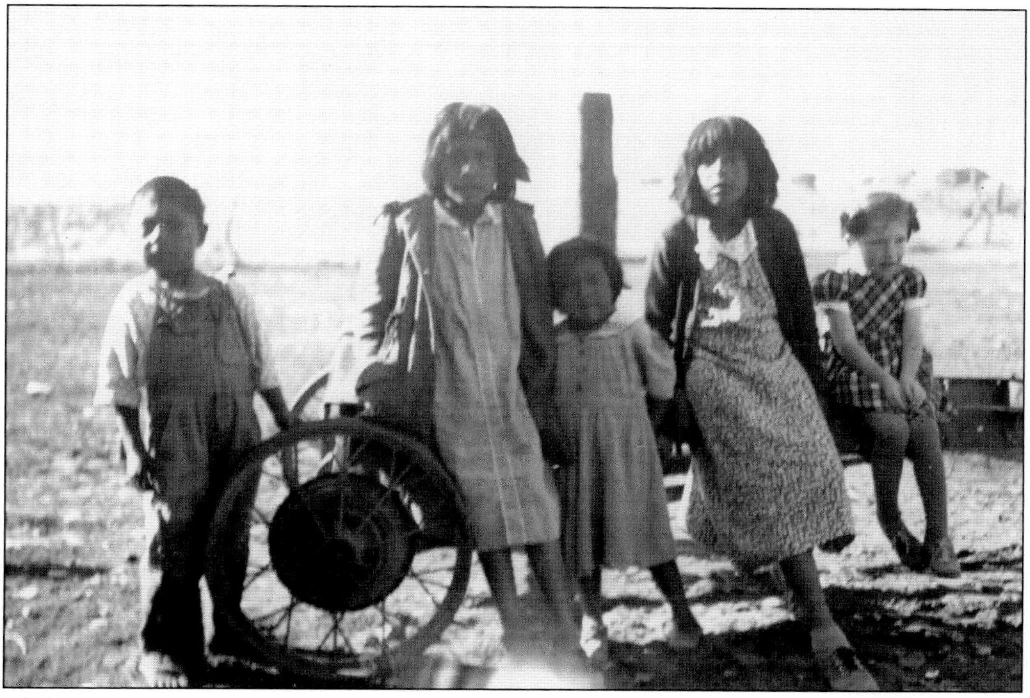

Children of Native American cotton pickers in La Palma, a few miles south of Coolidge, pose for a photograph sometime in the 1940s. The parents of these children most likely lived near Sacaton on the Gila River Indian Reservation adjacent to Coolidge to the north. (CHM.)

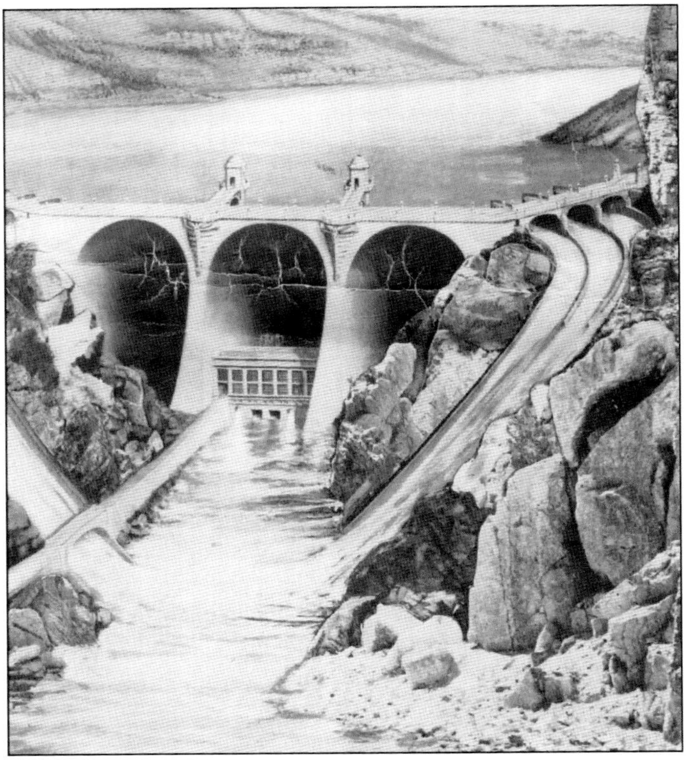

This artist's rendition of the future Coolidge Dam was sketched and published in May 1928 in the special Coolidge Dam edition of the *Florence Blade-Tribune* and the *Casa Grande Dispatch and Bulletin*. The prospect of harnessing the Gila River would bring hope to cotton farmers in the central valley region. (CHM.)

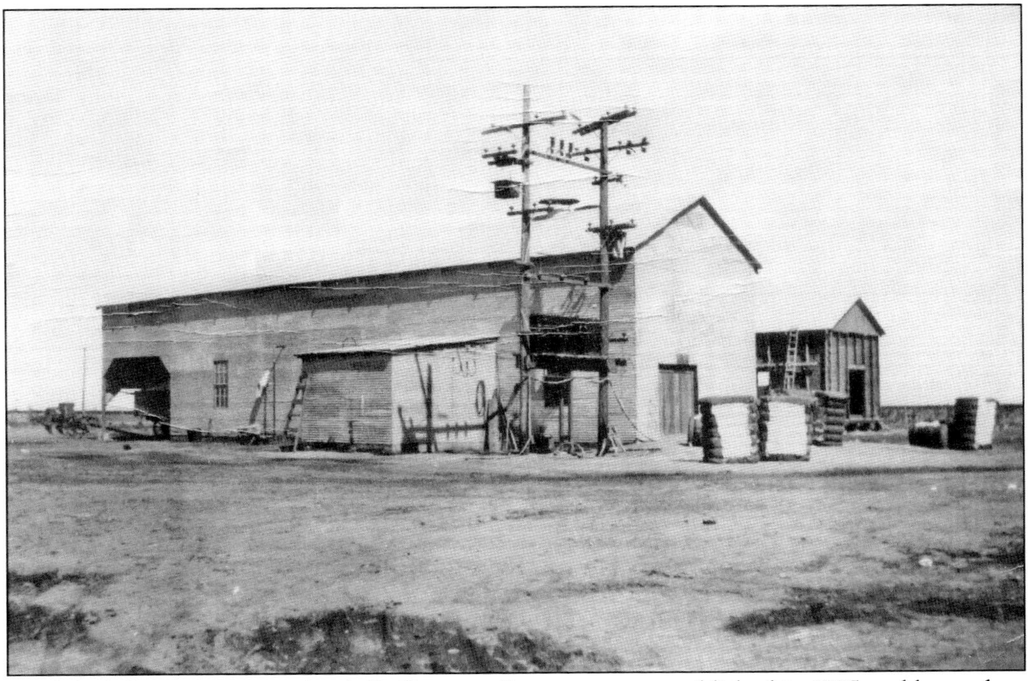

Coolidge's first cotton gin, the A.C. Ginning Company, was established in 1925 and located on Coolidge Avenue near the Southern Pacific Railroad tracks. Baled cotton can be seen in the photograph. Electrical power, which arrived in this part of Pinal County in 1923, was vital to operating the ginning machines. (CHM.)

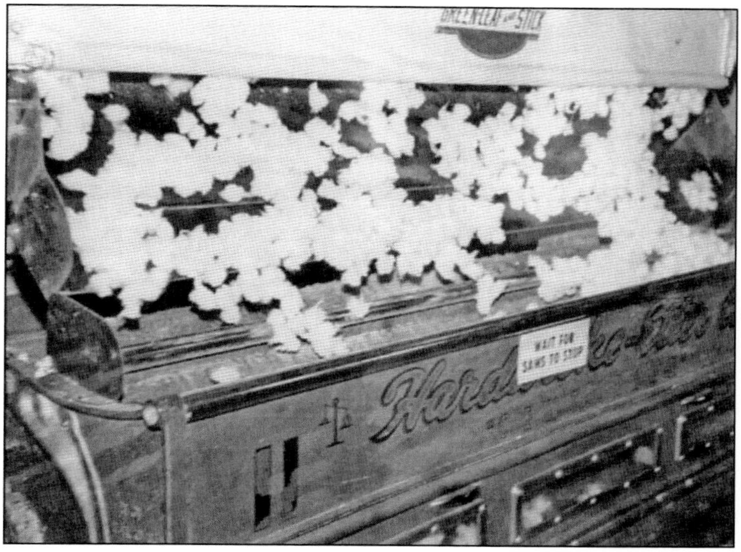

The ginning machine used a series of saw blades to separate and process the lint from the cotton seeds. Seeds would be processed into animal feed and oil. Other than the seeds and lint, any twigs and leaves were not to be placed inside the cotton sacks by the hand pickers. When the sacks were weighed in the field and any debris was observed, the picker's pay would be docked. (CHM.)

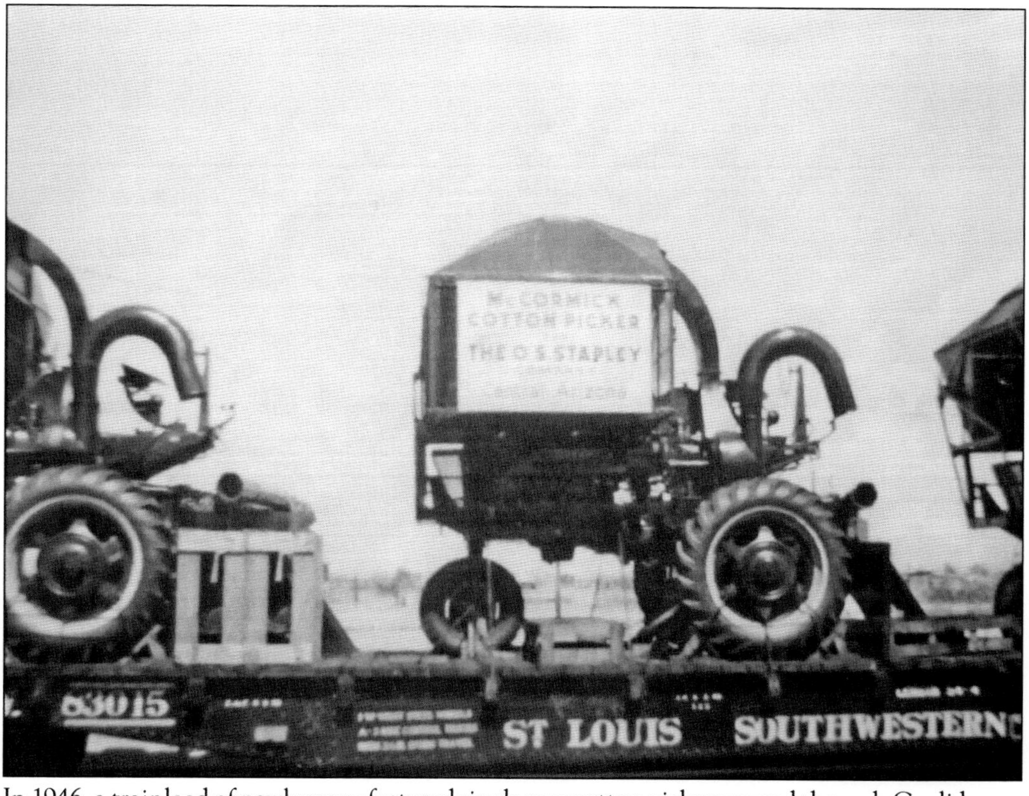

In 1946, a trainload of newly manufactured single-row cotton pickers passed through Coolidge on its way to Phoenix. The sign on this cotton picker reads, "McCormick Cotton Picker for the O.S. Stapley Company, Central Arizona." Stapley's was a hardware store located on Central Avenue in Coolidge across from Cohen's department store. (CHM.)

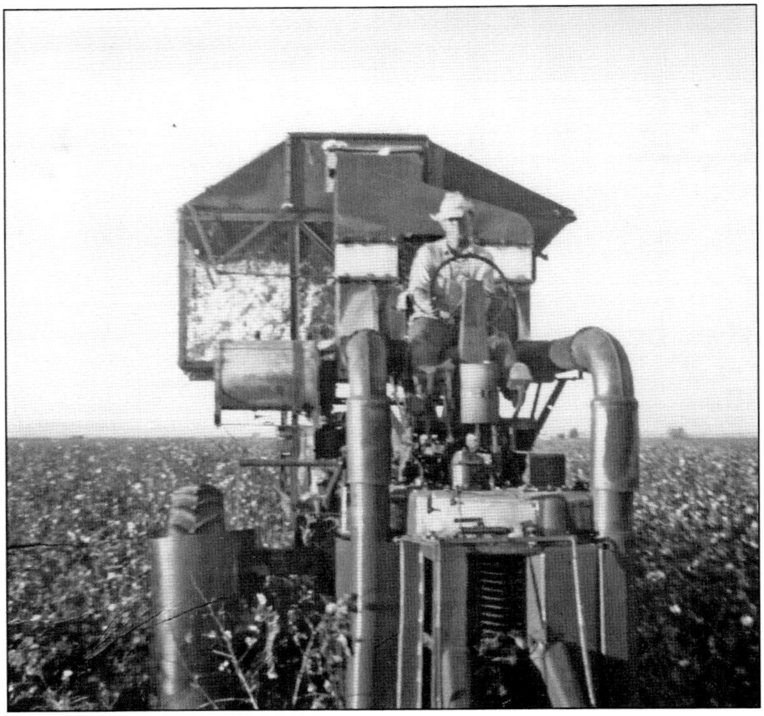

The single-row cotton picker manufactured by International Harvester was a boon to Pinal County cotton growers but sounded the death knell for local and migrant cotton pickers who either remained to search for other employment, moved on to other types of migrant work, or headed back to the community of their roots. Many African American migrants settled in nearby Randolph. (CHM.)

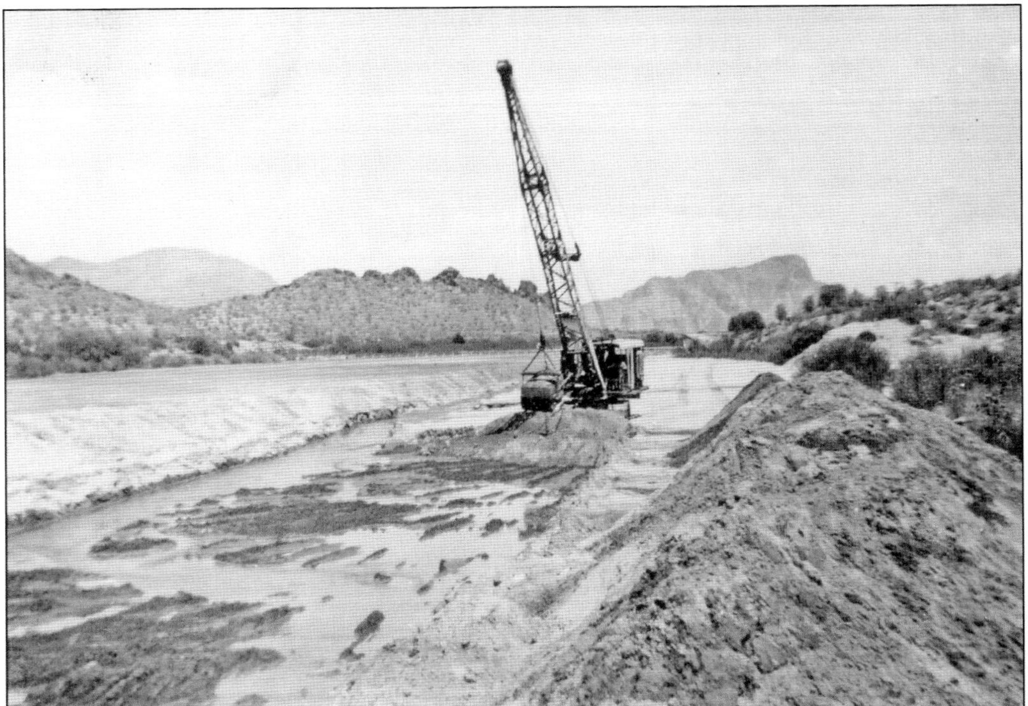

Large dredging machines were used to construct the San Carlos Irrigation Canal north of Coolidge on the Gila River Indian Reservation. Dianna Herrera, a longtime resident of the Indian community, remembers her father working on this canal and the construction of the Olberg Bridge across the Gila River nearby. (Dianna Herrera.)

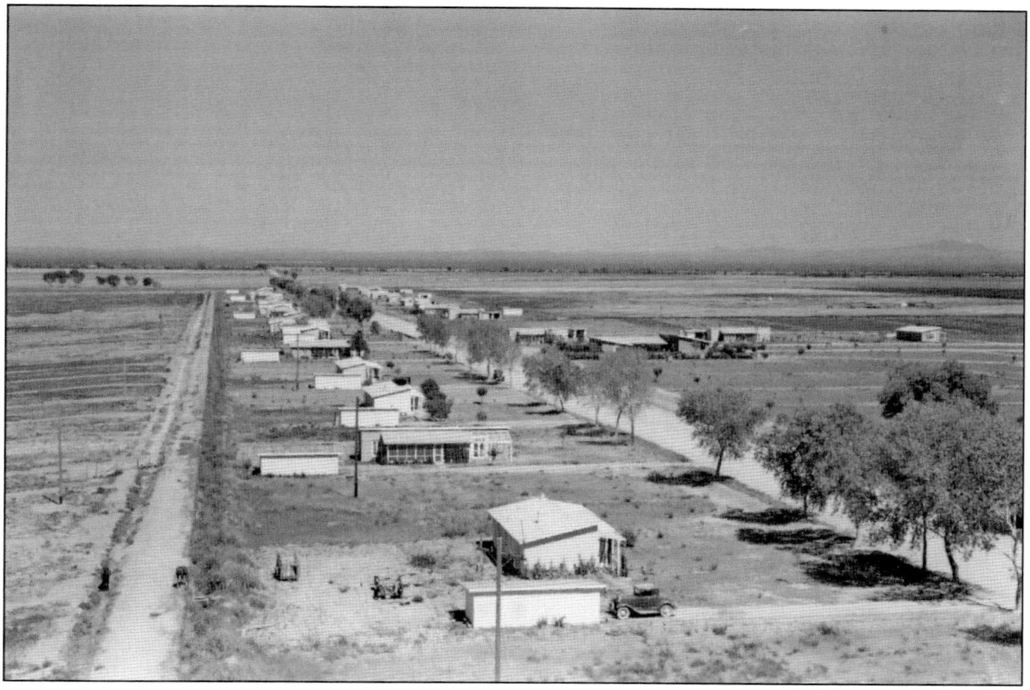

Casa Grande Valley Farms was one of the nation's first experiments in a self-contained communal agricultural farm a few miles east of Coolidge during the Great Depression. This aerial photograph looking east was taken by Russell Lee of the federal Farm Security Administration (FSA) in April 1940. The Anglo American community shared in the products of their labors and purchased their household goods at a government store located within the community. Valley Farms exists today as an unincorporated area for private property owners. (LOC.)

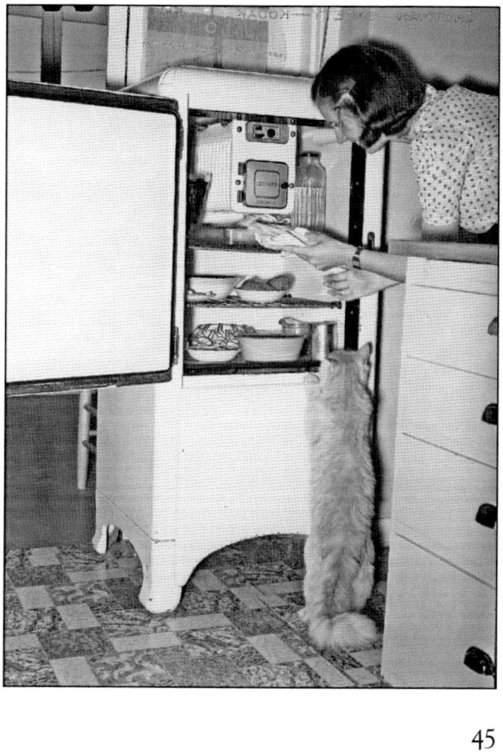

Each of the government-built homes at Casa Grande Valley Farms was fully furnished with a kitchen, appliances, and indoor plumbing. A farmer's wife selects food for the evening meal while the family cat peeks into the refrigerator for a tidbit. A community grocery and dry goods store was located in the community. Each month, a government paymaster gave each head of household a check for their work on the farm. (LOC.)

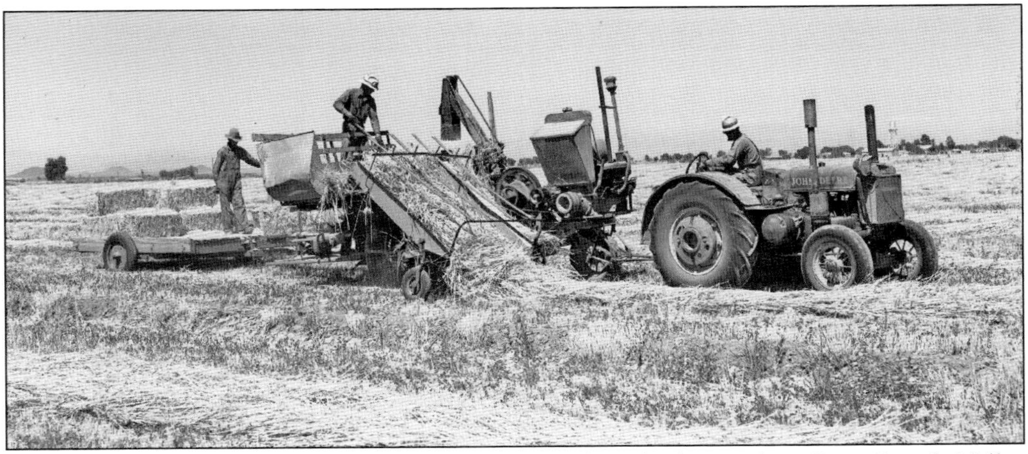

A chopping and picking machine gathers hay for feeding the livestock at Casa Grande Valley Farms. As a social experiment, the community was successful in providing a healthy environment for the entire family. Children were taught on-site in the government school, and Saturday night dances were held. Nevertheless, a few residents left the farm, one commenting that he did not like his chickens mixing in with everyone else's. Communal living was not for everyone. (LOC.)

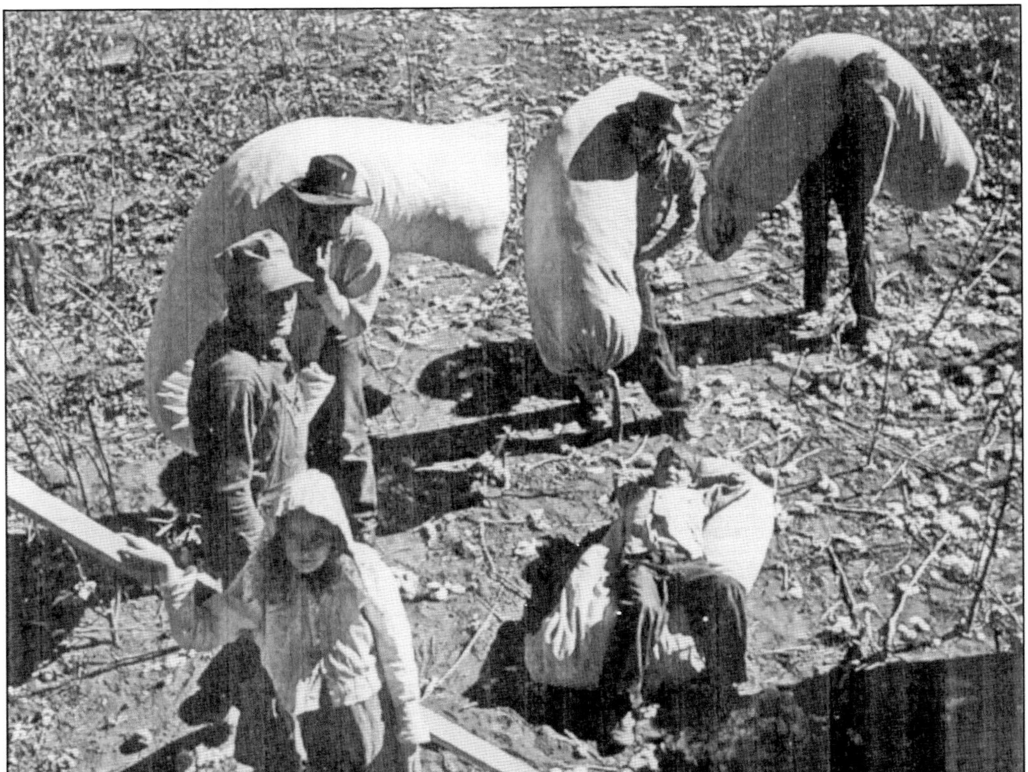

A family unit at Casa Grande Valley Farms picks cotton from their assigned fields. Before taking it into Coolidge for ginning, they weighed the cotton sacks on a tripod scale and then dumped the sacks into a wood-slatted wagon. It was a hard day's work before the introduction of the single- and multi-row cotton-picking machines that arrived after the Casa Grande Valley Farms experiment ended shortly after World War II. (National Archives.)

Five

Business Takes Hold

When the Homestead Act of 1862 was passed, it was not long after that the first Anglo attempted small-scale irrigation along the Gila River. In 1864, Amie W. White of Adamsville, a few miles east of present-day Coolidge, began digging ditches and diverting water from the river.

Later, in 1886, Dr. James Hurley, Thomas Davis, and George Brown began constructing 50 miles of canal to direct water to the Kenilworth district, where Davis and Judge Richard Sloan had converted a 1,700-acre ranch into a farm named after the Kenilworth Castle in England. The canal then continued past the Casa Grande Ruins area and on to Sacaton, north of the future townsite of Coolidge.

A first attempt to settle in what would become the town of Coolidge predates Richard J. Jones's establishment of the townsite by some 25 years. In 1899, Dr. Hurley and his wife, Ida, of San Bernardino, California, secured land claims amounting to some 480 acres north of the present town of Coolidge. The Hurleys had 320 acres of that claim cleared the following year for the purpose of farming, but a severe drought in 1893 put a stop to their plans, and they abandoned the project.

Other early settlers to the Coolidge area included Capt. J.D. Keating, Oliver H. Carpenter, and Len and Will Graham, all of whom patented land claims in and around the future townsite.

But, it was due to the foresight of Phoenix businessman Richard J. Jones and his wife, Alma, that engendered the inspiration to plat 80 acres into a future town that became known as the fastest-growing community in Arizona during the 1930s and 1940s.

The Wilbur Wuertz family was growing cotton before Coolidge Dam was built. Back in 1929, his father had 160 acres of land in South Dakota, and his grandparents had 100 acres near Coolidge but had retired to California. They offered to swap the land, and the move to Pinal County took place when his father started working at a cotton gin at Borree Corner west of Coolidge. A group of local farmers and the city attorney of Casa Grande had petitioned the state legislature to form an electoral district back in 1923 that allowed the sale of bonds to fund power lines into this part of Pinal County. It was that electrical power that ran the pumps to bring the water up to the fields for growing cotton.

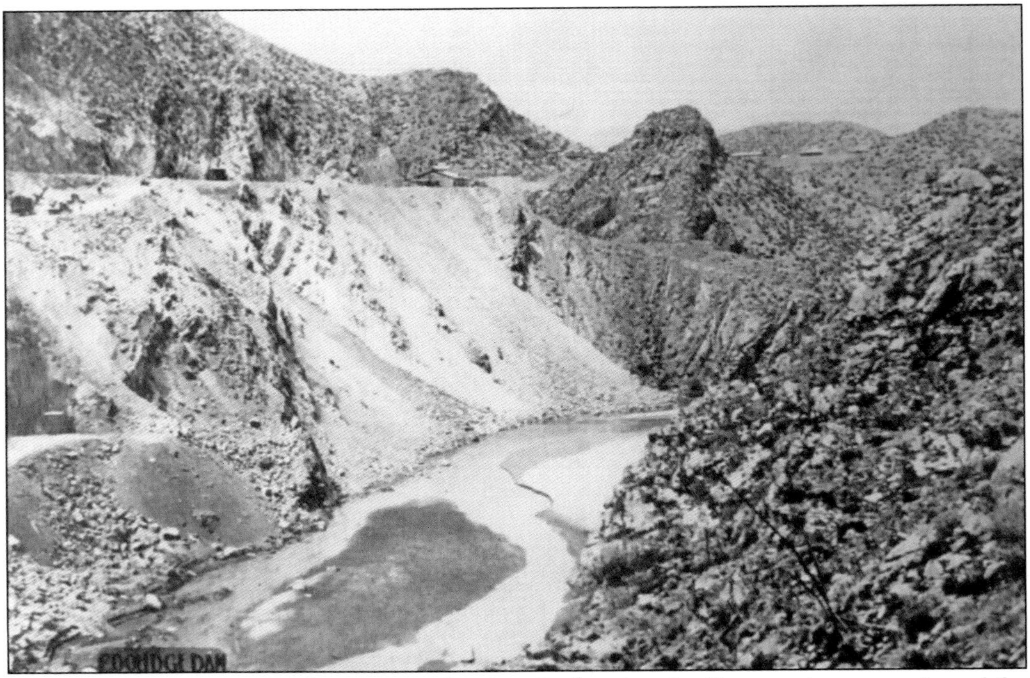

This spot on the upper Gila River in the San Carlos Apache Reservation was selected for construction of the Coolidge Dam around the time that the future townsite of Coolidge was platted by Richard J. Jones. By 1930, water below the dam was diverted to irrigation canals supplying 100,000 acres of desert with life-sustaining water from the newly named San Carlos Lake. (CHM.)

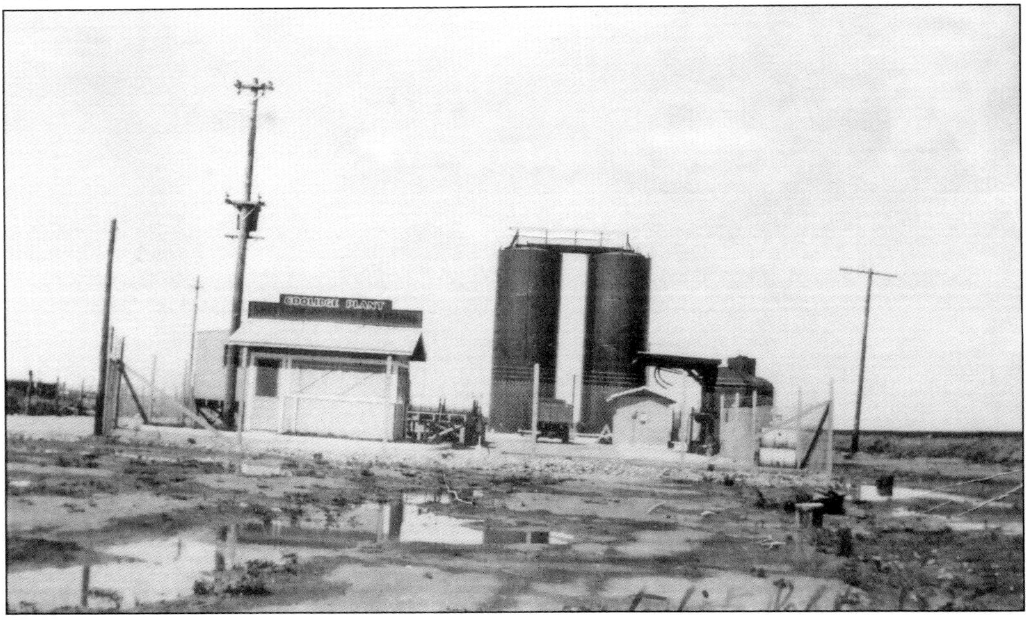

In March 1926, Shell, the first oil company in Coolidge, opened a plant on East Central Avenue adjacent to the Southern Pacific Railroad line. The Coolidge Service Station operated by Carl E. Douglas on the corner of Main Street and Coolidge Avenue pumped Shell gasoline and sold oil products to a growing population of car owners. (CHM.)

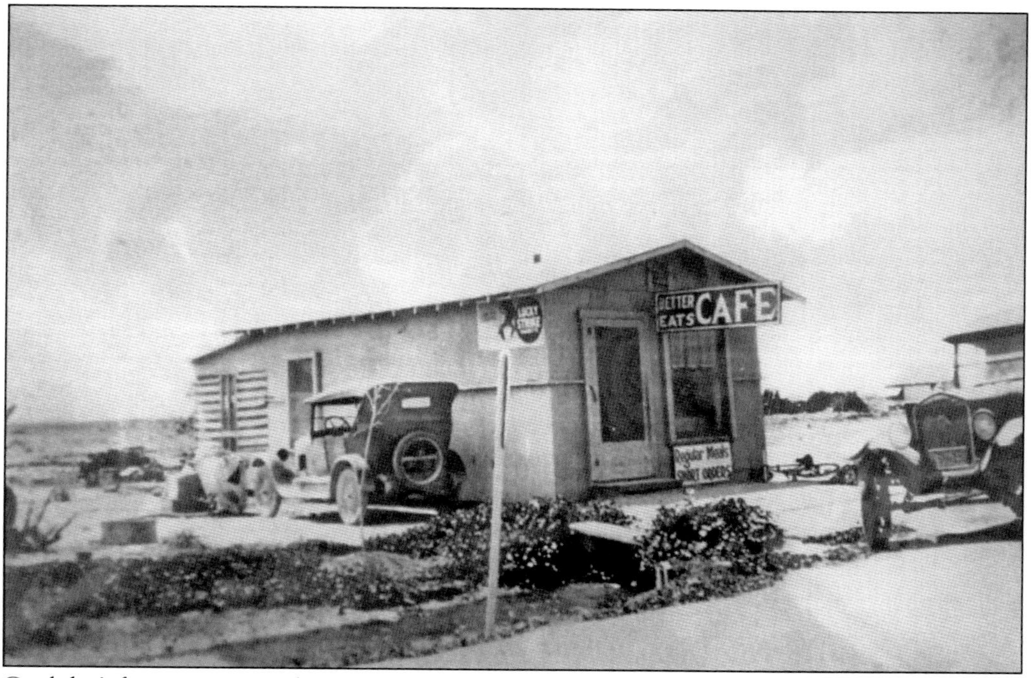

Coolidge's first restaurant, the Better Eats Café, opened in 1927 and was run by Ella Greenleaf. It was on the south side of Coolidge Avenue close to the railroad tracks and across the street from the A.C. Ginning Company. (CHM.)

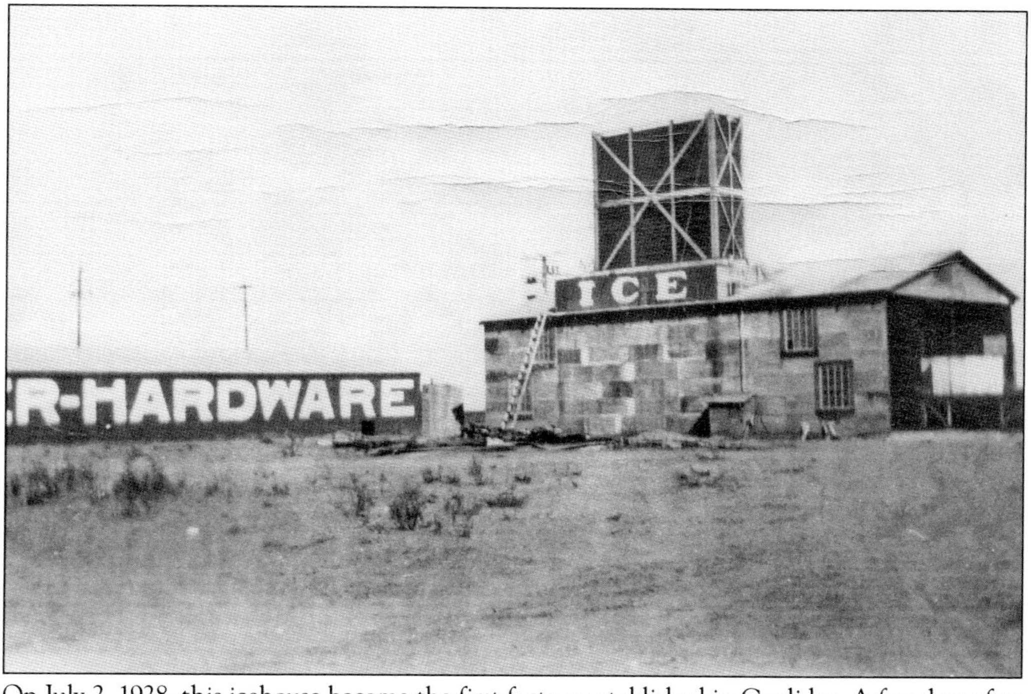

On July 2, 1928, this icehouse became the first factory established in Coolidge. A few days after opening, the owners gave a watermelon feed to 300 townsfolk, in effect, the entire population of the town. In February the following year, the facility, which was built by Richard J. Jones and Dr. W. Jackson, was sold to the Arizona Edison Company. (CHM.)

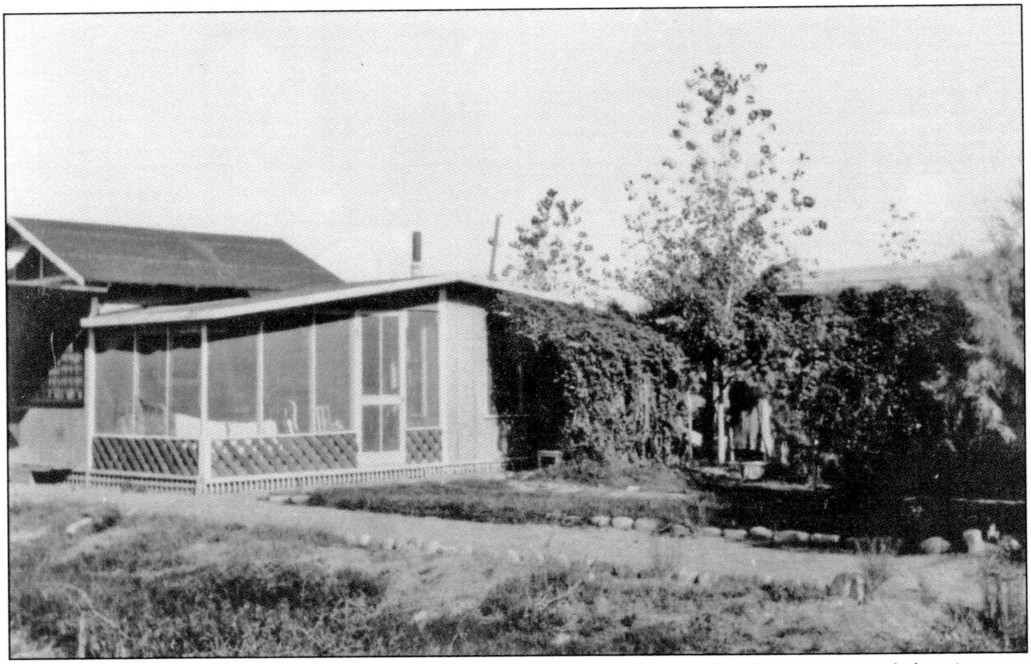

Dora Nutt became the first postmistress in 1926 and operated out of her home at Coolidge Avenue and Main Street. The first mail was sent out on August 20, 1926, to Alma Jones in Phoenix. The Nutt family lived in a house that had postal boxes mounted outside under an awning, pictured here on the far left. (CHM.)

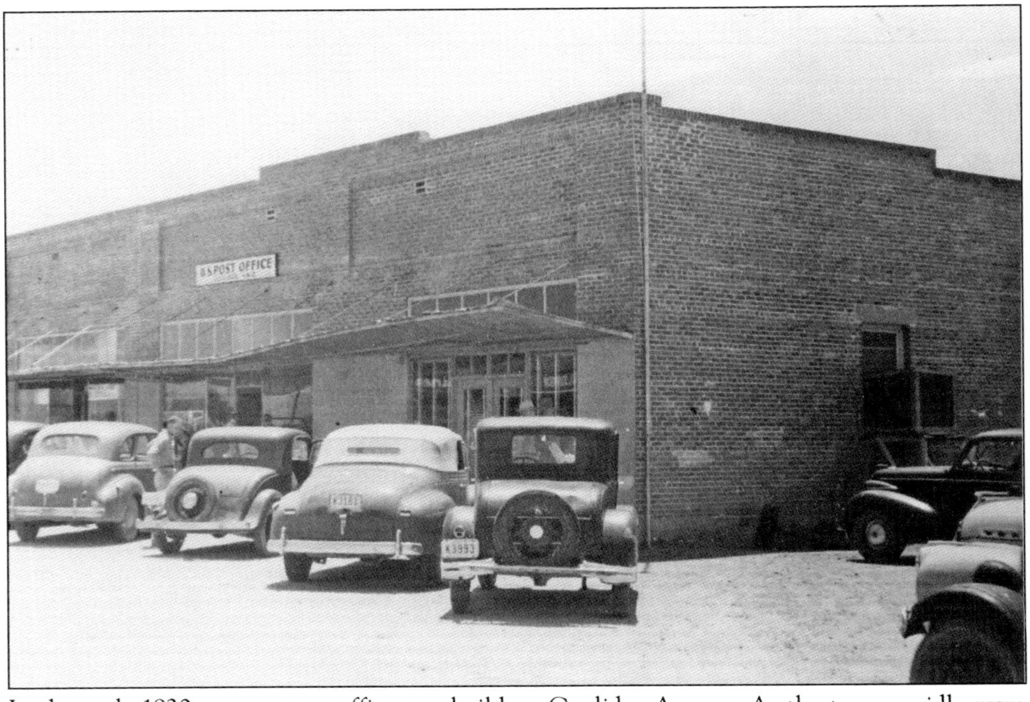

In the early 1930s, a new post office was build on Coolidge Avenue. As the town rapidly grew, the Nutts' outdoor postal facility required more spacious quarters. Coolidge Avenue and Main Street was becoming a hub of commercial activity. (CHM.)

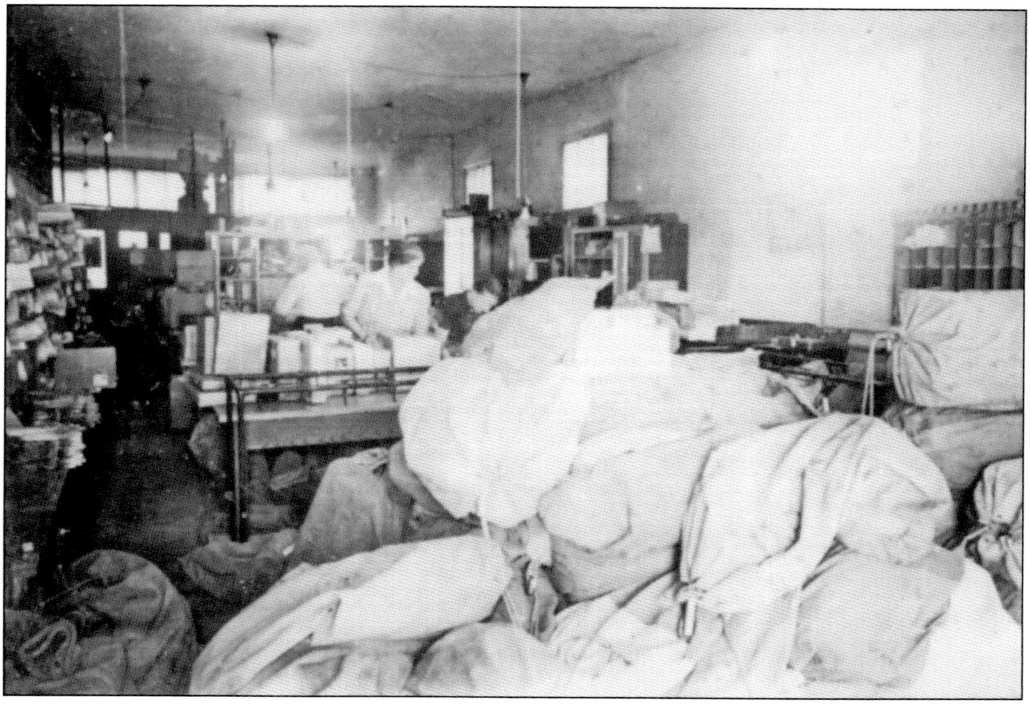

Mailbags stack up in the main sorting room of the Coolidge Post Office in the 1930s. (CCC.)

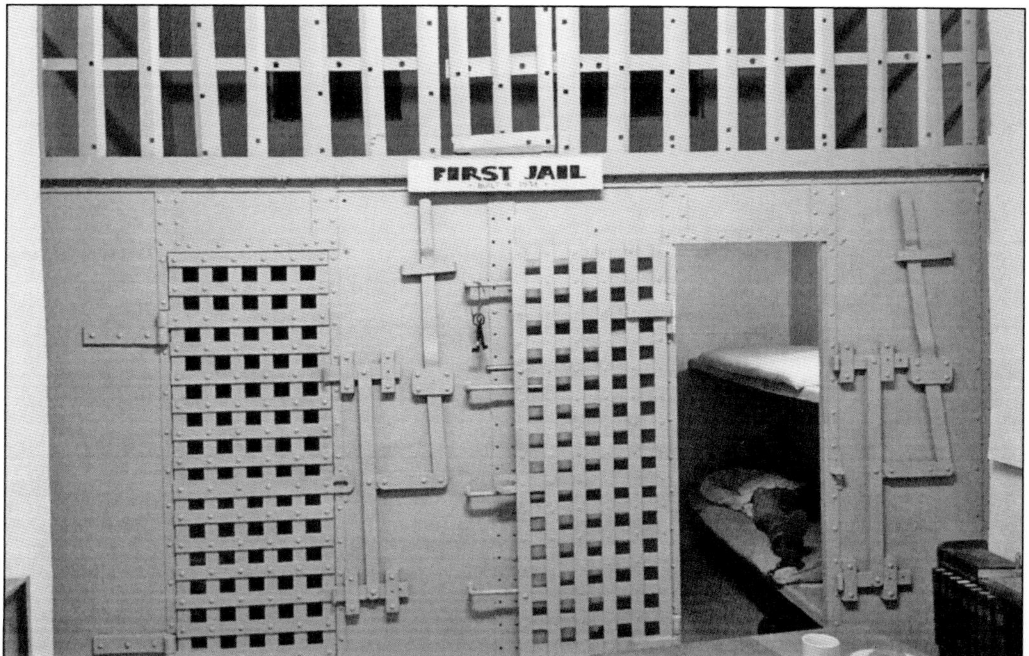

When the city of Coolidge began to grow in population, Sheriff Asa "Ace" Gardner needed a real jail to house prisoners. In 1935, the city fathers built the first courthouse and jail, thus relieving Gardner of having to house prisoners in a railroad boxcar. The first presiding justice of the peace was W.A. Thompson, and meals were provided to the inmates from town restaurants and certain charitable ladies of the community. (CHM.)

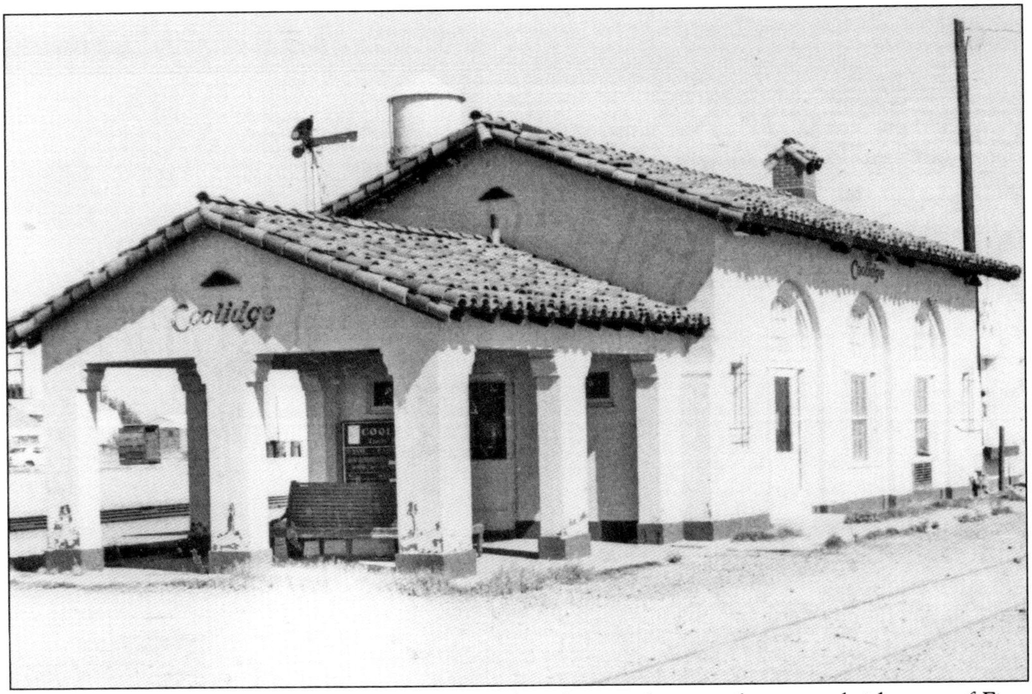

On February 1, 1931, the Southern Pacific Railroad opened a new depot trackside east of First Street, with M.L. Durham serving as ticket agent. Prior to the construction of the unique structure, the railway used a boxcar as the makeshift station. Years later, many Coolidge residents were upset when the historic station was demolished. (CCC.)

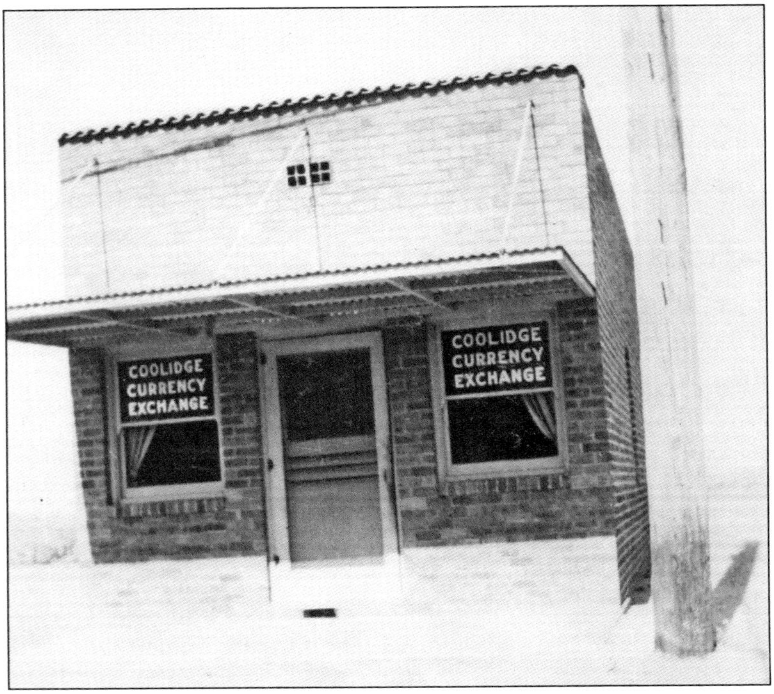

When the only local bank, Arizona Southwest Bank, closed following the Bank Panic of 1930–1933, a delegation from Coolidge visited the Valley Bank, a Phoenix-based institution that heavily invested in agriculture. They agreed to open a currency exchange that would not violate the federal ban on new banks. The exchange opened on June 1, 1933, north of the Masonic temple on Main Street. (Bank of the West.)

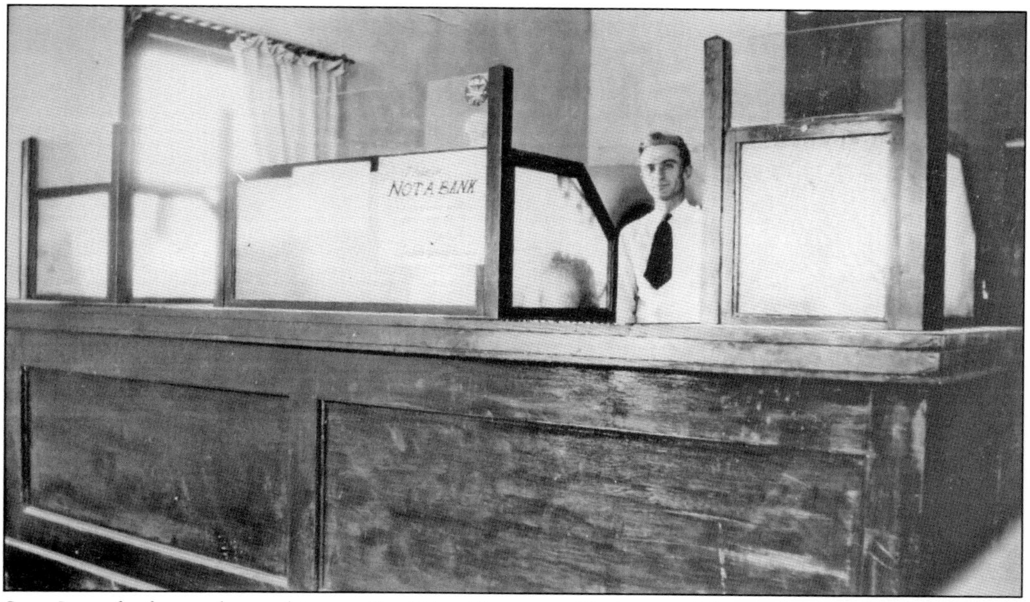

Sam Langford was the cashier at Coolidge Currency Exchange. To avoid violating federal law, the exchange held no deposits, made no loans, and assumed none of the responsibilities that made it a bank. Loan applications were forwarded to Phoenix and processed. In effect, it was a series of banking mailboxes receiving deposits for immediate deposit by mail to Valley Bank in Phoenix. (CCC.)

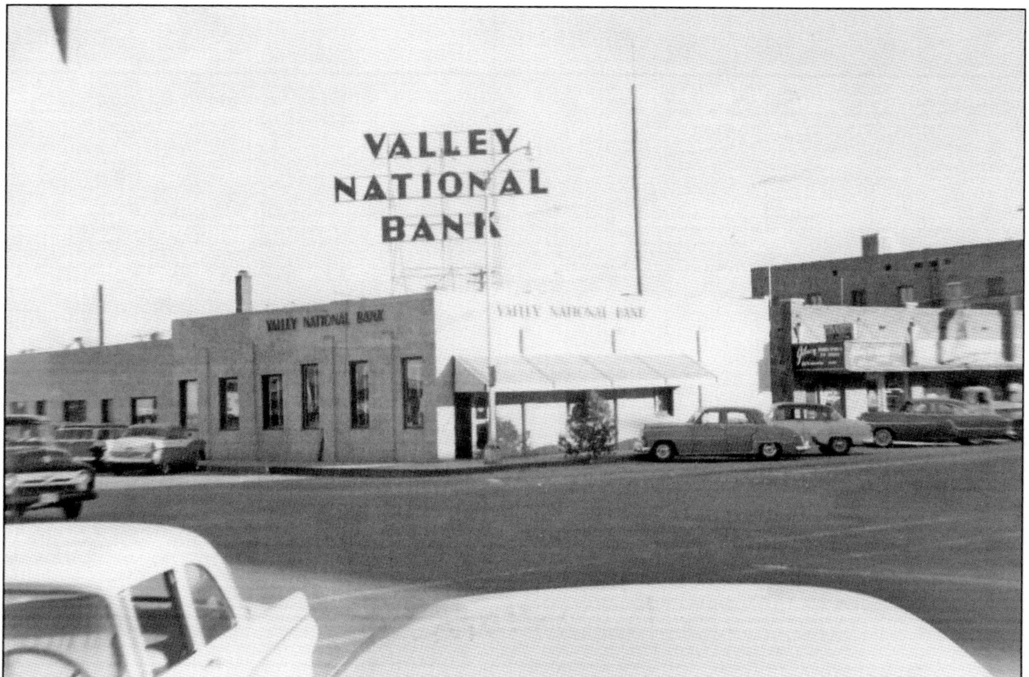

Once the currency exchange was no longer necessary, the facility became the Valley Bank and Trust Company. Once the federal Bank Act was amended and passed in 1933, Coolidge had an official bank on May 28, 1934. The bank continued to grow and was renamed the Valley National Bank, located on the corner of Main Street and Central Avenue. (Bank of the West.)

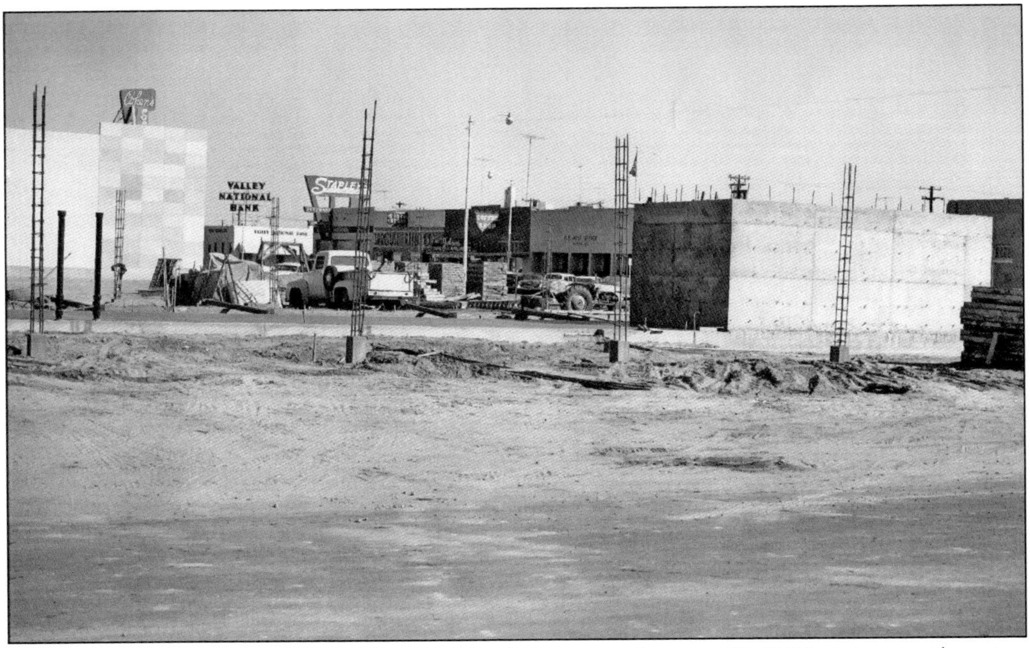

Construction of the new Valley National Bank began on January 17, 1959, at its new location on the northeast corner of Central Avenue and Third Street. The functioning Valley National Bank at 141 North Main Street can be seen in the distance, with Cohen's Popular Department Store on the far left. (Bank of the West.)

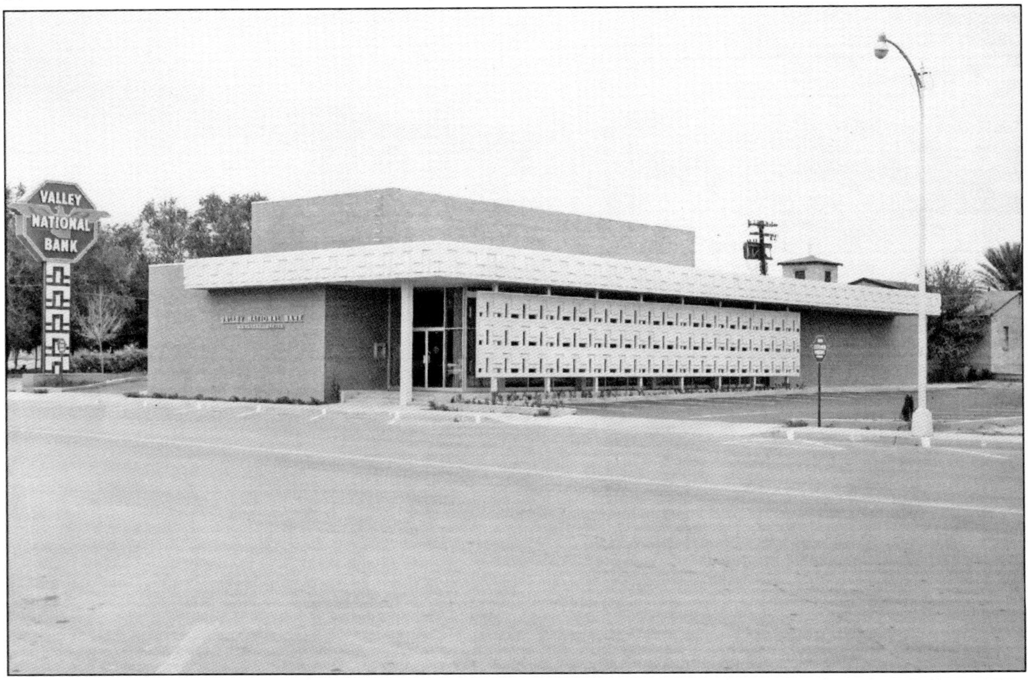

The just-completed Valley National Bank was designed in the architectural style of the 1950s known as Commercial Modernism. Except for the large sign on the left, the current Bank of the West has maintained the appearance of the structure. A tile mosaic mural adorns the north interior wall. (Bank of the West.)

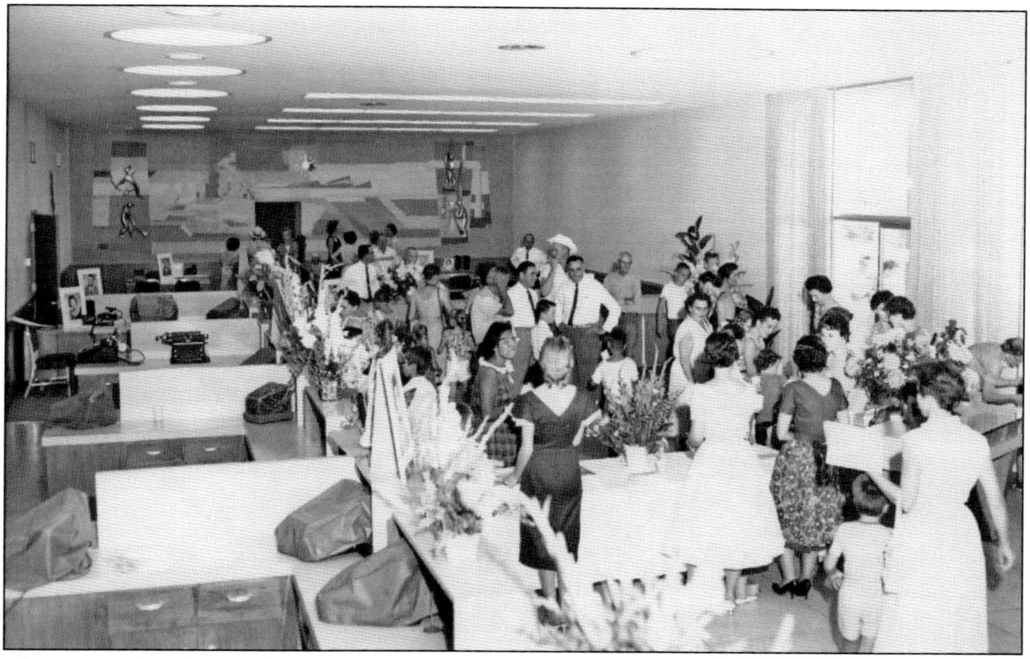

The new Valley National Bank was completed in July 1959 at 260 West Central Avenue. An open house for the bank's customers, city and business leaders, and the community at large was held on August 1, 1959. Today it is now a branch of Bank of the West. (Bank of the West.)

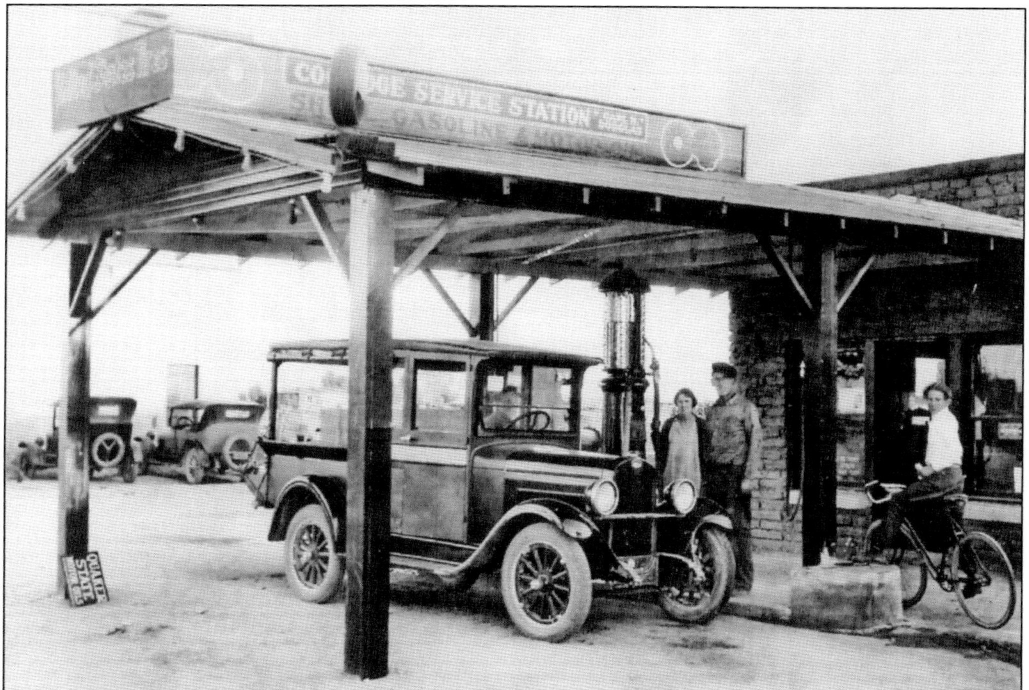

The Coolidge Service Station, owned by Carl H. Douglas, provided Shell Oil products to motorists at the corner of Main Street and Coolidge Avenue, beginning around 1928. Douglas lived in Florence and operated a service station there as well as one in Eloy and one in Casa Grande. (CHM.)

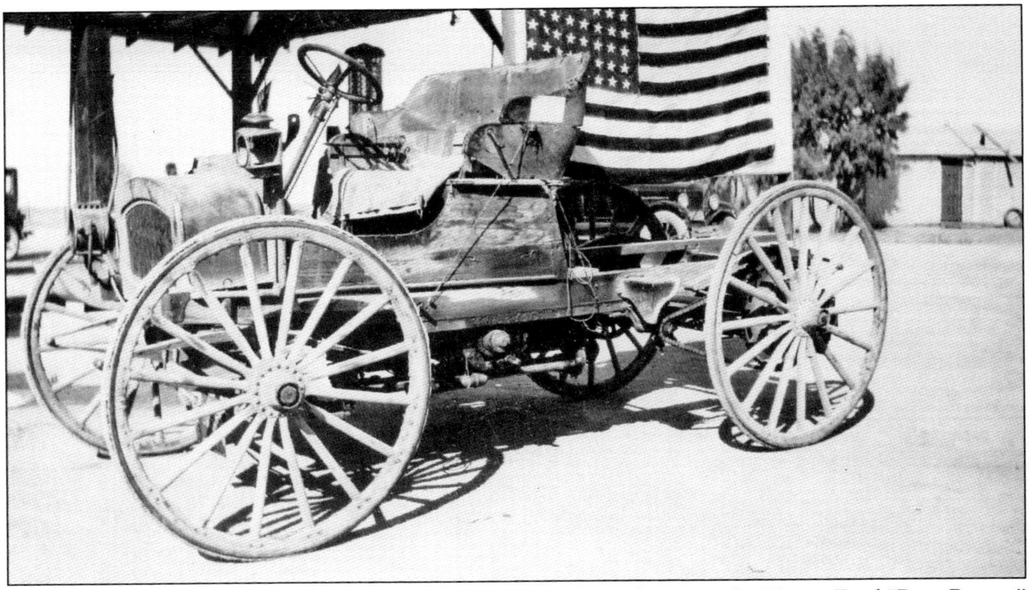

Carl H. Douglas, who owned the Coolidge Service Station, also owned a Henry Ford "Buzz Buggy," which he entered in the Pinal County Fair in 1928. The year before was the very first county fair, and it was held in Casa Grande. This year, the fair was held in Coolidge, and the Ford was an attraction for all in attendance. (CHM.)

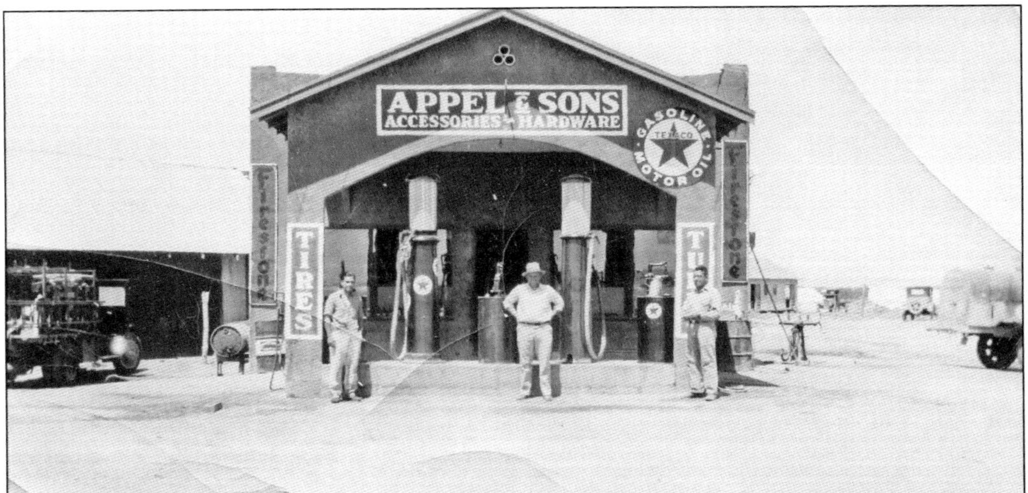

Service stations were cropping up all over Coolidge in the late 1920s as more and more people gave up their horse-drawn carriages for cars. Appel and Sons service station and garage was located a few miles west of town at Borree Corner on the extension of Coolidge Avenue. Also located at Borree Corner were a grocery store and a schoolhouse. (CHM.)

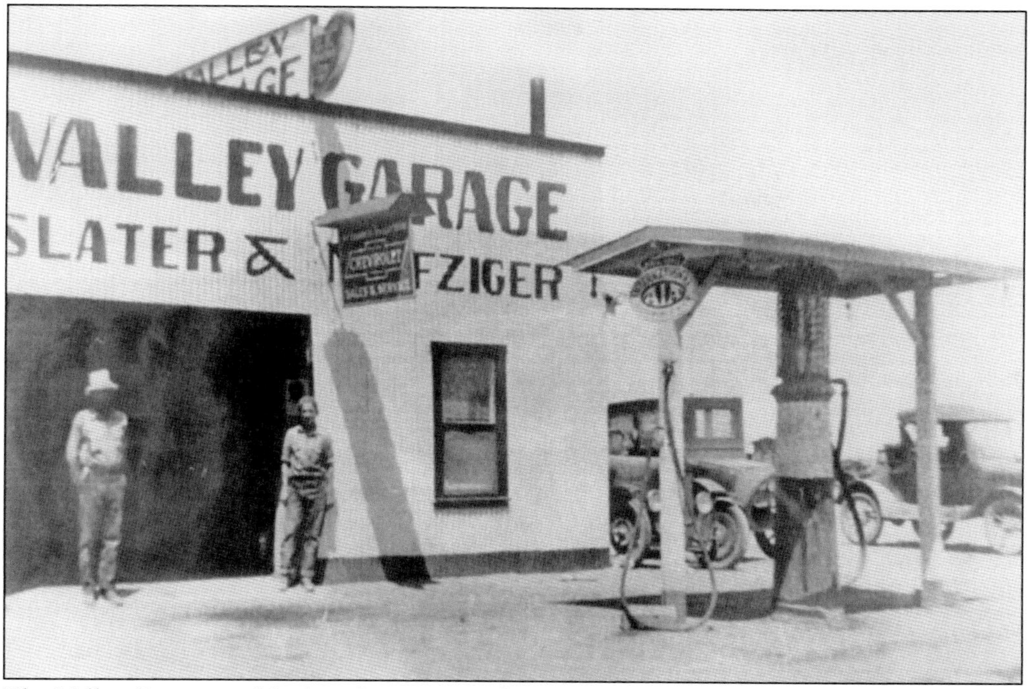

The Valley Garage on Harding Street opened in 1927 as Layman's Garage. Fred Slater was a co-owner of The Valley Garage, and most of the original building still stands today across the street from the Coolidge Historical Museum. (CHM.)

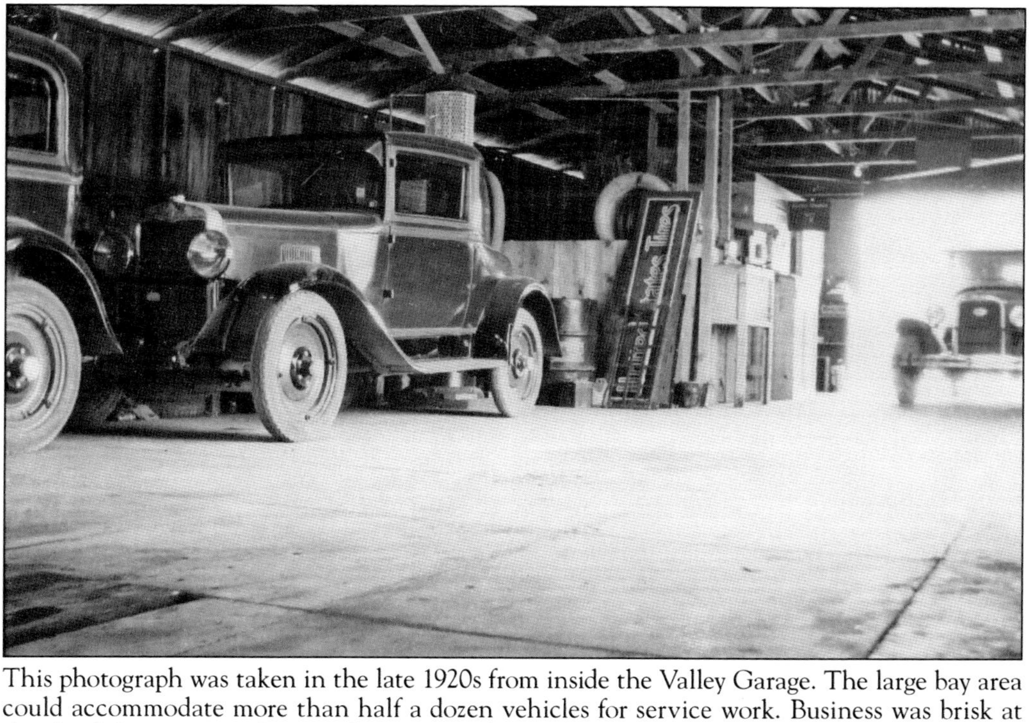

This photograph was taken in the late 1920s from inside the Valley Garage. The large bay area could accommodate more than half a dozen vehicles for service work. Business was brisk at the Coolidge garages when roads were just dirt and gravel. Cars and trucks needed constant maintenance on the county's rough roads. (CHM.)

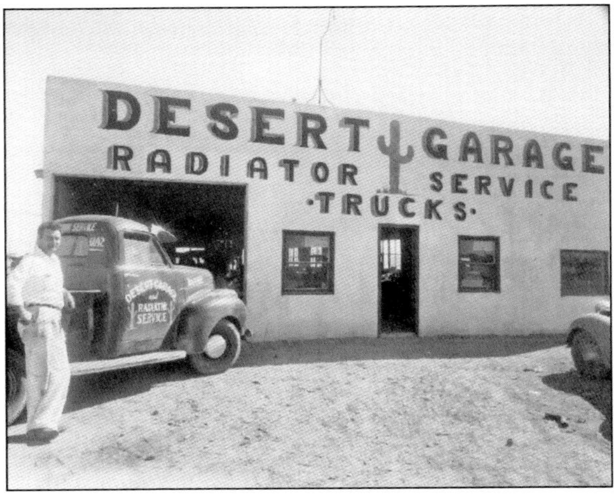

Elvin E. "Brownie" Brown moved to Coolidge in the early 1930s from Texas after serving in World War II and built Desert Garage Radiator Service in 1946. The building was located on the east side of Arizona Boulevard between Spruell and Taylor Avenues. In 1957, Ford Tractor rented the building, and later Coolidge Engine and Pump operated its business there. In the 1970s, it was a furniture store owned by Jim Rimmer, and then KB Bee's had a honey operation in the building. The place burned down in the late 1970s. (Jacque Hendrie-Henry.)

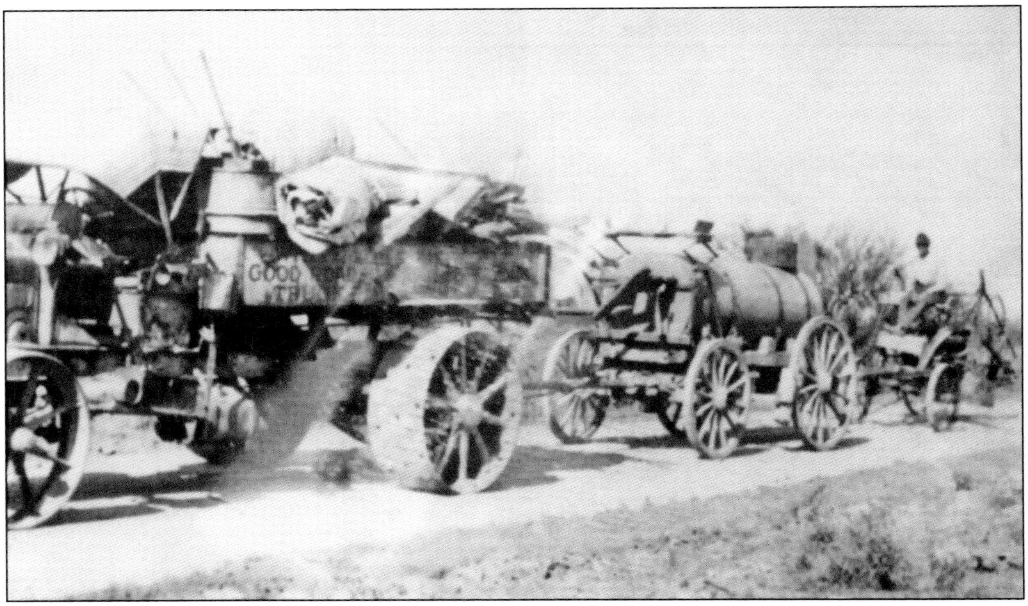

In 1916, the Pinal County Highway Department was moving its camp of road-building equipment, tents, and supplies along the Florence-Kelvin Highway east of Coolidge. Workmen lived on the road with their heavy equipment because the distance between communities was lengthy, and roadwork was slow and strenuous. The Florence-Kelvin Highway was the only route between the copper mine at Ray and the county seat. A 35-mile train ride was the only other means of transportation. (CCC.)

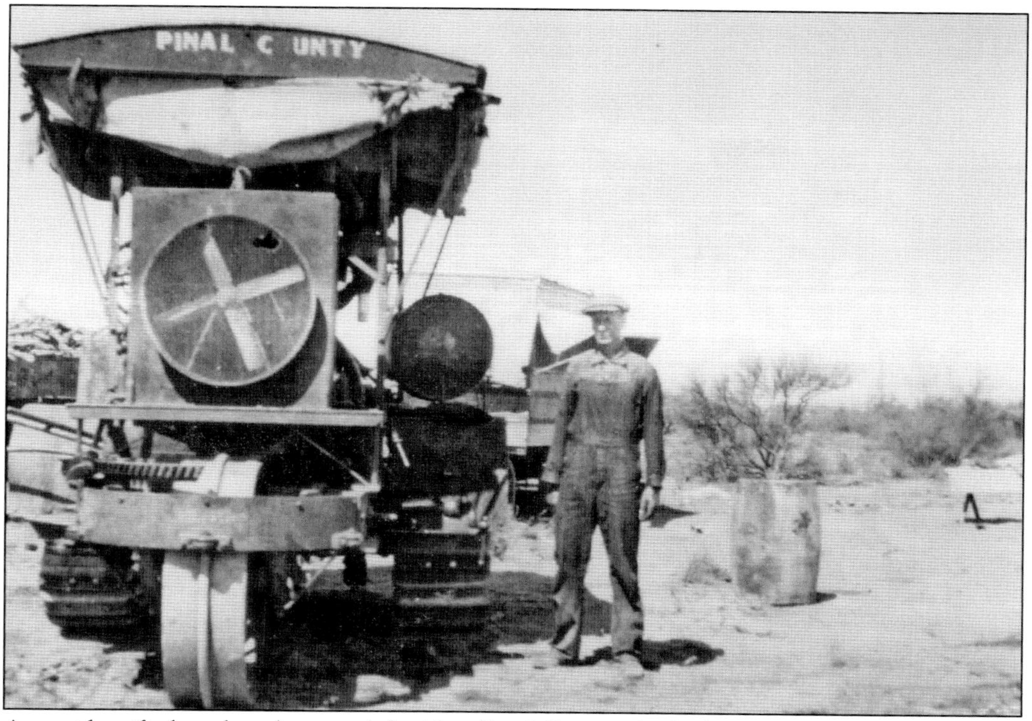

An unidentified road worker stands beside a Pinal County ditch cleaner sometime in the 1930s. Due to high winds and blowing dust, the ditches alongside the roads required constant maintenance and cleaning to remove excess dirt and tumbleweeds that accumulated. (CHM.)

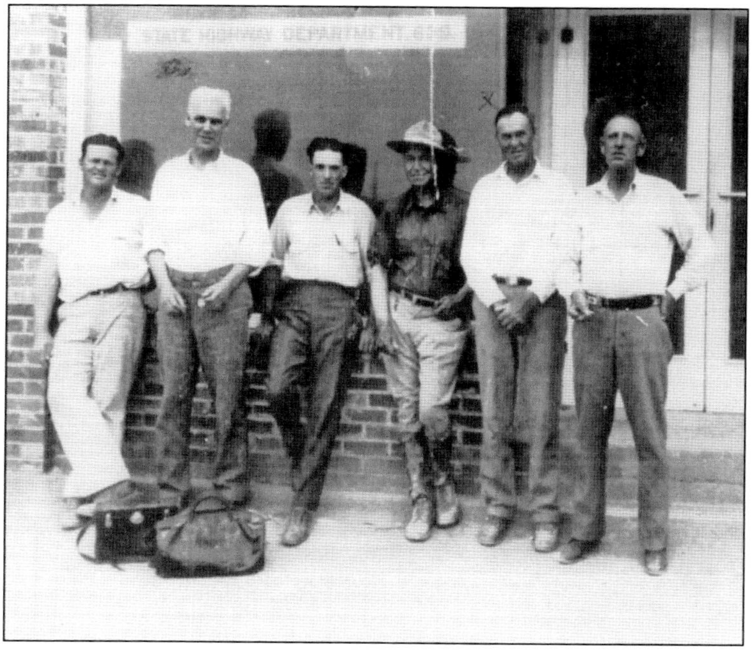

State highway department inspectors and supervisors were kept busy overseeing the building and maintaining of the thousands of miles of roadways in Arizona. Jacob Chesley arrived in Coolidge in 1928 (second from right) to work for the department that maintained an office in nearby Florence. The department was then moved to Coolidge in 1963. (CHM.)

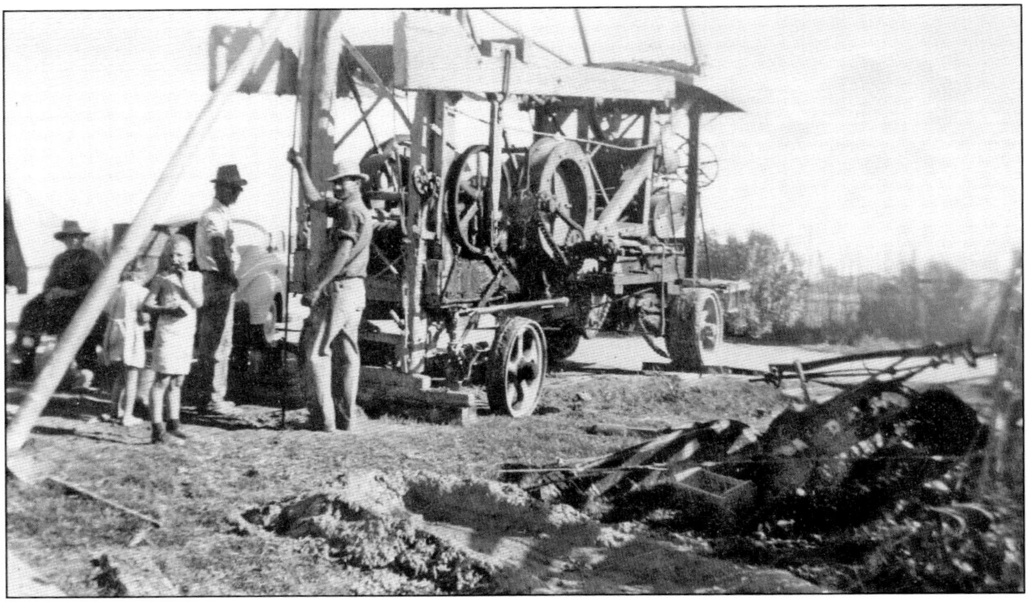

Chester Carter moved his family to Coolidge from Lawton, Oklahoma, in 1934. He set up a much-needed drilling business in Pinal County that he operated well into the 1950s. In Lawton, he operated a grocery store, but when the Great Depression hit and customer credits could not be called in, he packed up and moved to Arizona. From left to right are Chester's father Anthony, daughter Josephine, son Gene, assistant McKinley "Mud" Magnus, and Chester. (Gene D. Carter.)

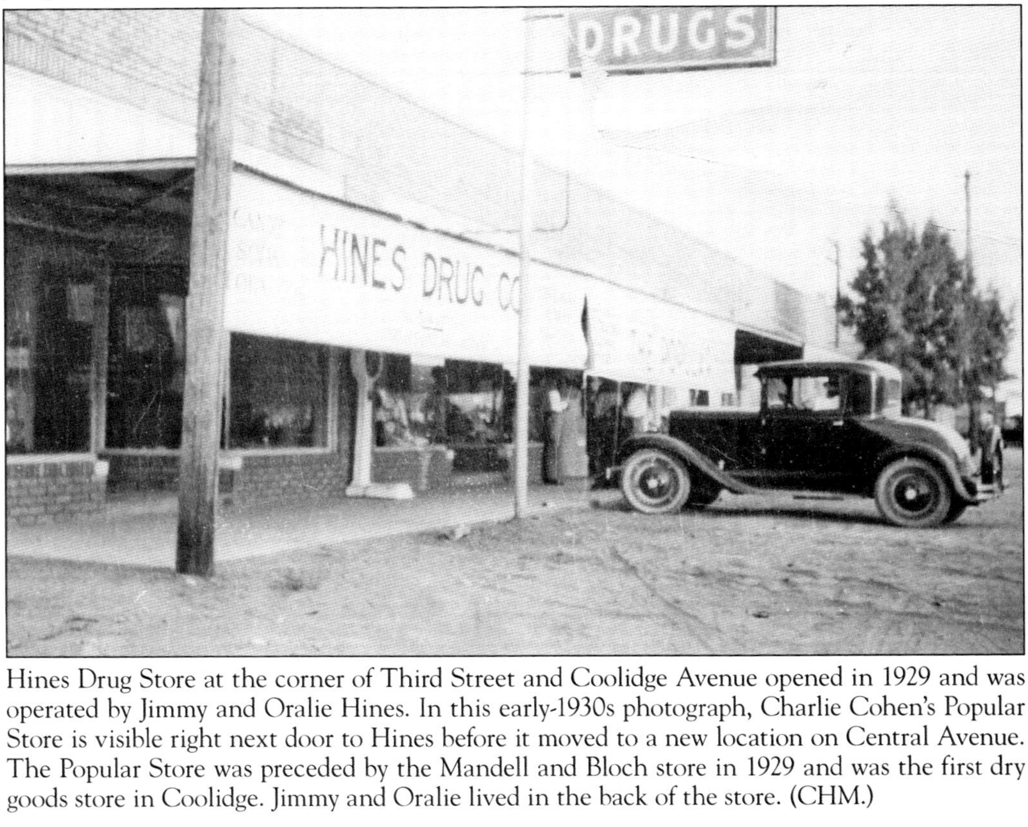

Hines Drug Store at the corner of Third Street and Coolidge Avenue opened in 1929 and was operated by Jimmy and Oralie Hines. In this early-1930s photograph, Charlie Cohen's Popular Store is visible right next door to Hines before it moved to a new location on Central Avenue. The Popular Store was preceded by the Mandell and Bloch store in 1929 and was the first dry goods store in Coolidge. Jimmy and Oralie lived in the back of the store. (CHM.)

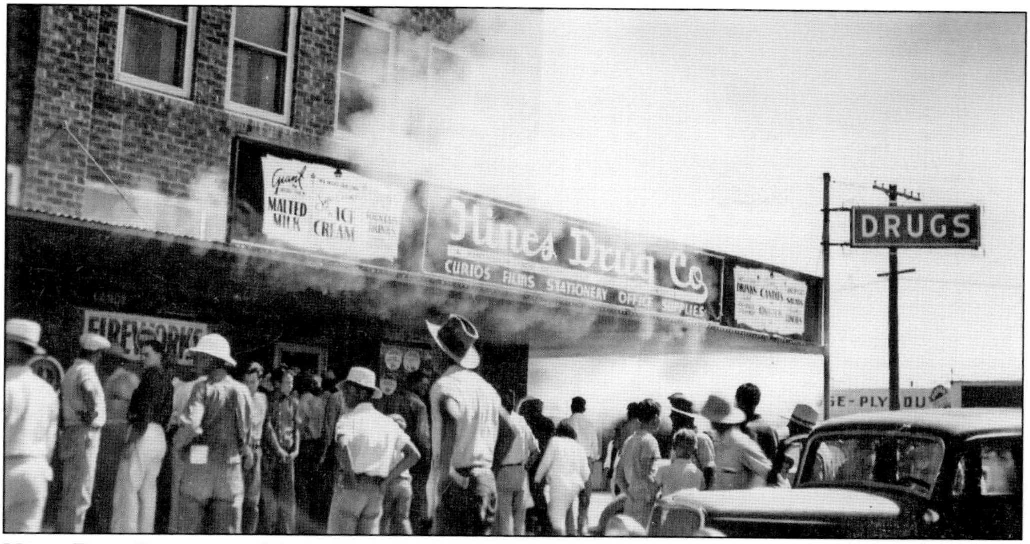

Hines Drug Store moved from the corner of Main Street and Coolidge Avenue to the northwest corner of Main Street and Central Avenue below the San Carlos Hotel. Sometime in the 1940s, a fire started in the drugstore, caused by either hot cigar ash dropped by the store porter or static electricity from a feather duster setting off fireworks. The building still stands today as the Open Hands Veterans Outreach Center thrift store. (CHM.)

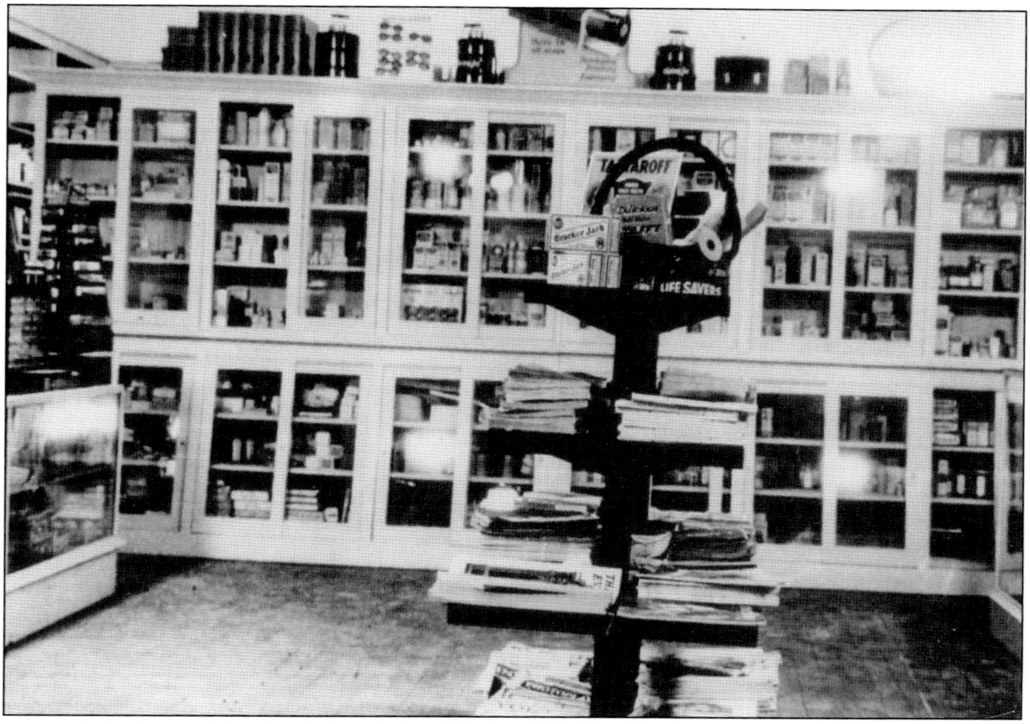

Hines Drug Store was a spacious facility that included a large lunch counter as well as a fully stocked pharmacy. Co-owner Oralie Hines studied for and passed the pharmaceutical exam and became a licensed pharmacist. She and her husband, Jimmy, both worked together in the store. Oralie remembers when Coolidge was the fastest-growing city in Arizona between 1930 and 1940, when the population increased to 3,200. (CHM.)

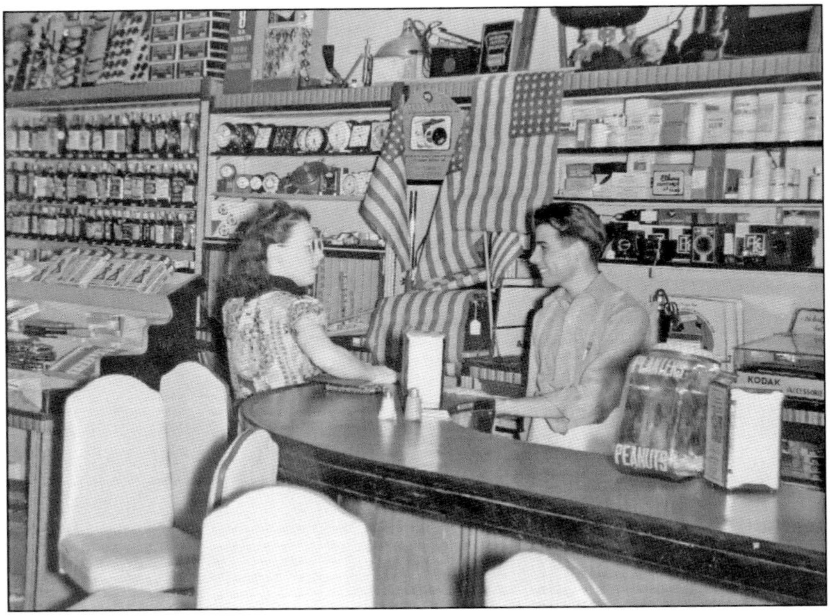

In the 1940s, the Hines soda fountain counter was a popular place for customers young and old to hang out. The store was well stocked with household and personal goods, drawing local shoppers and shoppers from nearby communities as well. (CHM.)

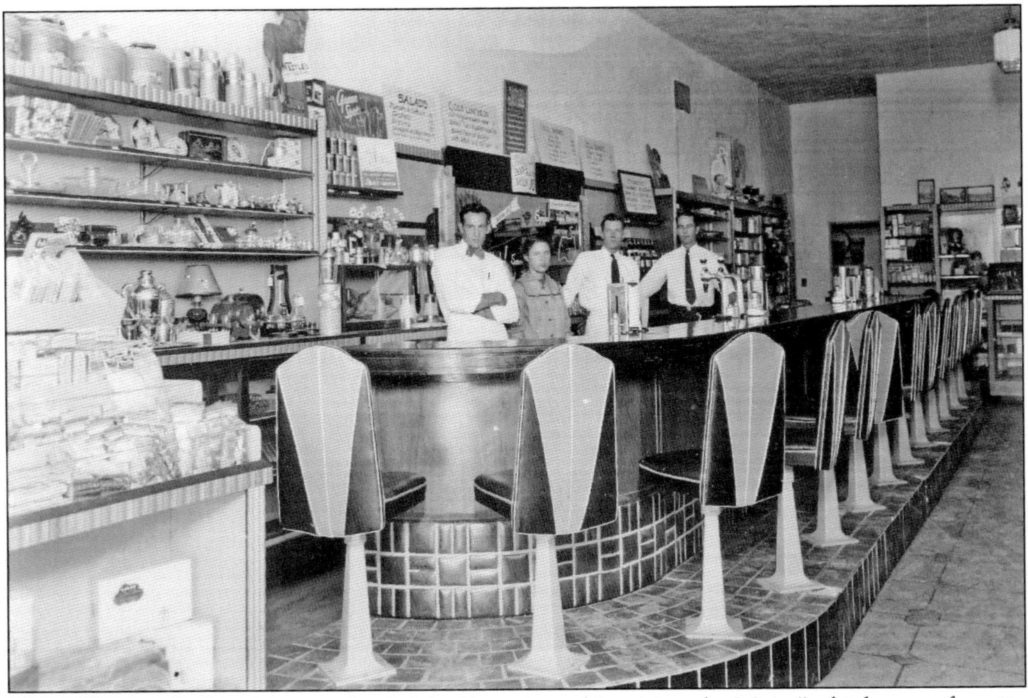

The 1950s was the beginnings of rock 'n' roll music and "cruising the Main," which was a favorite Saturday-night tradition among Coolidge youth when they drove the loop from Main Street, to Central Avenue, to Arizona Boulevard, to Coolidge Avenue and back. A favorite stop was the soda fountain counter at the Hines Drug Store on the corner of Central Avenue and Main Street. (CHM.)

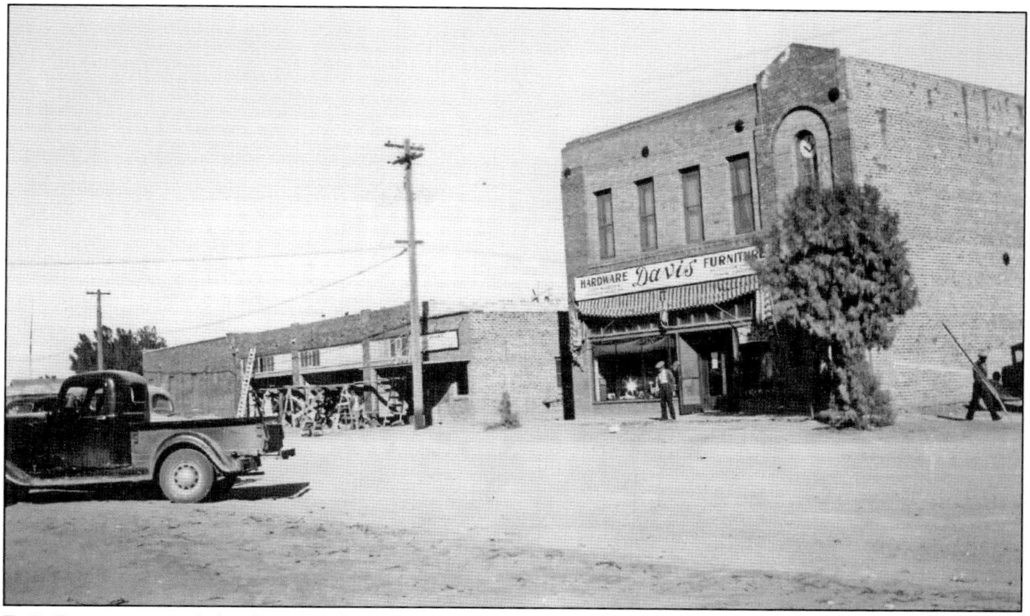

D.S. Davis opened the first hardware and furniture store in Coolidge in December 1928. In this photograph, the store is housed in the lower level of the Masonic lodge, erected in 1930. Lodge activities initially took place on the second floor. Richard J. Jones was installed as the first worshipful master. Alma Jones was installed as the first worthy matron of the Eastern Star in 1931. (Hansen Engineering and Surveying.)

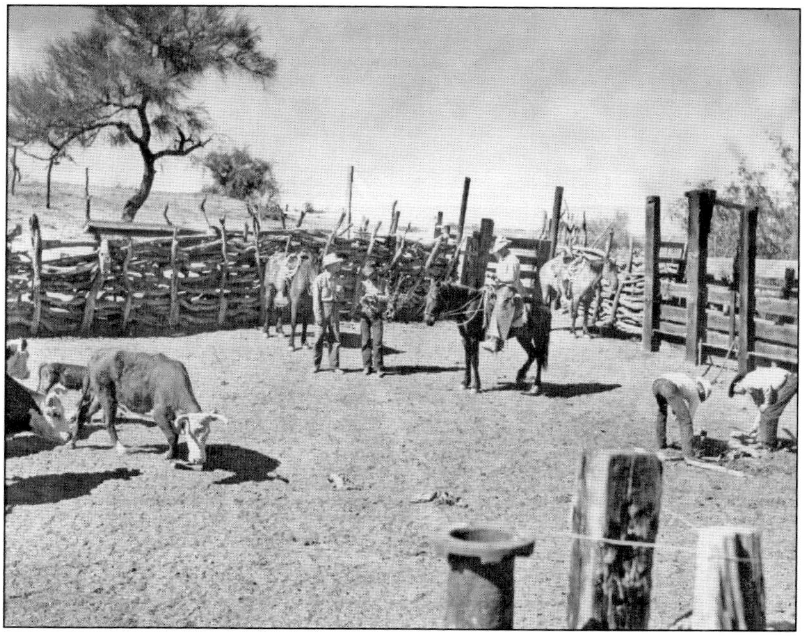

Cattle ranching was still a major industry around Coolidge in the 1930s, even as cotton was developing as a major crop. Ranch hands prepare a fire to heat the branding irons on a ranch, possibly the Balcomb Ranch, south of Coolidge. (CHM.)

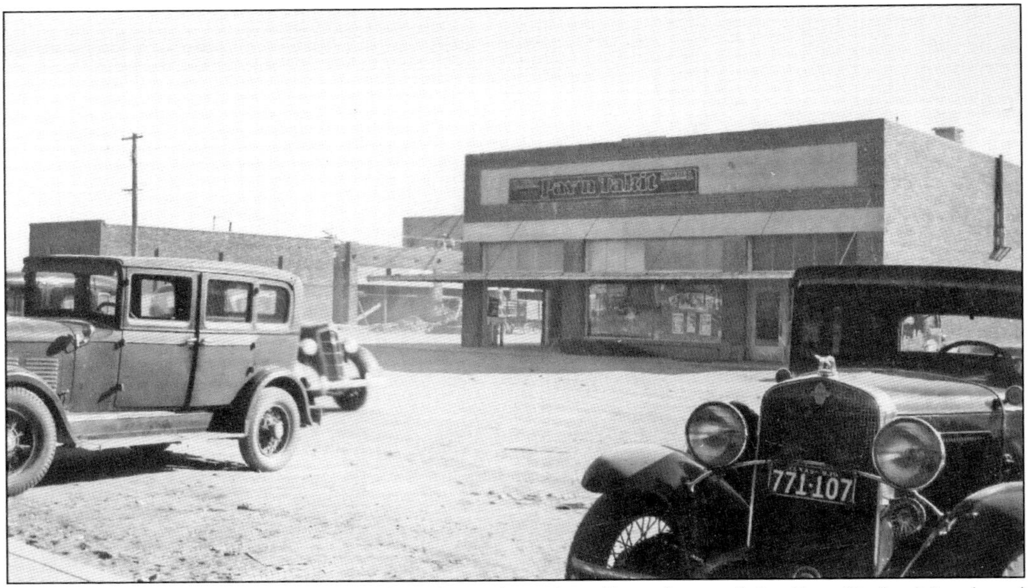

This early-1930s photograph was taken from the sidewalk in front of the San Carlos Hotel and looks toward the intersection of Central Avenue and Main Street. The Safeway Pay 'n' Takit grocery is on the corner and later became the location of Stapley's hardware store. (CHM.)

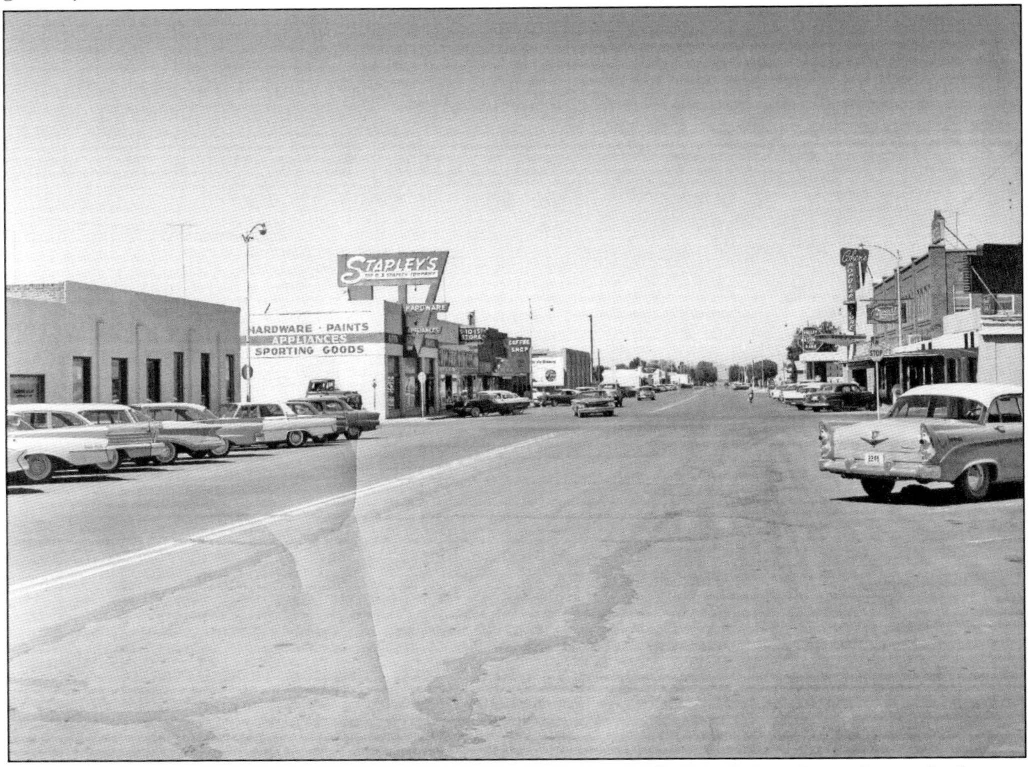

Central Avenue in Coolidge has always been an important thoroughfare from the early days to today. In 1963, this photograph was taken looking west from First Street. Stapley's hardware store is on the southwest corner of Central Avenue, and Main Street is opposite the San Carlos Hotel. Farther down on the right is the large marquee of Cohen's Popular Department Store. (CHM.)

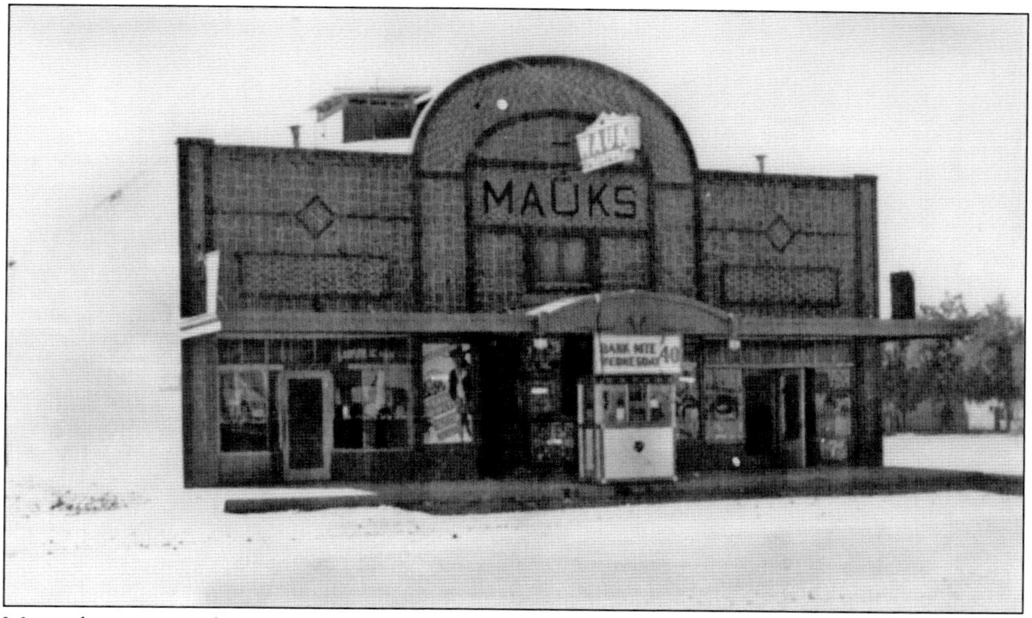

Movie-house mogul George Mauk built the theater in Coolidge on Main Street in 1935 and showed the first movie on April 7. This later became the Studio Theater, and the radio studios of KCKY were located on the second floor. Before Mauk built this theater, he previewed Coolidge's first moving picture show on November 2, 1928, in the community clubhouse. The flamboyant Mauk later became a US marshal. (Joseph Reed Chesley.)

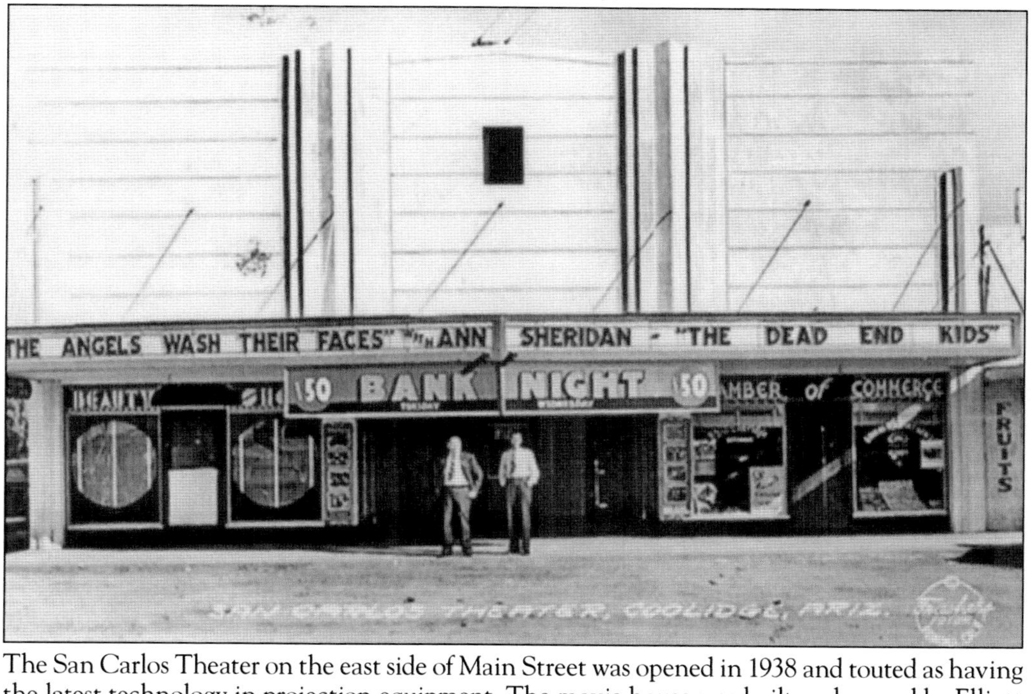

The San Carlos Theater on the east side of Main Street was opened in 1938 and touted as having the latest technology in projection equipment. The movie house was built and owned by Elliott Long of Safford. Able to accommodate 850 people, the theater had upholstered seats and a modern air-cooling system that completely changed the air in the building every three minutes. (Joseph Reed Chesley.)

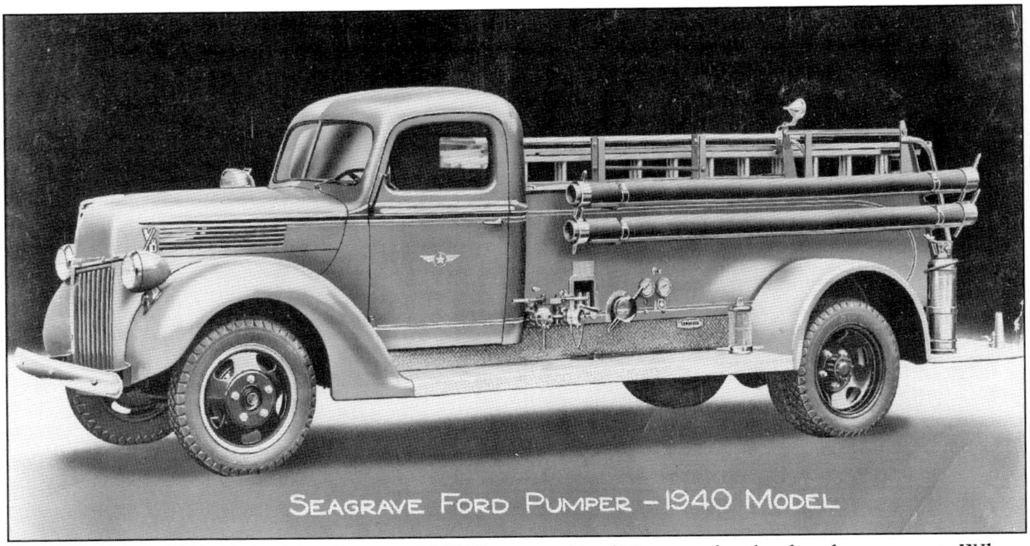

The City of Coolidge purchased a new 1940 Seagrave Ford Pumper for the fire department. When it was delivered on August 1, 1940, the city realized it needed to build a new firehouse to protect the shiny new marvel. A location on Central Avenue in the southeast corner of San Carlos Park was selected. (CHM.)

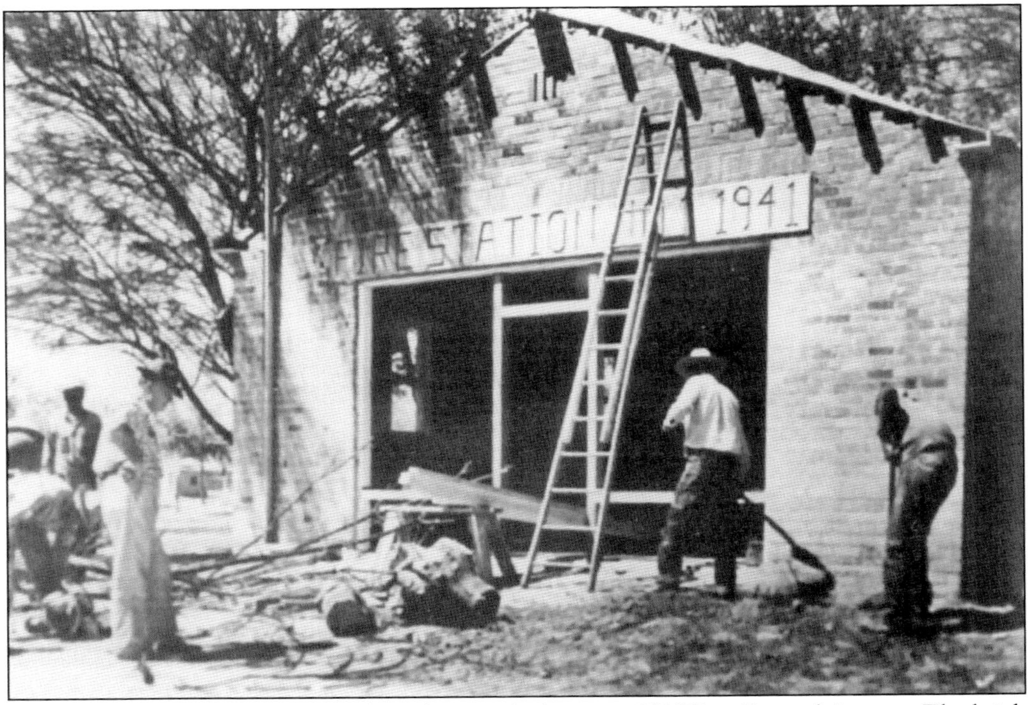

Finishing touches are being placed on the new firehouse at 320 West Central Avenue. The brick structure later became the location of the Coolidge Chamber of Commerce offices when a larger, more modern fire station was built two blocks away on First Street. (CCC.)

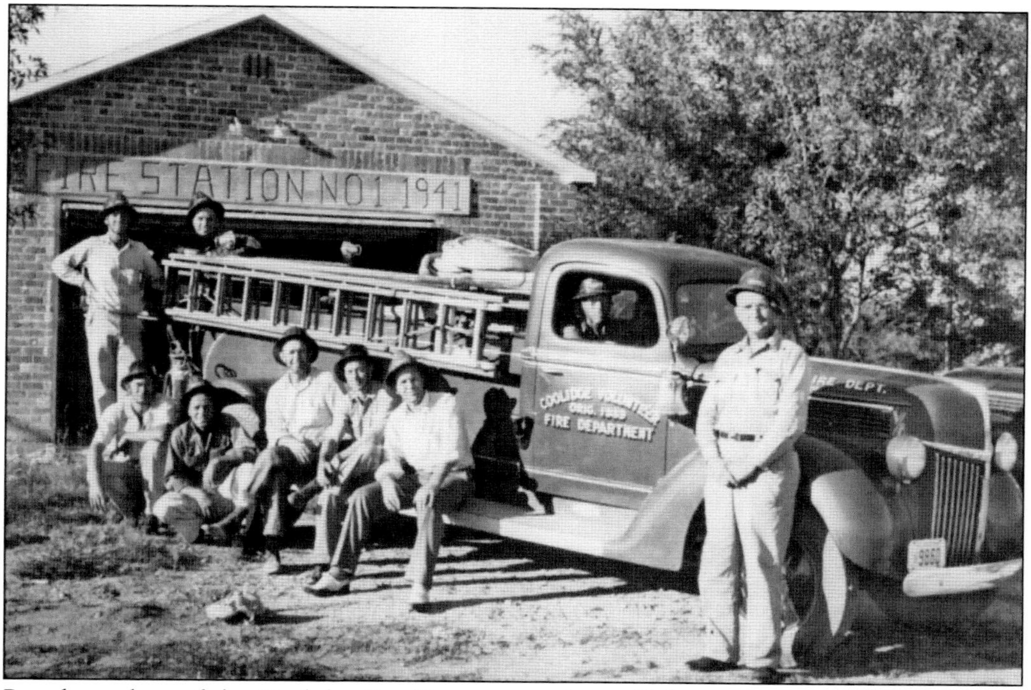

Proud members of the Coolidge Fire Department show off their new pumper in front of the recently completed Fire Station No. 1. When a new station was built years later, the Coolidge Chamber of Commerce moved in. The building was vacated by the chamber of commerce in early 2015. Future plans are to restore the building as a fire museum to house the old fire truck that still operates. (CCC.)

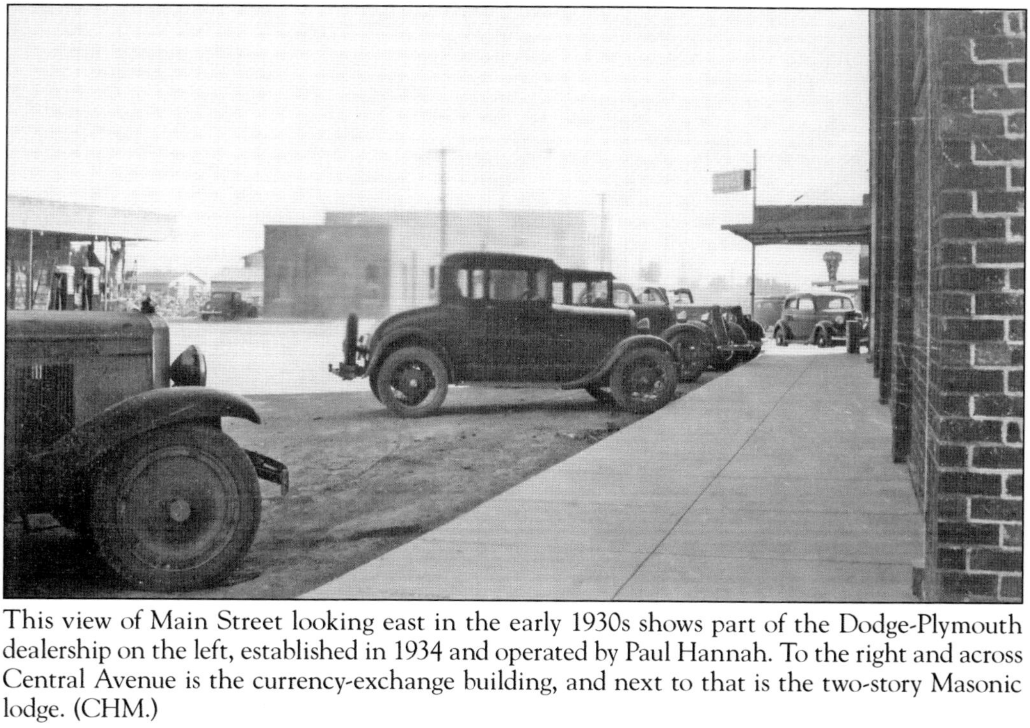

This view of Main Street looking east in the early 1930s shows part of the Dodge-Plymouth dealership on the left, established in 1934 and operated by Paul Hannah. To the right and across Central Avenue is the currency-exchange building, and next to that is the two-story Masonic lodge. (CHM.)

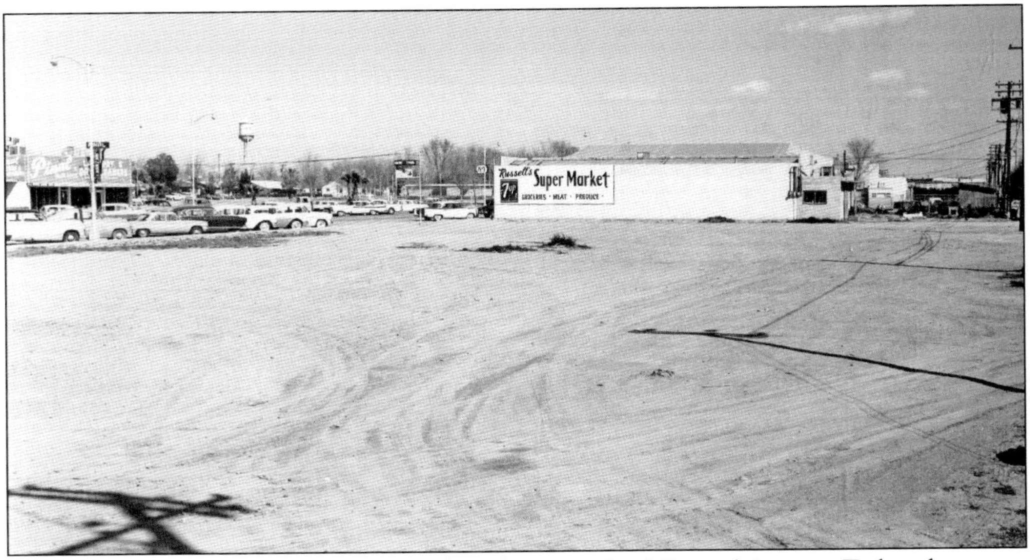

Russell Shope's Super Market was located on the east side of Central Avenue. Today, the empty lot next to it includes the Compass Bank. Russell's son Tom took over operation of the market when it became Shope's IGA and relocated on South Arizona Boulevard near the Coolidge wye intersection. Tom Shope served several terms as mayor and is now a justice of the peace. He still owns and operates the IGA supermarket. (CHM.)

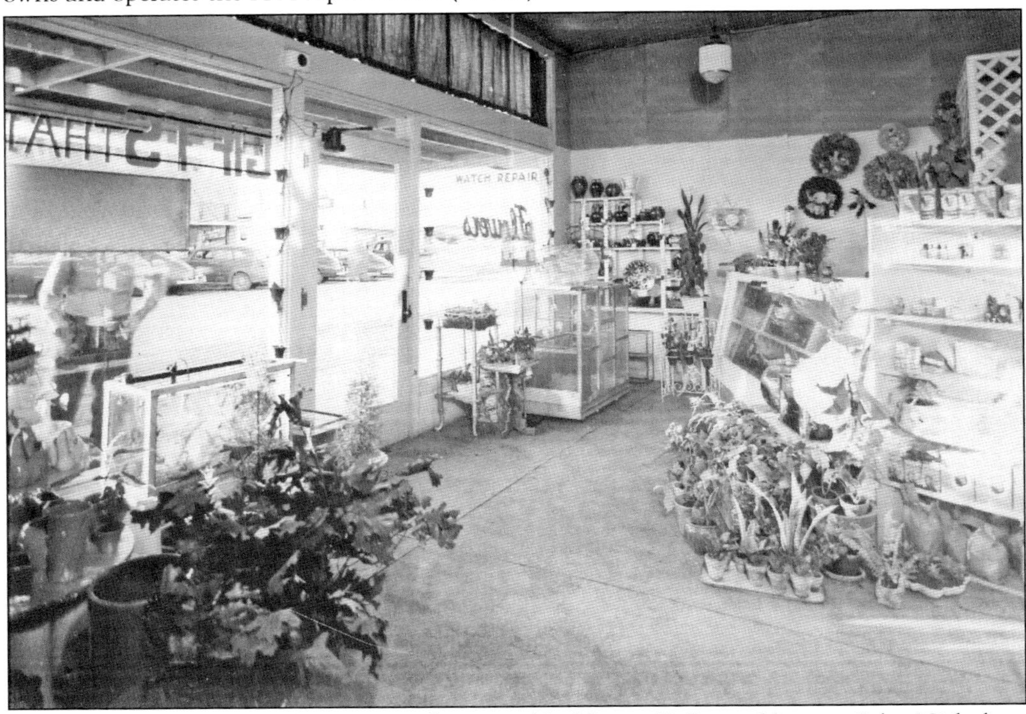

A grocery store was opened in 1938 and operated by Naomi Kalko and her son John Nicholson at 333 South Main Street. In 1942, Pam Meadows turned the store into a flower shop. This is a view from inside the shop looking out onto Main Street sometime in the late 1940s. The shop is still open and being operated by her son John Meadows and granddaughter Nancy "Rusty" Meadows-Heikes. (John W. Meadows.)

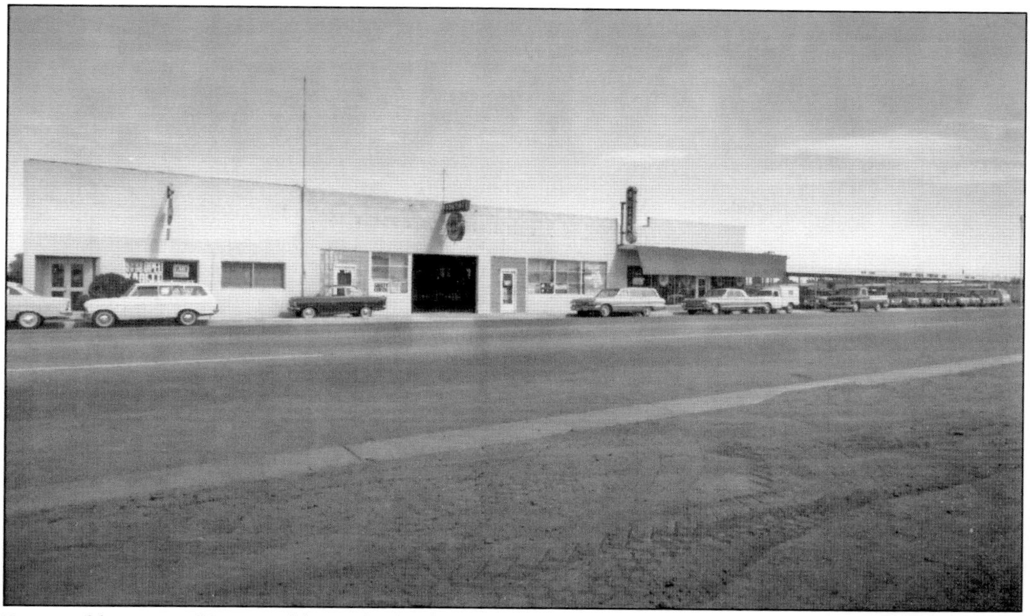

Pictured here is a 50-year-old car dealership opened in Coolidge by Jay and Evelyn Hendrie after moving from Clare, Michigan, in 1949. The Hendrie Buick Pontiac and GMC dealership was located at 716 South Arizona Boulevard when Joe Forehand began selling cars in Coolidge after World War II had ended and invited his friend and former business partner in central Michigan to join him. (Jacque Hendrie-Henry.)

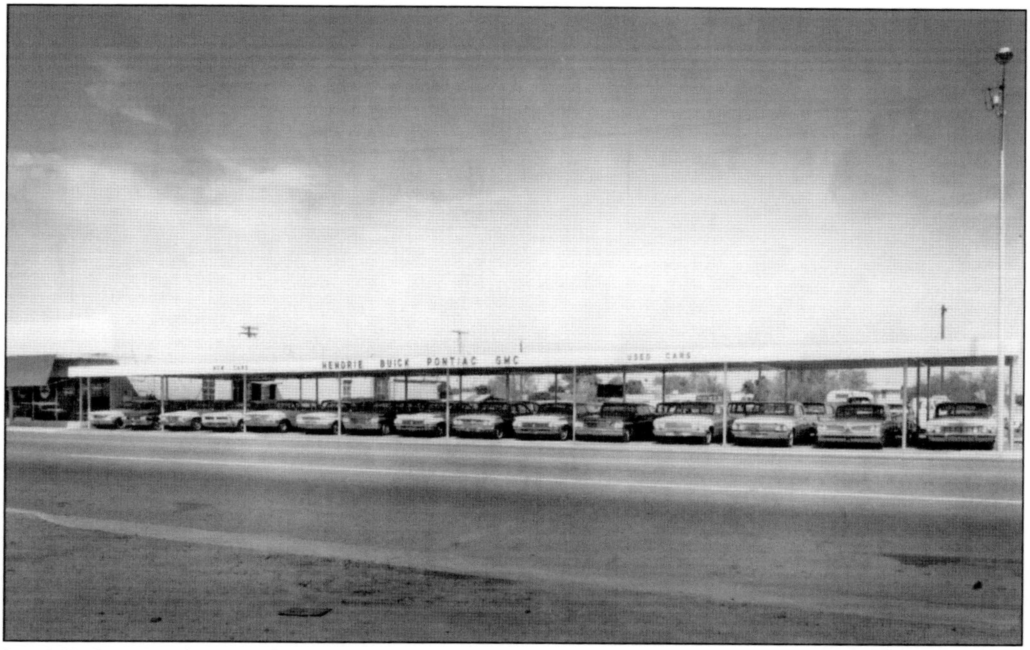

In 1950, Jay Hendrie purchased Joe Forehand's interest in the Buick agency after making modern improvements by adding a Visualiner machine for front-end alignments, a wheel-balancing machine, a steam-cleaning service for engines, twin hoists, headlight-alignment apparatus, and a dust-free spray area for painting. In 1999, Sean Lawley of Sierra Vista purchased the dealership, and it became Lawley Buick Pontiac GMC Truck. Lawley's has since closed. (Jacque Hendrie-Henry.)

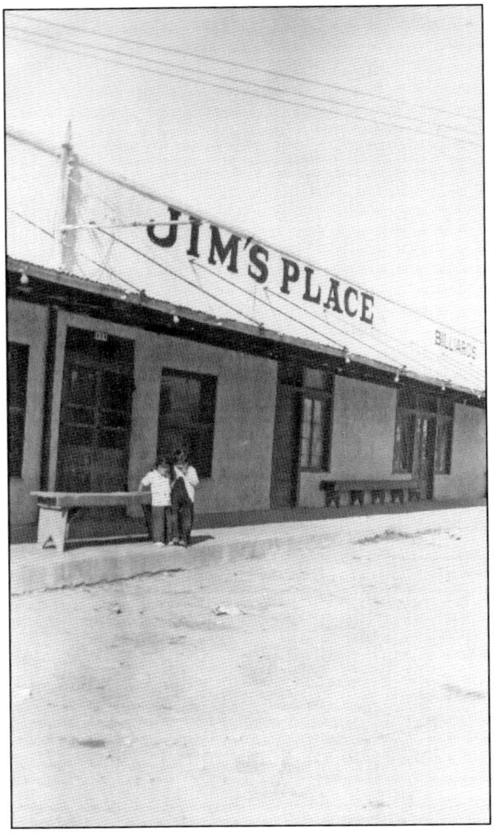

Jim's Place was the first business operated by the Jesus Garcia family, which moved to Coolidge in 1933. The oldest son of Jesus, Santiago "Jimmy" Garcia, operated the bar on Main Street at Lincoln Avenue shortly after returning from World War II. Jimmy became a successful businessman and served on the Coolidge City Council. (Irma Garcia Salazar.)

Welen and Florian "Shorty" Unger (right) took possession of the former San Carlos Club in 1948 with three other owners at 168 South Main Street. Unger soon bought out the other partners and changed the name of the bar to Shorty's. The business moved to Central Avenue in 1959, where it remains today. The original Main Street building still stands as the offices of the Open Hands Veterans Outreach Center. (Paul Unger.)

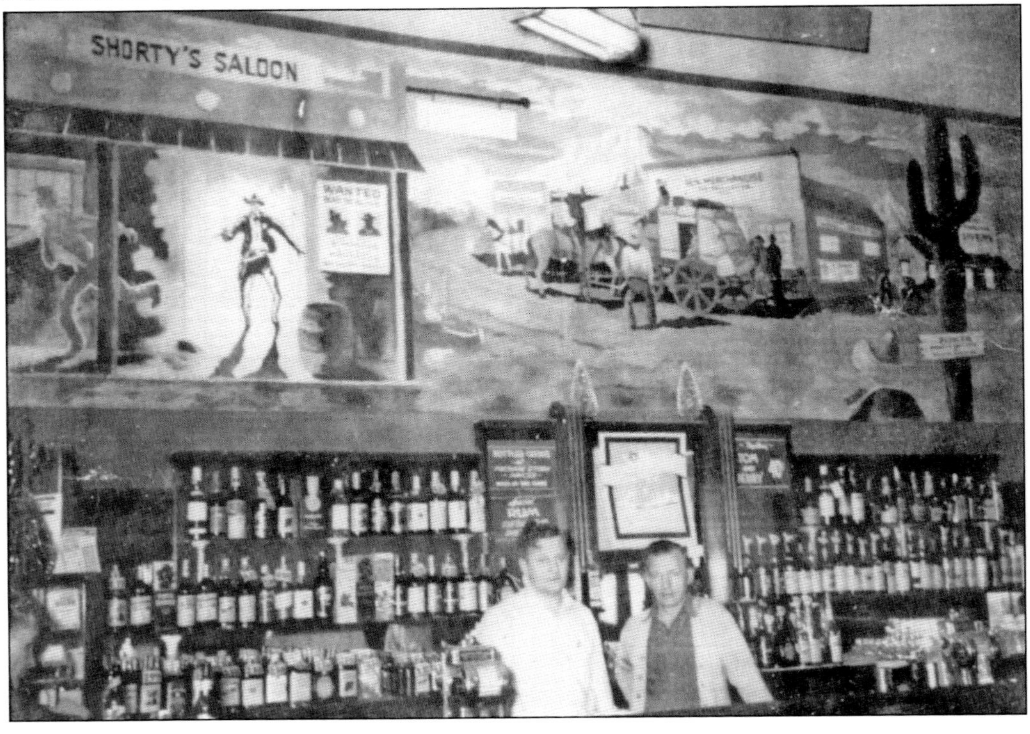

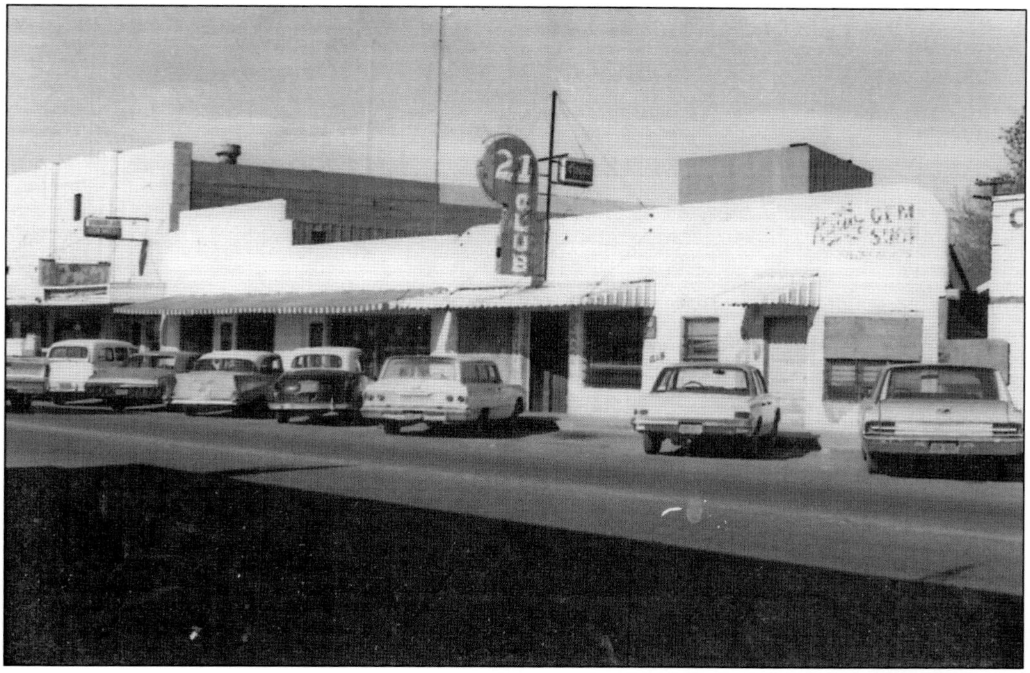

The 21 Club was located on the east side of the 300 block of Main Street. Also on Main was Hayduke's Confectionery store, which also served as the depot for Continental Bus Lines. The Coolidge Flower Shop was also located on the 300 block, just to the east. (John W. Meadows.)

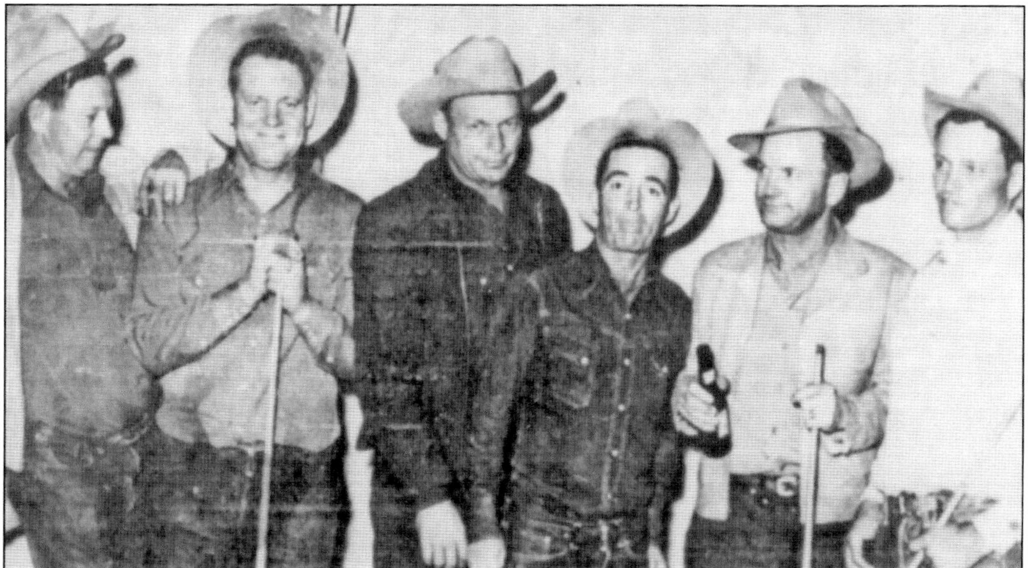
Regulars at the 21 Club who enjoyed the pool tables and cold beer are, from left to right, Jack Nichols, Earl McEuen, Ivan Jones, H. Ramsey, Ben Scott, and Sam McKinney. The bar closed in 2009. (CHM.)

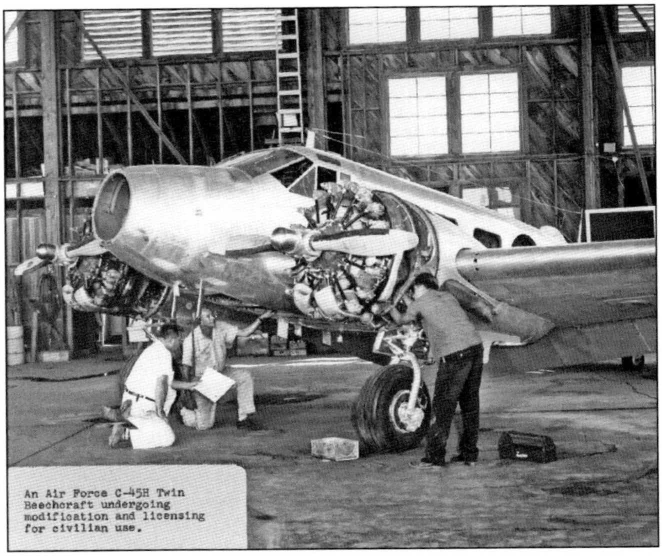

In 1960, the Coolidge Airport was the location of Thompson Aviation Sales. The 120-foot-by-80-foot World War II–era hangar was used for modification and licensing of the Air Force C-45H twin-engine Beechcraft. The airfield was declared surplus by the War Department on November 30, 1945, and transferred from Pinal County to the City of Coolidge on March 2, 1959. From 1962 to 1992, the facility was used for Cessna T-37 jet training. The airport and hangar are still active today. (ASL No. 05-6903.)

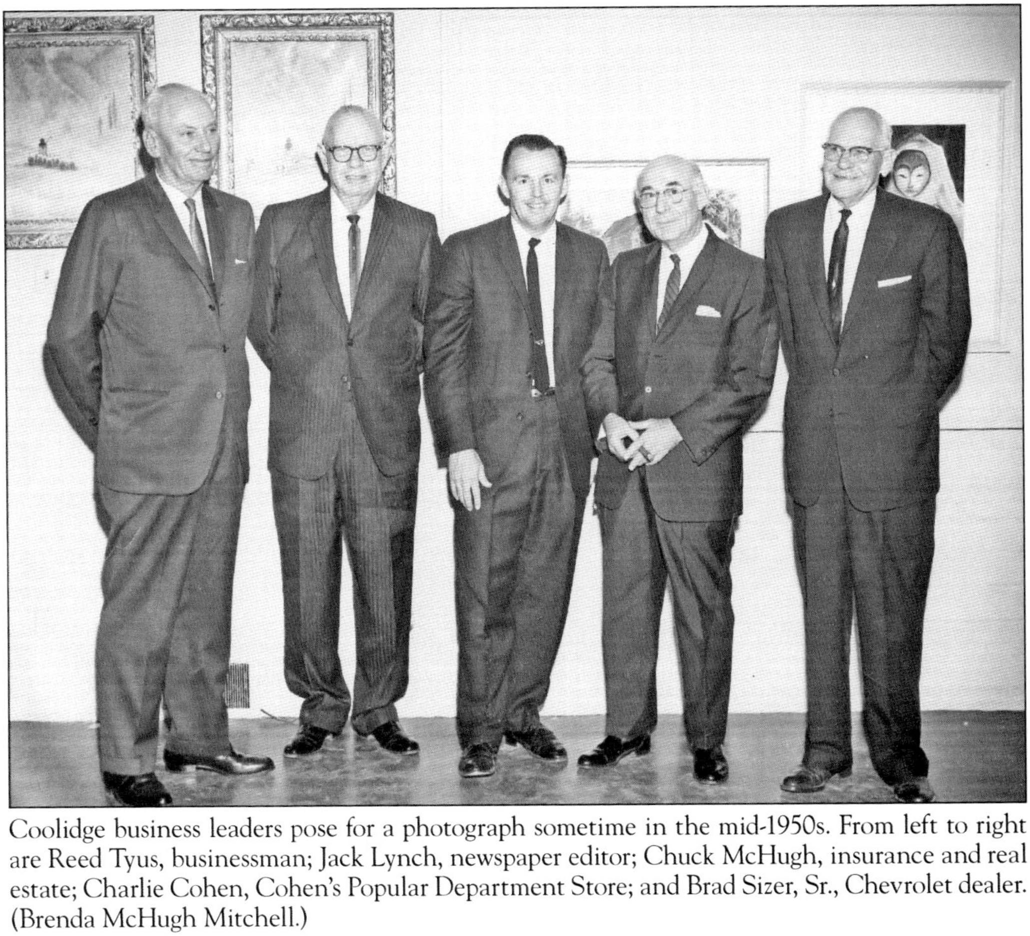

Coolidge business leaders pose for a photograph sometime in the mid-1950s. From left to right are Reed Tyus, businessman; Jack Lynch, newspaper editor; Chuck McHugh, insurance and real estate; Charlie Cohen, Cohen's Popular Department Store; and Brad Sizer, Sr., Chevrolet dealer. (Brenda McHugh Mitchell.)

Pictured here in September 1945 are members of the Coolidge City Council being sworn in. From left to right are Raymond Shoaf, the notary public administering the oath, Mayor A.D. Taylor, and councilmen Dr. R.V. Campbell, C.W. Lewis, R.W. Chadborn, L.O. McMillin, Carl McFarland, and George Ware. (CCC.)

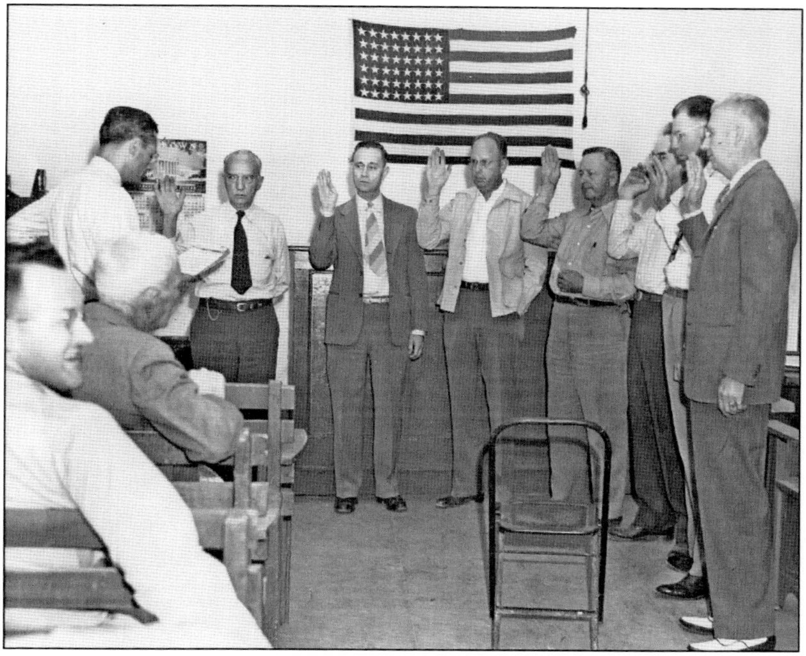

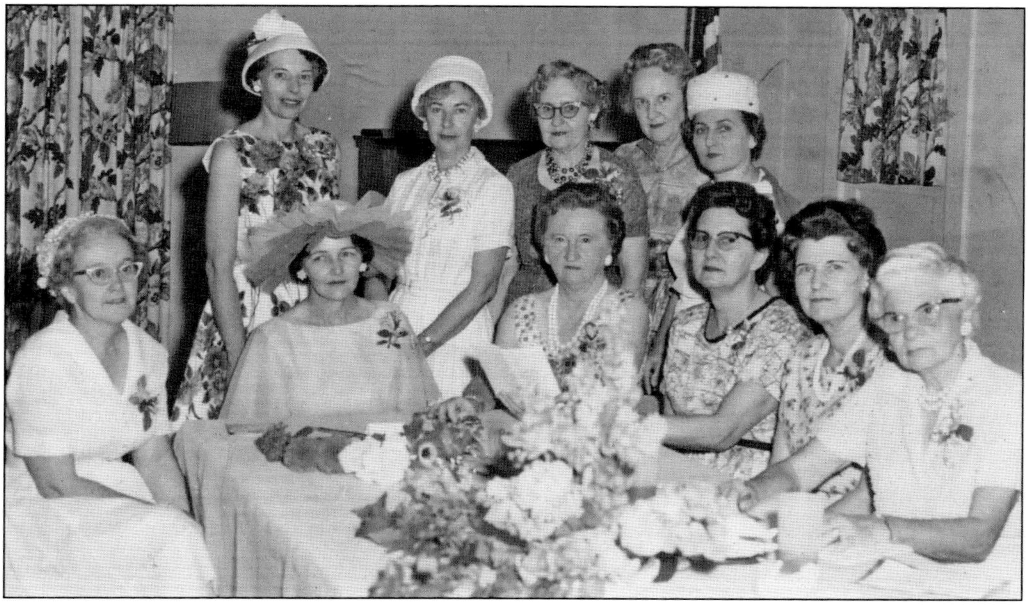

The new officers of the Coolidge Women's Club were installed on May 28, 1963. Pictured here are, from left to right (first row) Mrs. E.L. McManus (corresponding secretary), Mrs. Henry Wang (treasurer), Mrs. W.J. Robinson (director of music), Mrs. Clyde Burnside (installing officer), Mrs. Kruse Davis (house committee), and Mrs. C.A. Christenson (house committee); (second row) Mrs. Wells Moore (first vice president), Mrs. Fred Goode (president), Mrs. J.G. Waggoner (secretary), Mrs. C.B. Shiflet (auditor), and Mrs. Ben Slocum (second vice president). (CCC.)

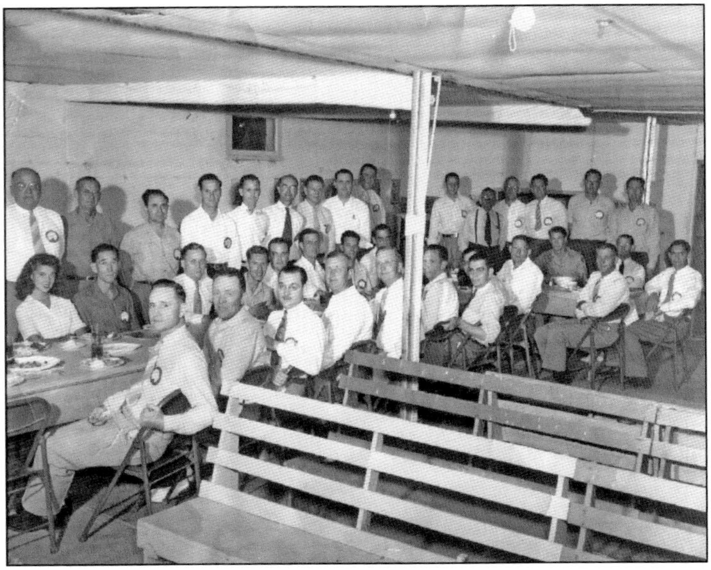

The Coolidge Lions Club was founded in March 1929 with Dr. H.E. Pinkerton presiding as the first president. This photograph was taken in October 1944 during one of its regular dinner meetings. The fraternal organization was significant in its service work to the community. The club also operated the Lions Den at the Kenilworth School, where ice cream and candy were dispensed during special events. (CHM.)

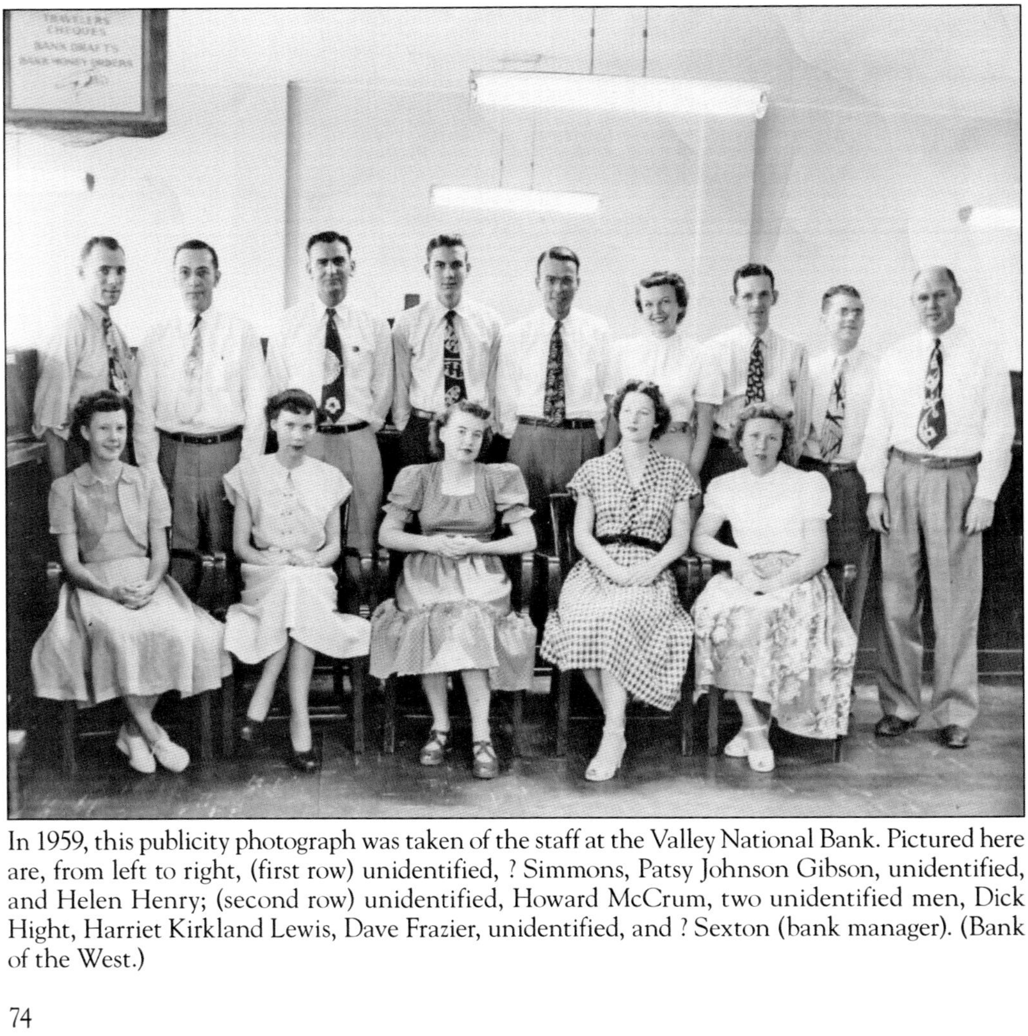

In 1959, this publicity photograph was taken of the staff at the Valley National Bank. Pictured here are, from left to right, (first row) unidentified, ? Simmons, Patsy Johnson Gibson, unidentified, and Helen Henry; (second row) unidentified, Howard McCrum, two unidentified men, Dick Hight, Harriet Kirkland Lewis, Dave Frazier, unidentified, and ? Sexton (bank manager). (Bank of the West.)

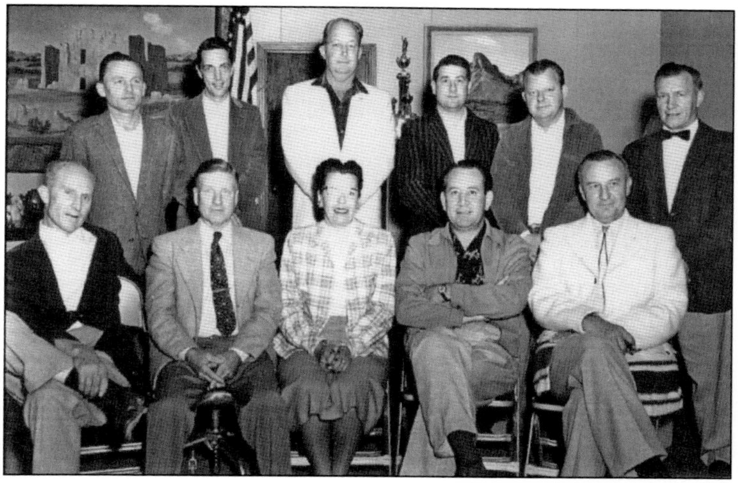

These Coolidge community leaders in the 1950s included, from left to right, (sitting) Reed Tyus, Glenn Willing, ? Anderson, Tag Guayante, and Jay ?; (standing) Tom Anderson, Brad ?, unidentified, ? Beckman, unidentified, and Florian "Shorty" Unger. (CHM.)

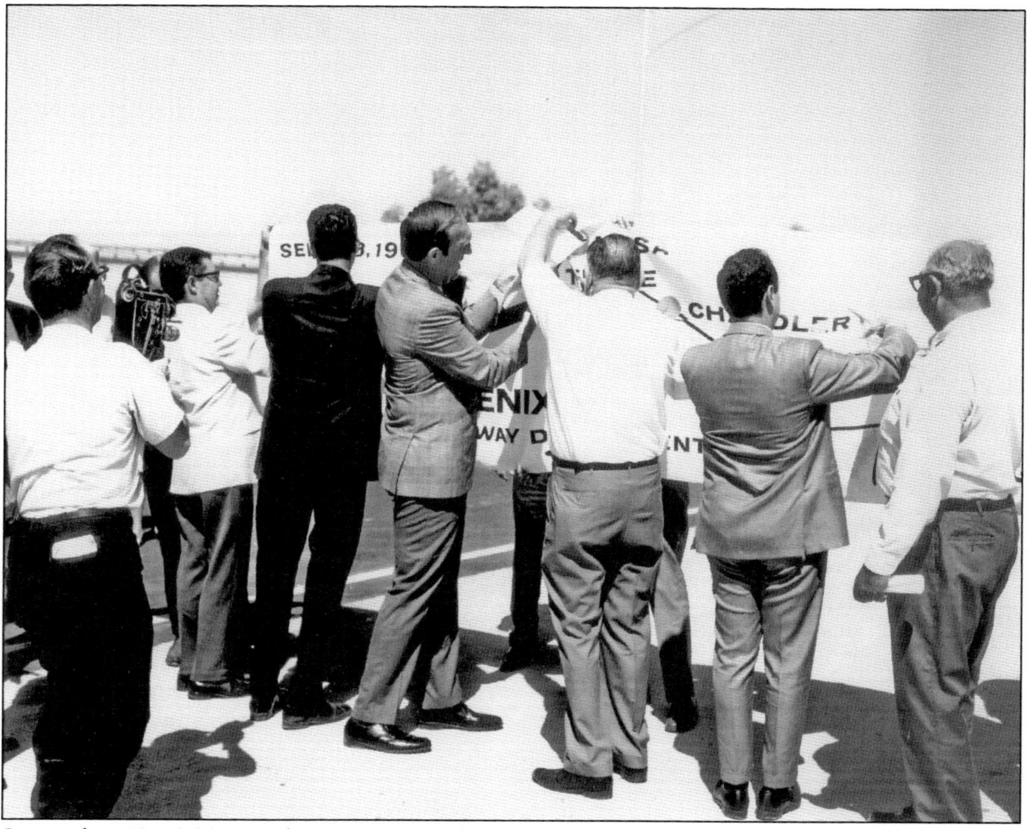

September 18, 1966, was the momentous day that the new Interstate 10 from Casa Grande to Phoenix was opened and dedicated, marking the beginning of traffic bypassing Coolidge. The ribbon-cutting included, from left to right, Phoenix mayor Milton Graham, Tucson mayor James Corbett Jr., Tempe mayor Elmer Bradley, Casa Grande mayor Jimmie Kerr, Coolidge mayor Sigmund Lieberman, and Chandler mayor George Nader. (ASL No. 04-5648.)

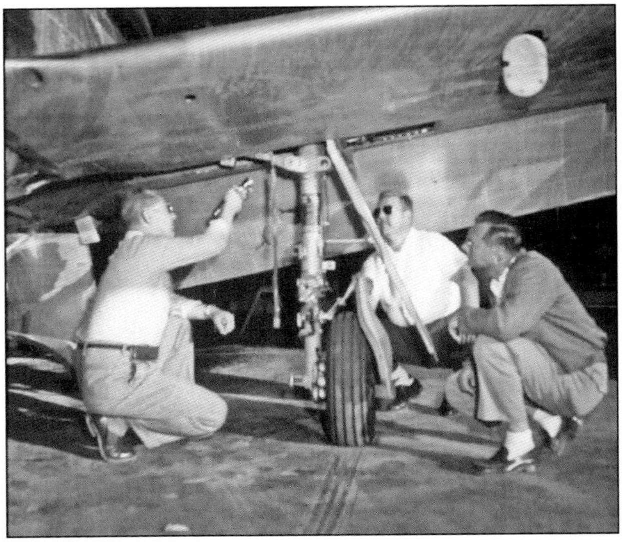

In the 1960s, Thompson Aviation Sales used the Coolidge Municipal Airport hangar to refurbish Air Force C-45H Beechcraft trainers for civilian use. In the spring of 1943, the airfield served as an auxiliary operating base for Williams Air Force Base in Mesa. In 1945, the War Department declared the airbase surplus property and transferred it to Pinal County in 1950. The City of Coolidge acquired the airport in 1959. Today, monthly fly-ins, including the Coolidge Lion's Club pancake breakfasts, are held on the first Saturday from October to May. (ASL No. 05-6908.)

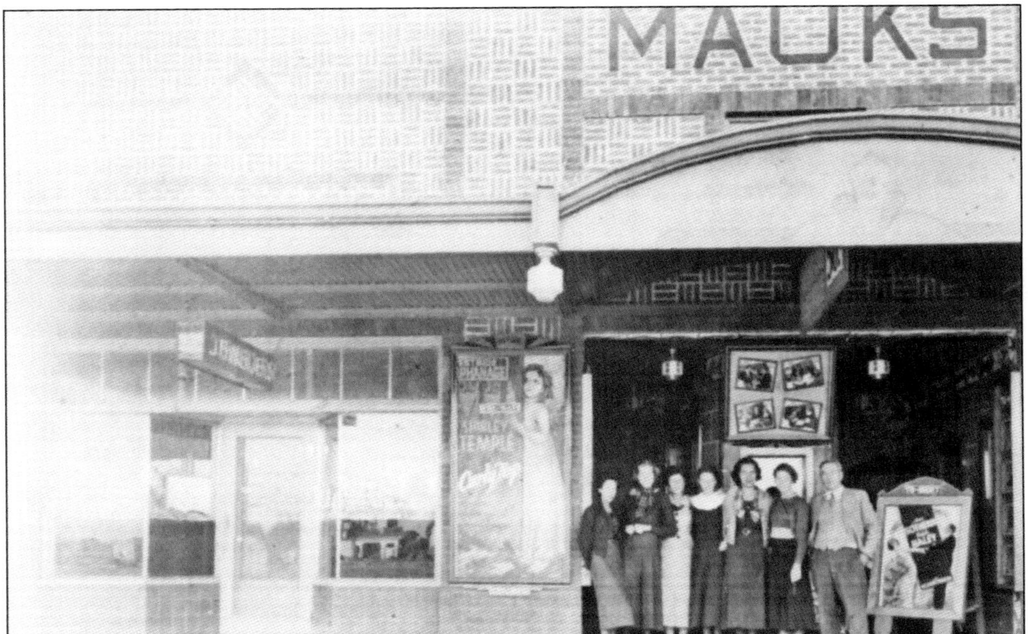

Mauk's was the first theater in Coolidge. The posters in this 1935 photograph show that *Curly Top* with Shirley Temple and *The Girlfriend*, starring Ann Southern and Jack Haley, were the movies on exhibit. Miller Jewelry store is on the left in this snapshot of Main Street. (CCC.)

Six

Education is Paramount

When new settlements and organized communities are established, one of the paramount responsibilities of parents is the education of their children. Early in the history of the Coolidge community, schools were established to educate the children in what was referred to as the three *R*s: "reading, 'riting, and 'rithmetic." One- and two-room schoolhouses were built with whatever materials could be acquired. Many schools were constructed in and around Coolidge, but two of the most important were the Kenilworth School, a few miles east of Coolidge, and Coolidge Union High School.

In 1895, Len Graham donated part of a claim he made in 1891 to the newly formed Kenilworth School District No. 6, and Frank Carpenter, son of early pioneer Oliver H. Carpenter, became the first schoolteacher at Kenilworth. The site was on two stagecoach lines, one running from Florence to Casa Grande and the other from Tucson to Phoenix. In 1915, when Florence Union High School opened, Kenilworth students continued on to Florence after graduating from the eighth grade. In 1970, Coolidge Union High School District annexed Kenilworth after a controversial and heated debate. A few decades later, the buildings were saved from demolition when Coolidge Christian Schools began leasing the property in 1990. Today, Calvary Church occupies the property.

Up until 1936, students from Coolidge who attended Kenilworth were required to continue on to Florence High School until the citizens pressured the county school superintendent to hold an election for a separate Coolidge Union High School District. Chester L. Kenworthy sold 20 acres of land for the new Coolidge school for $8,500. The school opened on September 9, 1936, and the first principal was Clinton M. Magum, who hired five teachers that first year.

During the months the school was under construction, Coolidge students at Kenilworth were allowed to attend temporary classes at various locations in Coolidge rather than being bused to Florence. Within two years, Coolidge became the largest high school in Pinal County, with an operating budget of $35,435, and Coolidge students attending the University of Arizona had scholarship rankings 19 points above the state average.

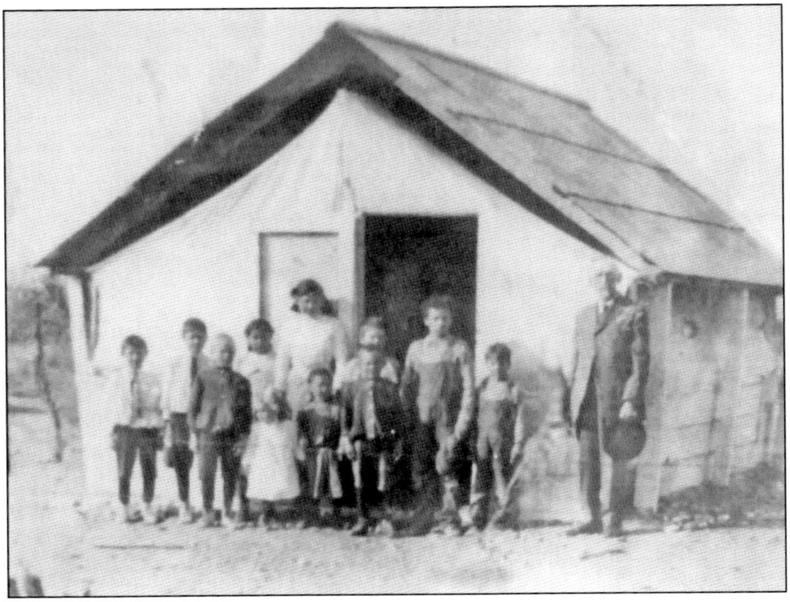

A one-room schoolhouse was established north of the future Coolidge townsite across Highway 87/287 and north of the Casa Grande Ruins. Children from nearby farms and ranches were sent there. (CHM.)

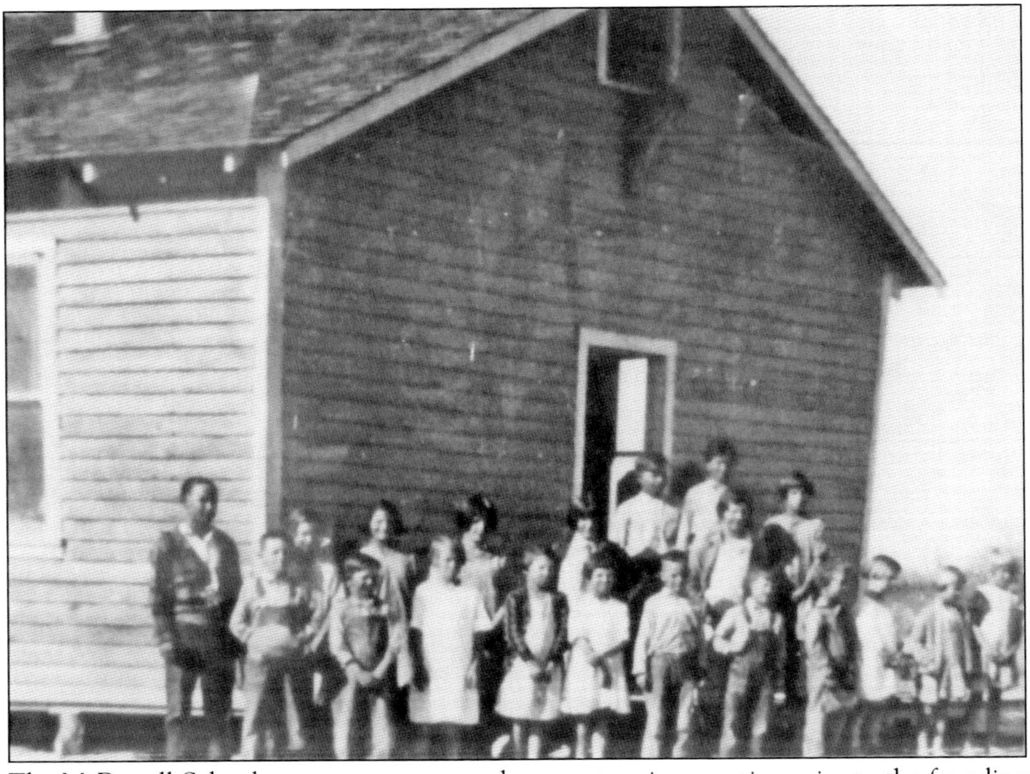

The McDowell School was a one-room wooden structure in operation prior to the founding of the townsite of Coolidge in 1925 and was located on the east side of the S-curve of Eleven Mile Corner Road several miles southwest of town. This photograph was purportedly taken in 1920. (CHM.)

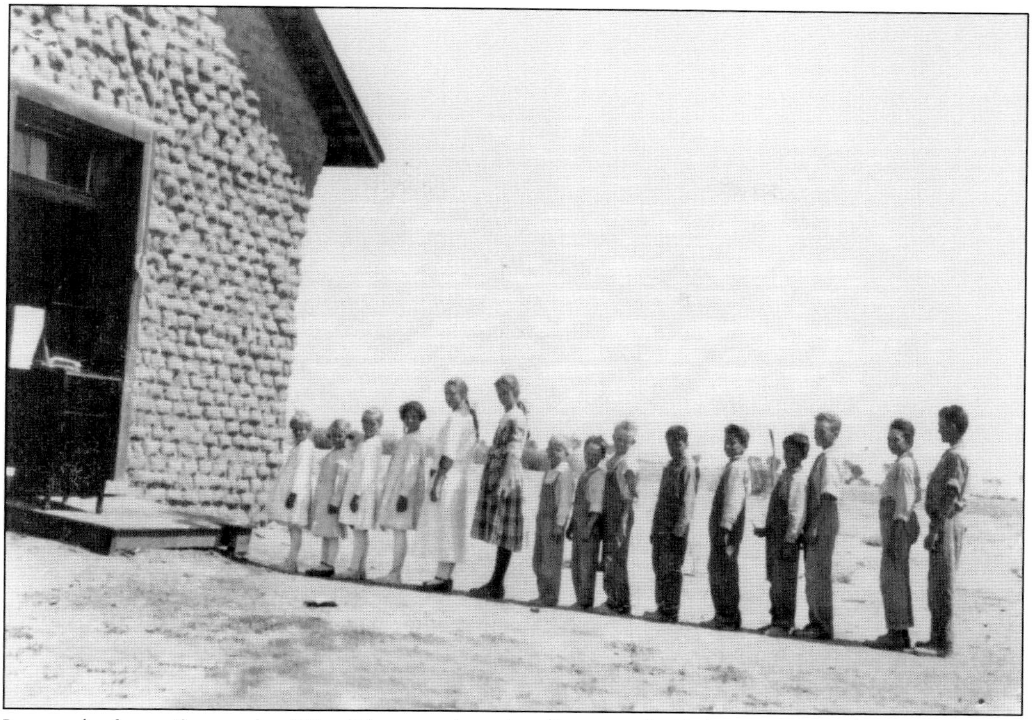

Located a few miles south of Coolidge was the schoolhouse at La Palma, operated by the Nazarene Church, which also held services in the building. The original school was built by hand with sun-cured adobe blocks by the H.C. Hess family, who also grew watermelons that they shared with friends and neighbors with a big watermelon feed each fall. (CHM.)

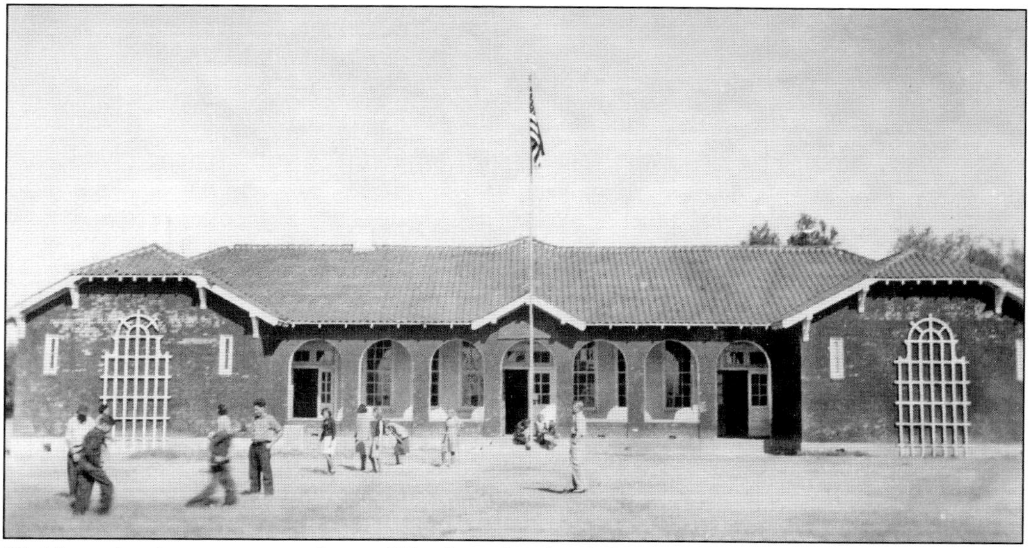

Children play during recess in front of Kenilworth School, facing south a few miles east of Coolidge. The adobe building shows the adobe bricks prior to the application of the exterior stucco surface. Many children walked several miles to the school or rode their horses and tied them up under the trees behind the schoolhouse. In the early years, Kenilworth had no electricity or running water. Children were given the duty of carrying water from a nearby farm in buckets to pour into a large metal container. (CHM.)

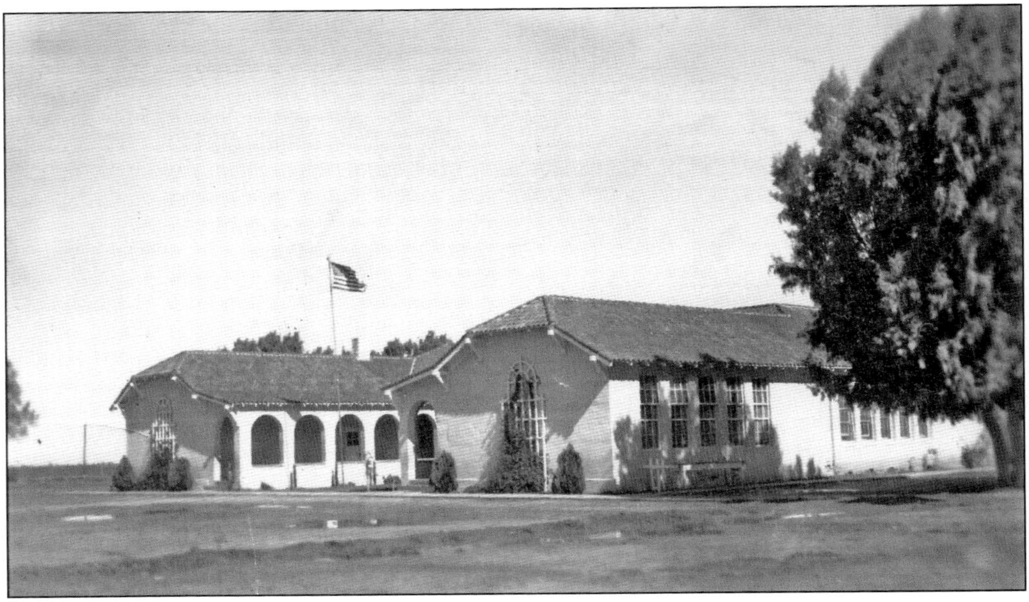

White stucco material was later used to cover the adobe blocks and reflect the heat of the sun. By the mid-1940s, enrollment reached 210 students, and between 116 and 178 meals were served in the cafeteria during that time. The principal was Harry Culbert. The school building also housed an auditorium, and Kenilworth became a community center for dances and other community gatherings. (CHM.)

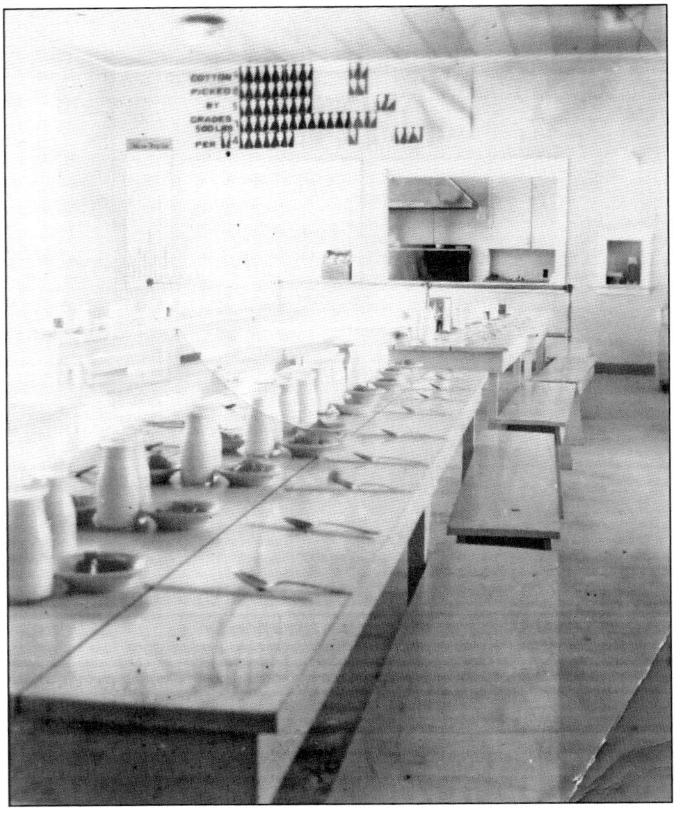

The Kenilworth cafeteria was spartan but clean. The poster on the wall reads, "Cotton Picked by Grades." Each symbol represents 500 pounds of cotton, with the grades posted fourth through eighth. The seventh grade is in the lead with 7,500 pounds of cotton picked during the harvest sometime in the 1940s. (CHM.)

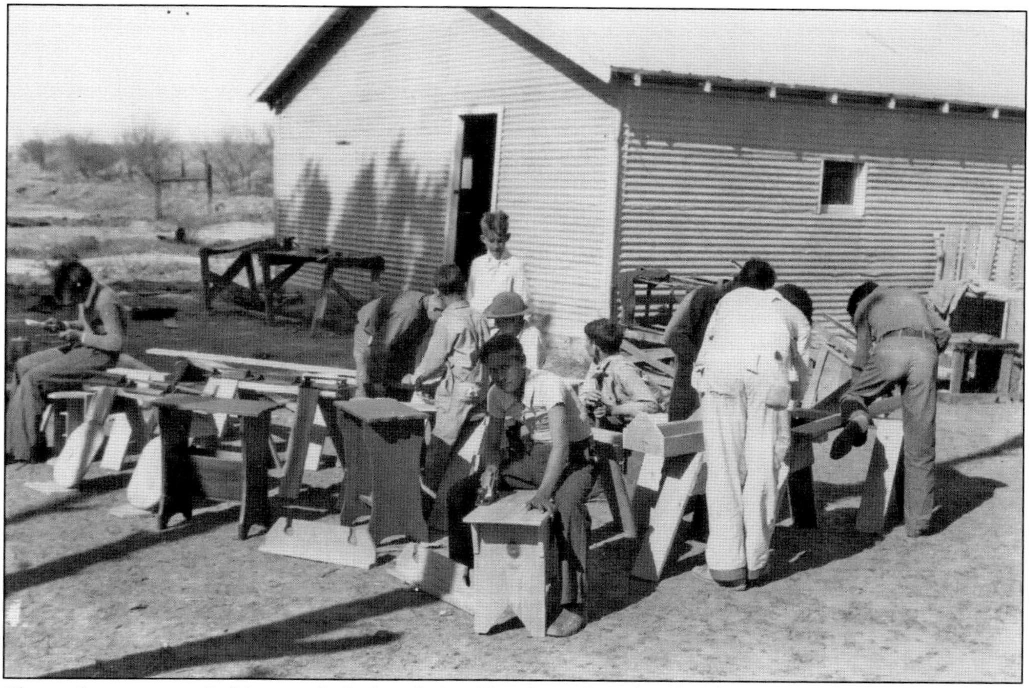

Shop classes were held outside behind the Kenilworth School, where boys learned carpentry and the use of hand tools. The students are constructing wooden end tables that were cut by handsaws, assembled, sanded, and painted. The objects made in shop classes became useful items for each child's home. (CHM.)

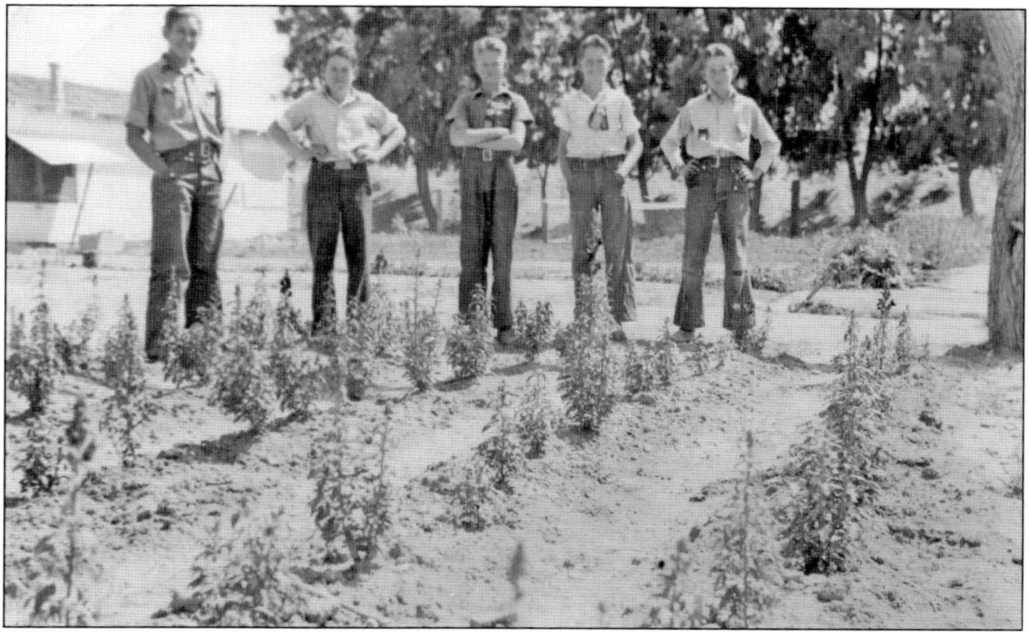

The 4-H Club was an important activity at Kenilworth Elementary School. Besides raising livestock, students planted a large garden behind the schoolhouse. The irrigation canal can be seen behind the boys. Students who road their horses to school tied them to the trees in the background. (CHM.)

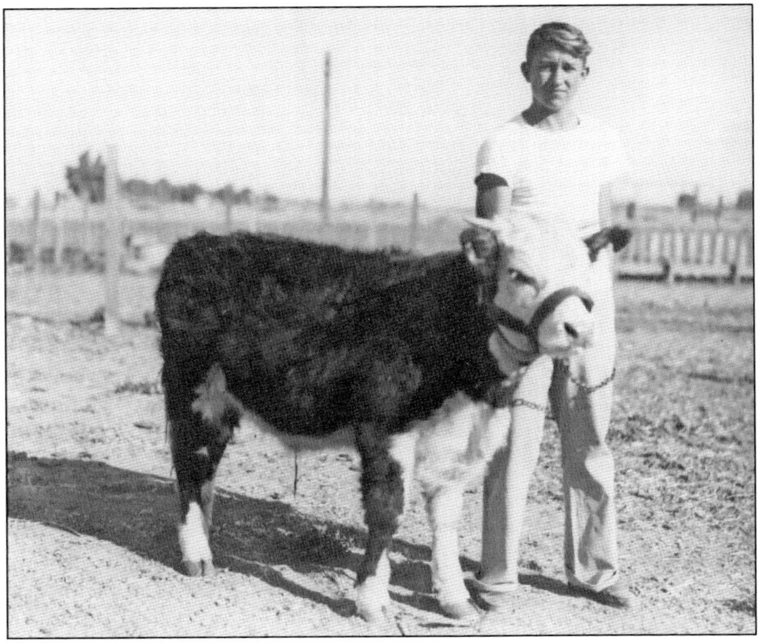

One of the most devoted members of the Kenilworth Junior Farmers 4-H Club was Gene Carter, who raised this Hereford calf that he entered in the 4-H fair. Young Carter's interest in livestock stayed with him, and he later attended the veterinary school at Colorado State University and practiced both large- and small-animal veterinary medicine in Coolidge and nearby Casa Grande. (CHM.)

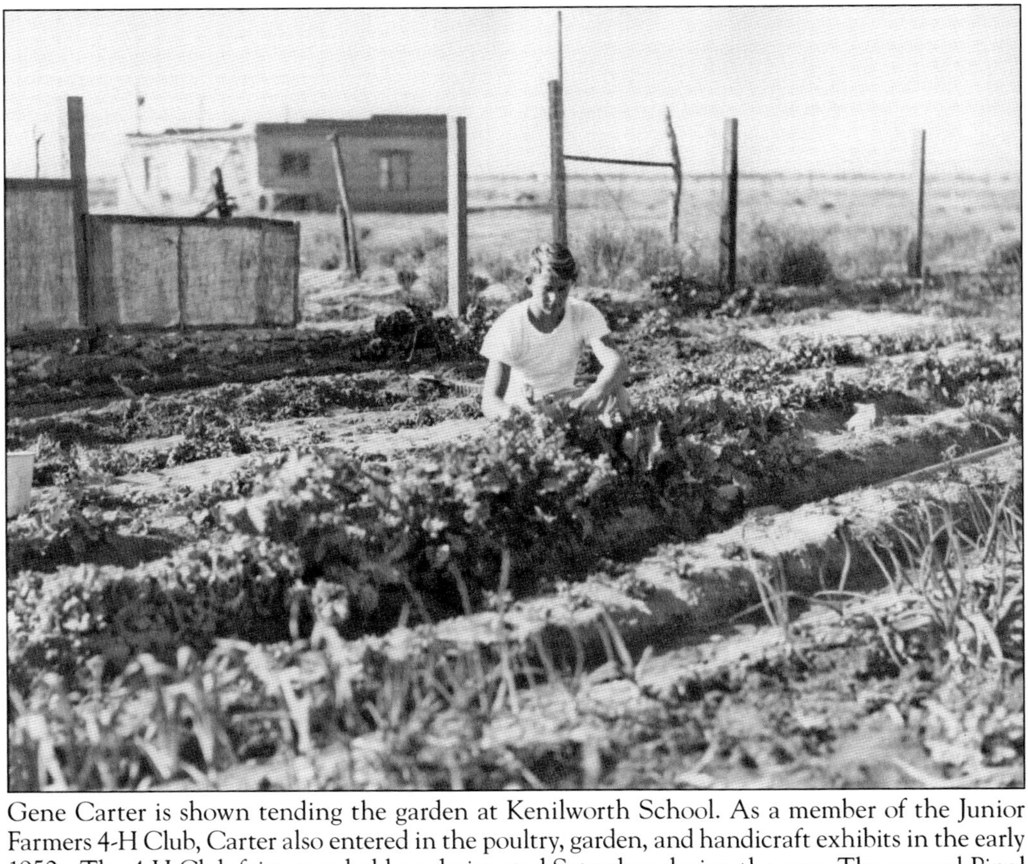

Gene Carter is shown tending the garden at Kenilworth School. As a member of the Junior Farmers 4-H Club, Carter also entered in the poultry, garden, and handicraft exhibits in the early 1950s. The 4-H Club fairs were held on designated Saturdays during the year. The annual Pinal County Fair was also a regular showcase of 4-H Club projects. (CHM.)

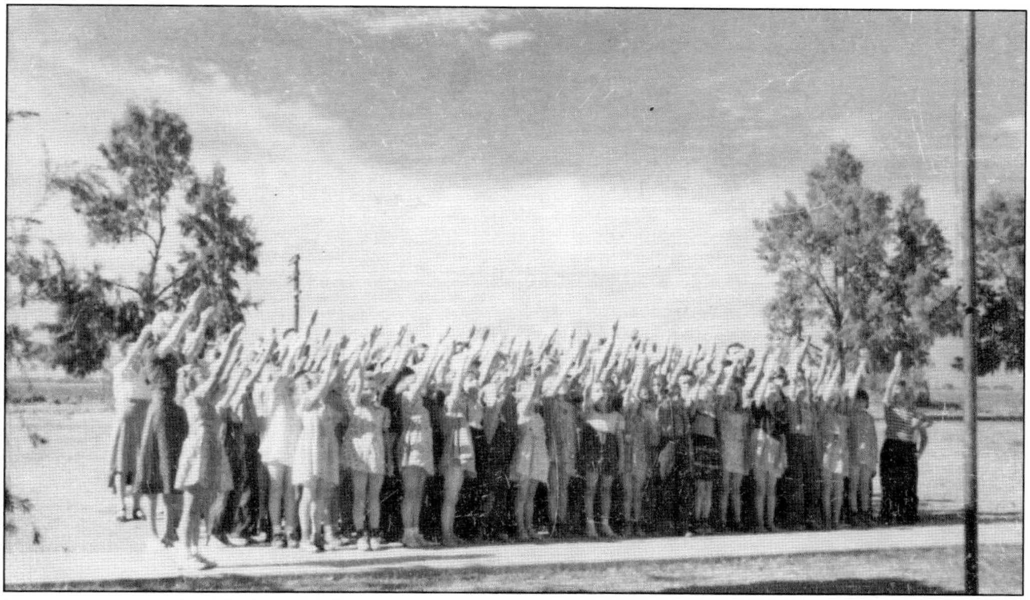

Every morning, the Pledge of Allegiance was recited at the flagpole in front of Kenilworth School. Many schools around the country used the Bellamy salute, named after the Christian socialist Baptist minister Francis Bellamy, beginning in 1892. The salute to the flag began with palm facing down and ended with the palm facing up after the arm was raised. Because the salute resembled the Nazi salute, on December 22, 1942, Congress changed the American flag salute to the hand over the heart. (CHM.)

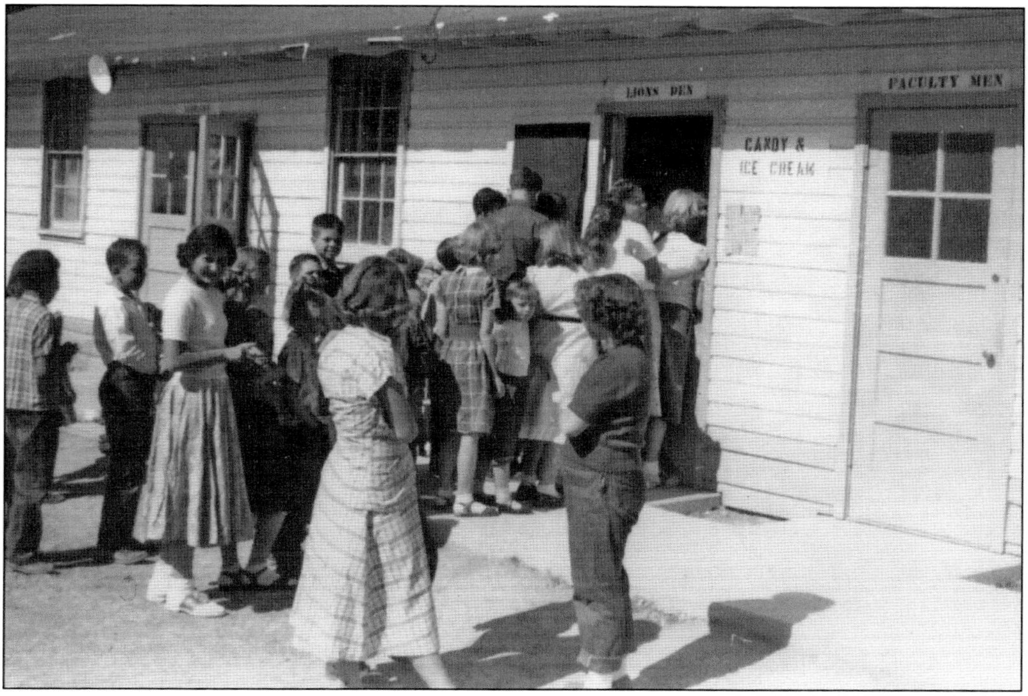

In the 1950s, the Lion's Club operated a snack bar at Kenilworth School called the Lion's Den. During special events such as the Saturday 4-H Club fairs, students and adults would line up to purchase ice cream and candy. (CHM.)

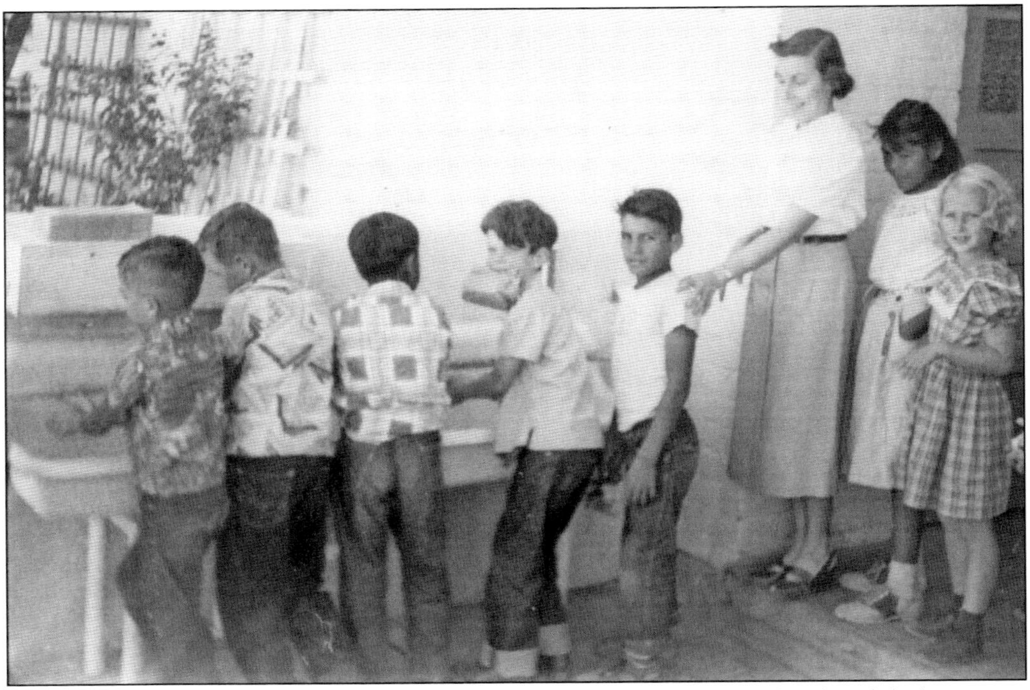

Kenilworth students line up under the direction of their teacher to wash their hands before eating lunch in the school cafeteria. The fourth boy from the left is holding the lunch his mother packed between his teeth while washing. Good hygiene was always taught in the schools. (CHM.)

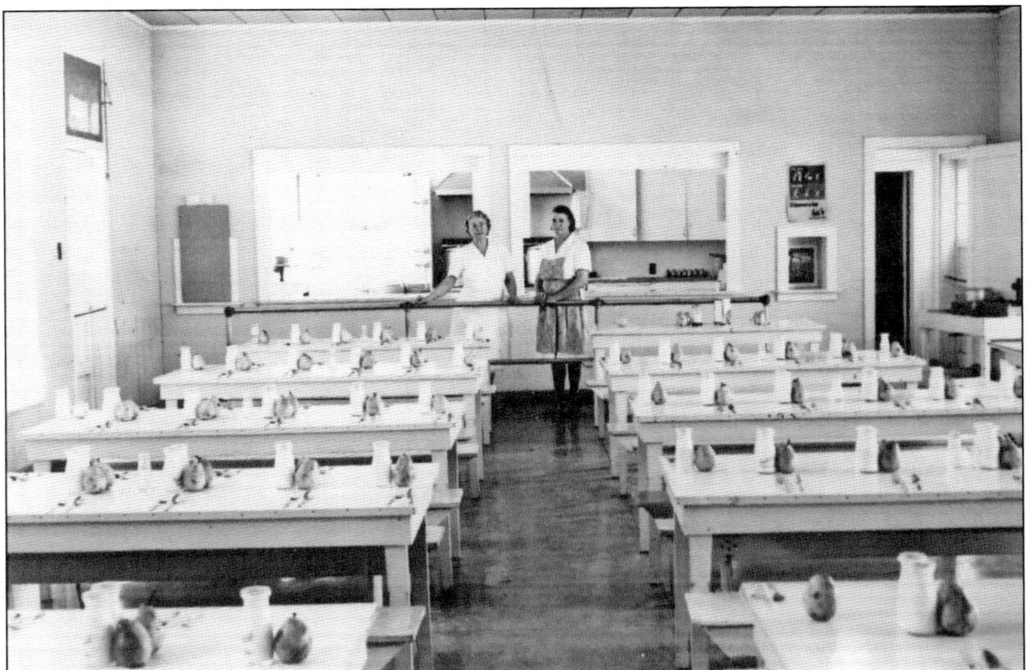

The kitchen staff at Kenilworth School always kept the cafeteria orderly and sparkling clean for the students at the elementary school. Many of the children came from families from the Casa Grande Valley Farms resettlement project nearby. (CHM.)

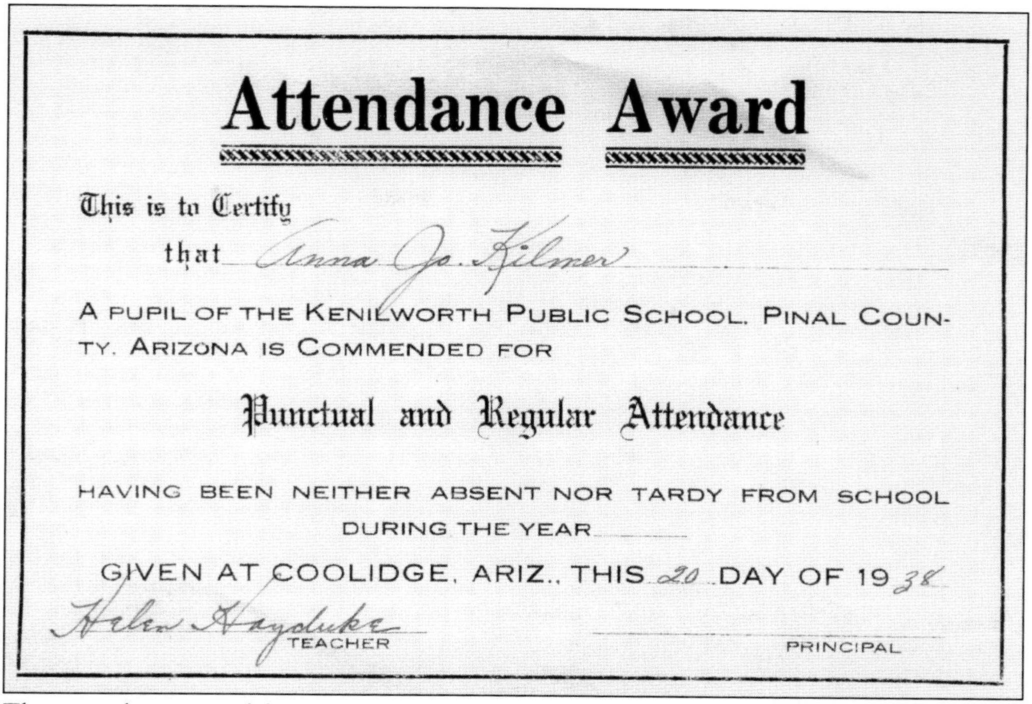

Attendance Award

This is to Certify

that Anna Jo. Kilmer

A PUPIL OF THE KENILWORTH PUBLIC SCHOOL, PINAL COUNTY, ARIZONA IS COMMENDED FOR

Punctual and Regular Attendance

HAVING BEEN NEITHER ABSENT NOR TARDY FROM SCHOOL DURING THE YEAR ______

GIVEN AT COOLIDGE, ARIZ., THIS 20 DAY OF 1938

Helen Hayduke
TEACHER

PRINCIPAL

This attendance award for Anna Jo Kilmer shows that she was in regular attendance with no absences or tardiness for the entire 1937–1938 school year. The certificate was signed by her teacher Helen Hayduke. Students at Kenilworth were regularly rewarded for good grades, behavior, and attendance. (CHM.)

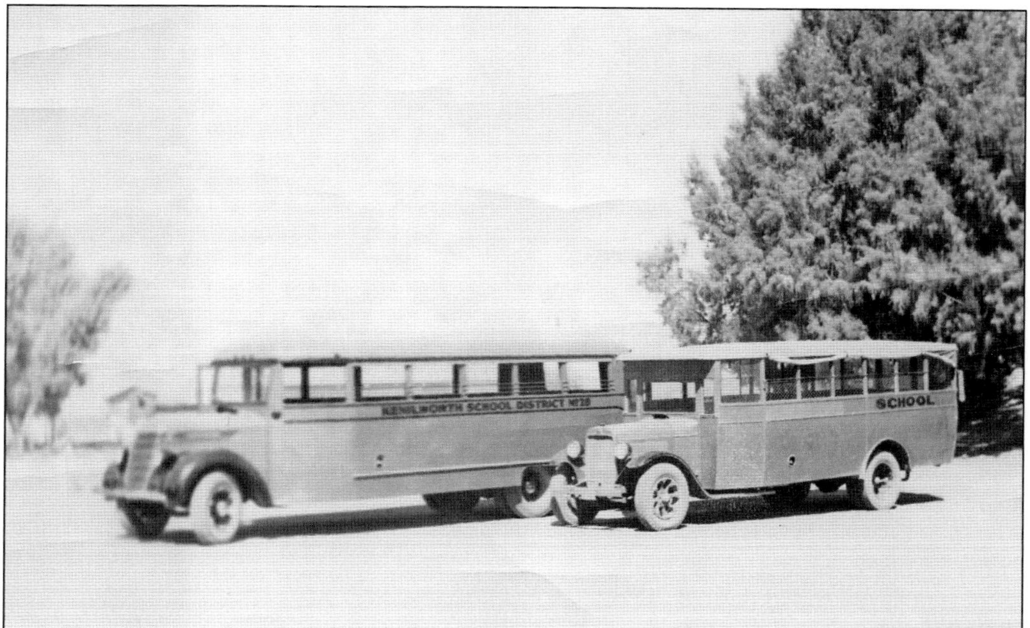

Two of the school buses for the Kenilworth Elementary School are parked near the tamarack trees behind the schoolhouse sometime in the 1930s. (CHM.)

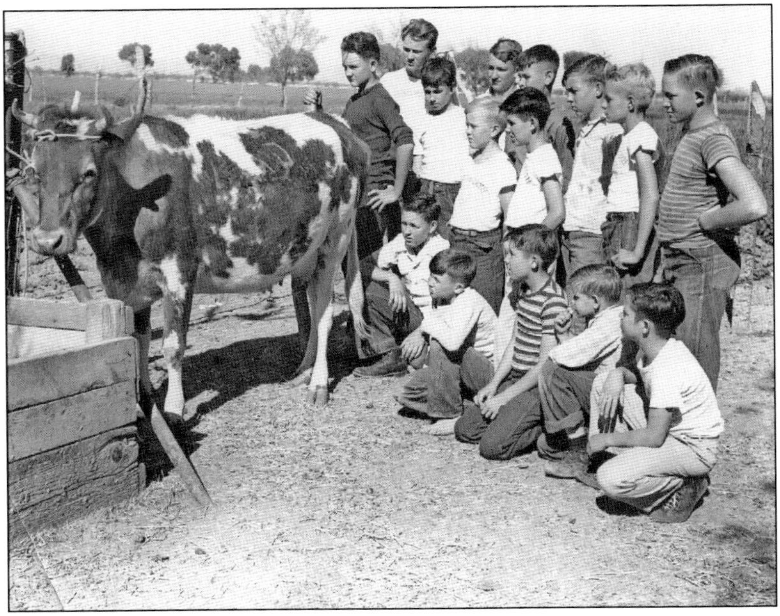

Members of the Future Farmers 4-H Club at Kenilworth observe the proper care, health, and conformation of a dairy cow on the school grounds. Standing to the right of the tallest boy in the back row is Gene Carter of Coolidge. (CHM.)

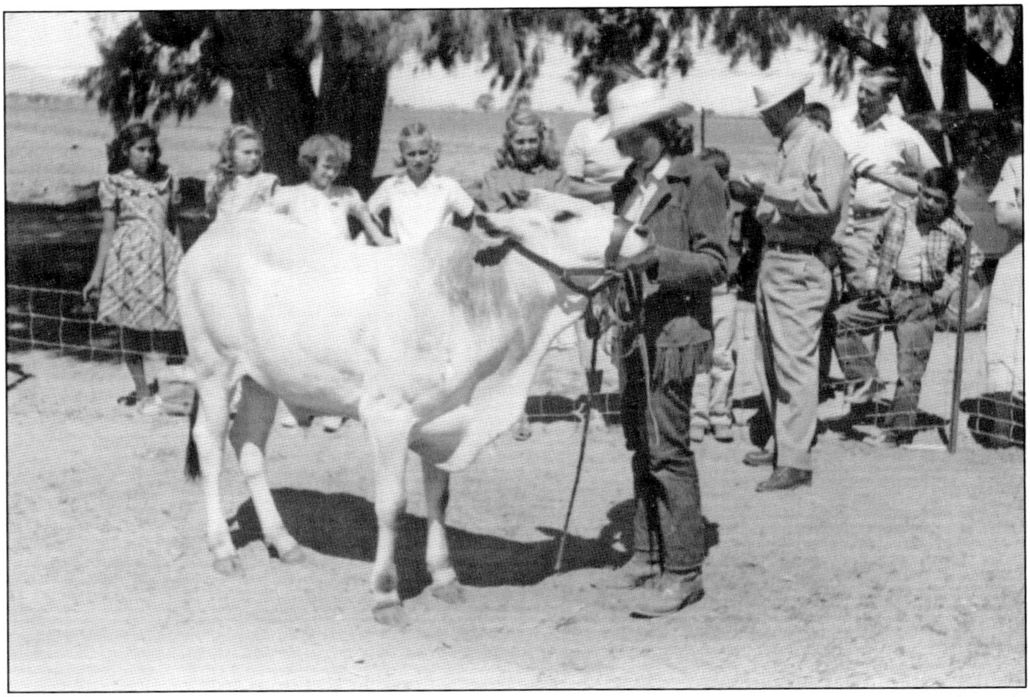

Livestock judging during the Saturday 4-H Club fairs was held on the grounds of Kenilworth School. This unidentified girl is proudly showing her Brahman calf. The nearby Casa Grande Valley Farms operated 4,000 acres of farmland that brought families with children to enroll in the rural school. (CHM.)

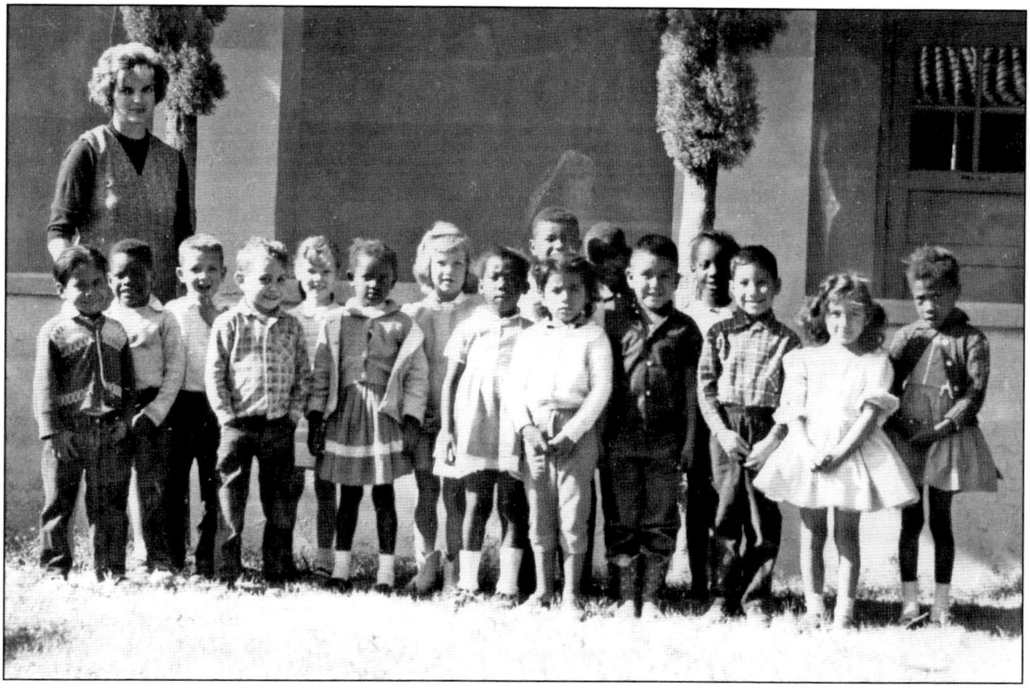

This April 9, 1964, photograph of Darla Maddock's kindergarten class at Kenilworth School shows the ethnic diversity of her students. From left to right are Robert Tristan, Donell Newton, Tom Cathemer, Scott Lewis, Terry Woods, Doren Jordan, Sandra Keller, Elnora Mathis, Wilbert Muldrow, Marcia Garcia, Robbie Dosty, Jerry Webb, Lovina White, Karlos Garcia, Rosa Murrieta, and Maxine Reece. (CCC.)

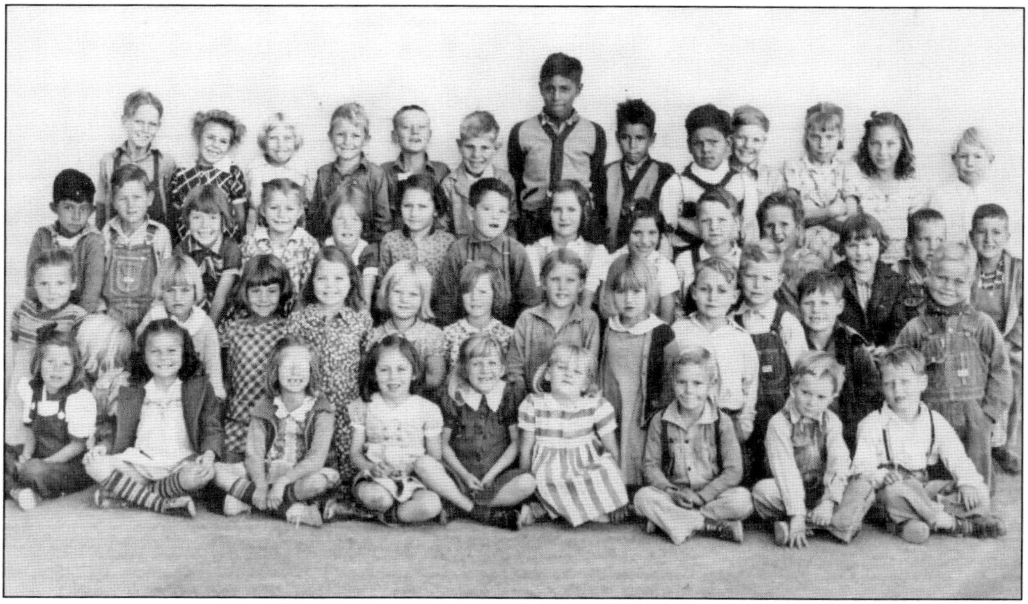

The first-grade class at Kenilworth in 1939 depicts a full class of cheerful students, including Gene Carter (standing, fourth from the left). Upon graduating from eighth grade, Coolidge residents would attend Coolidge High School instead of Florence Union because the Coolidge school opened in 1935, allowing students from that town to stay in Coolidge. (Gene D. Carter.)

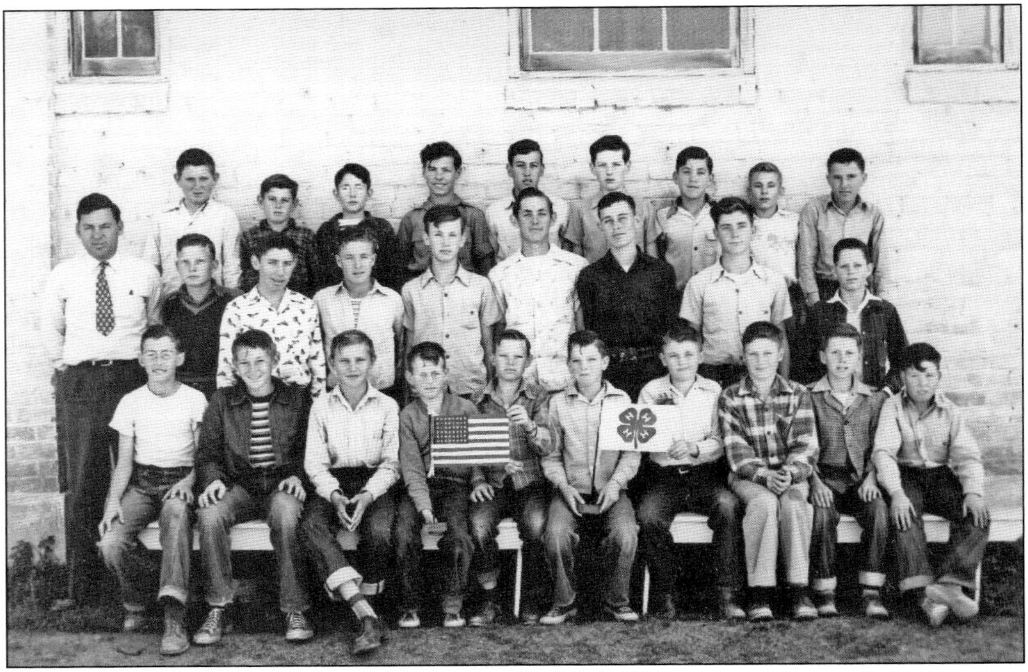

In the late 1940s, the boys of the Future Farmers 4-H Club display their patriotism with the American flag and the official 4-H Club symbol. Club members maintained an extensive garden on the school grounds, as well as livestock that were kept in pens in the back of the school. (CHM.)

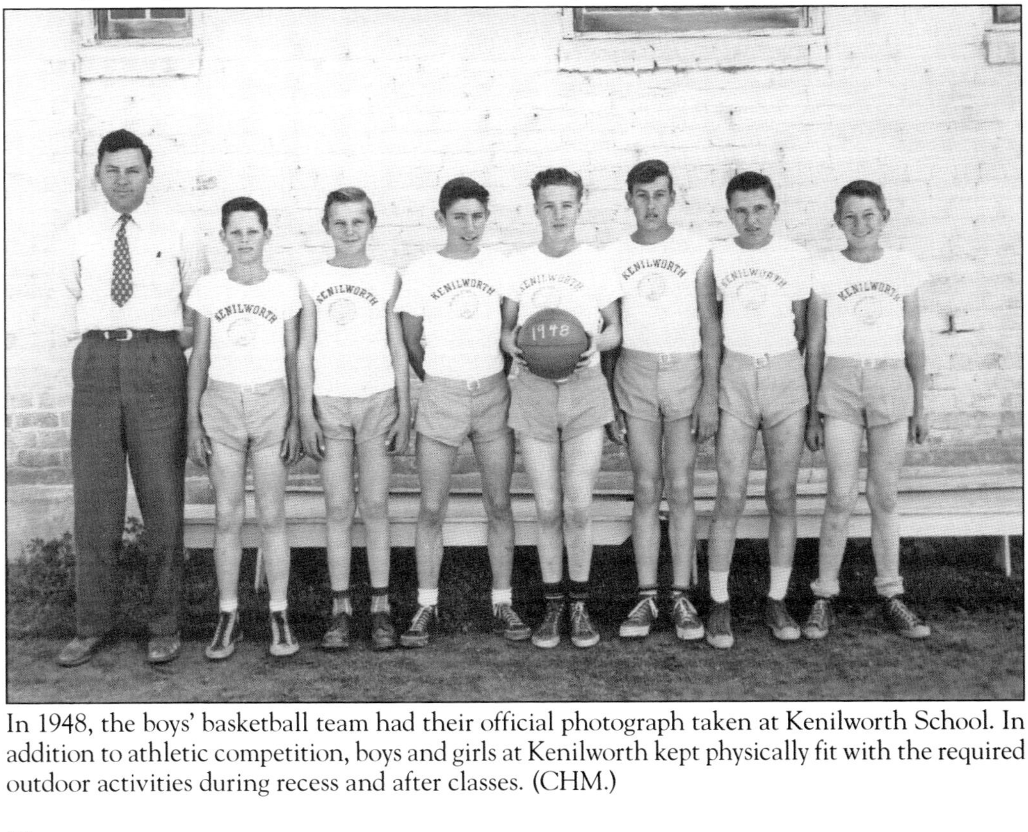

In 1948, the boys' basketball team had their official photograph taken at Kenilworth School. In addition to athletic competition, boys and girls at Kenilworth kept physically fit with the required outdoor activities during recess and after classes. (CHM.)

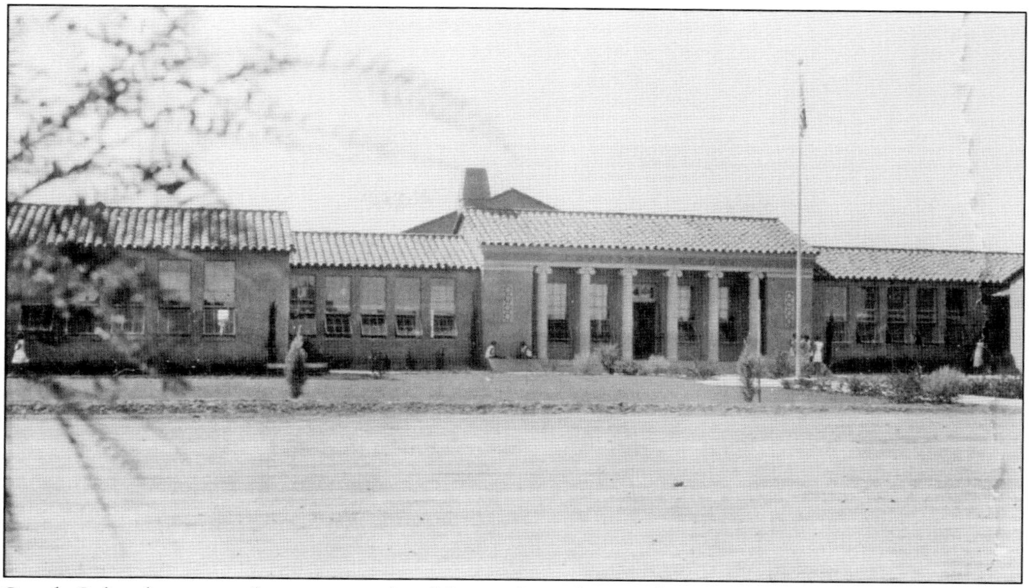

South School was an elementary school located on the southeast corner of Roosevelt Avenue and Fourth Street. The school opened in 1931 and closed in January 1976, when students were moved to West Elementary School at Coolidge Avenue and Seventh Street. All that remains today of South School are the six Roman columns marking the entrance to an apartment complex. (CHM.)

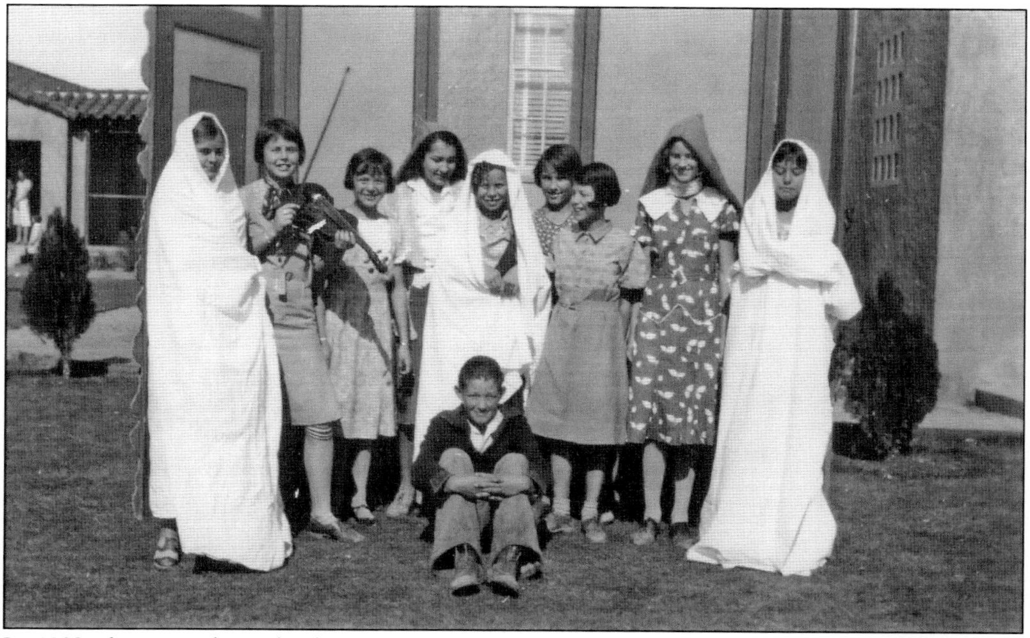

In 1933, the seventh-grade class at South School participated in the play *The Ghost House of Rockville*. Seated on the ground is Bob Blakely; standing from left to right are Geraldene Rowe, Mary Jan Fench, Marjorie Claire Talla, Barbara Gwens, Hazel Weaver, Willie Crane, Virginia Knox, Mabel Lee, and Anna Nichols. (CHM.)

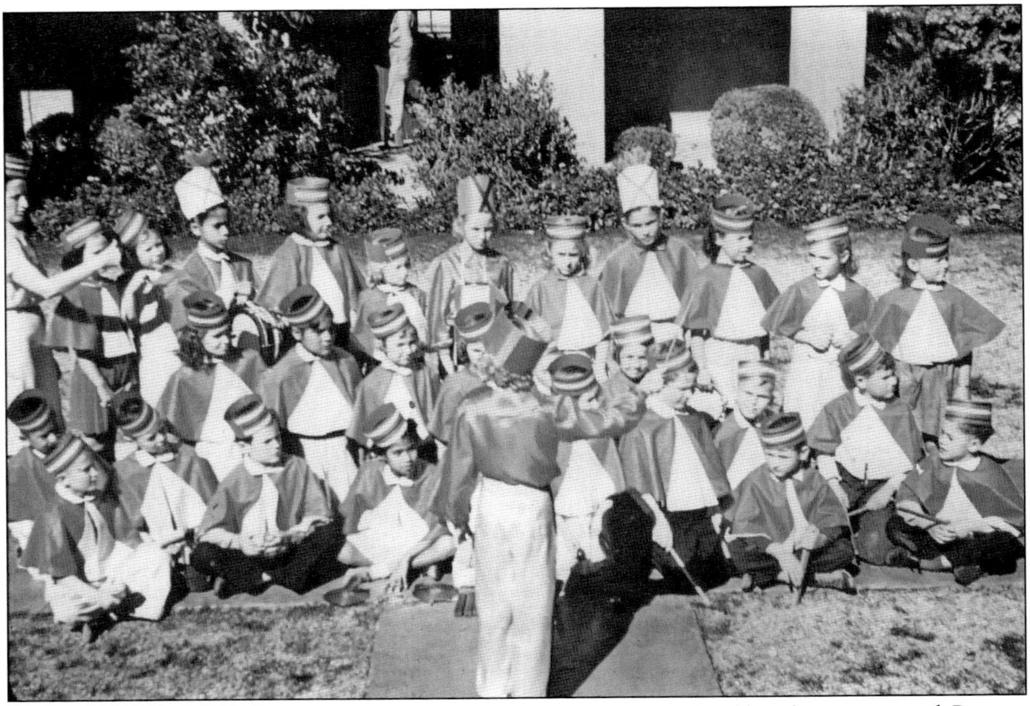

In 1936, five years after South Elementary School opened, the first school band was organized. Parents assisted in making the uniforms for the children, who played musical instruments such as tom-toms, triangles, flutes, and bells. A young member of the band poses as the director. (CHM.)

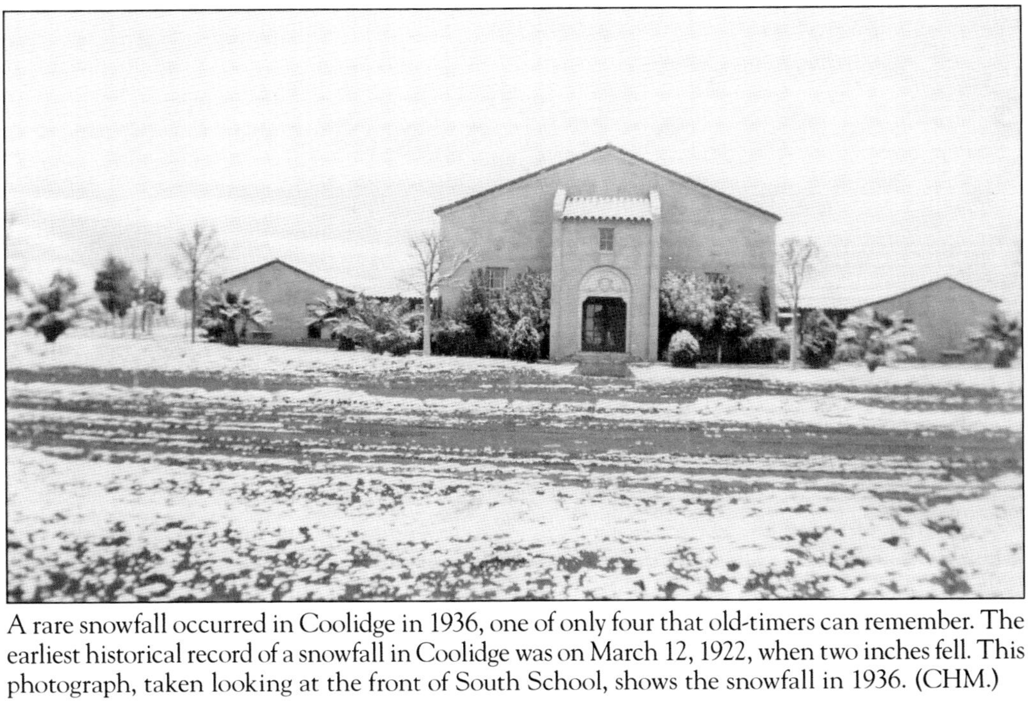

A rare snowfall occurred in Coolidge in 1936, one of only four that old-timers can remember. The earliest historical record of a snowfall in Coolidge was on March 12, 1922, when two inches fell. This photograph, taken looking at the front of South School, shows the snowfall in 1936. (CHM.)

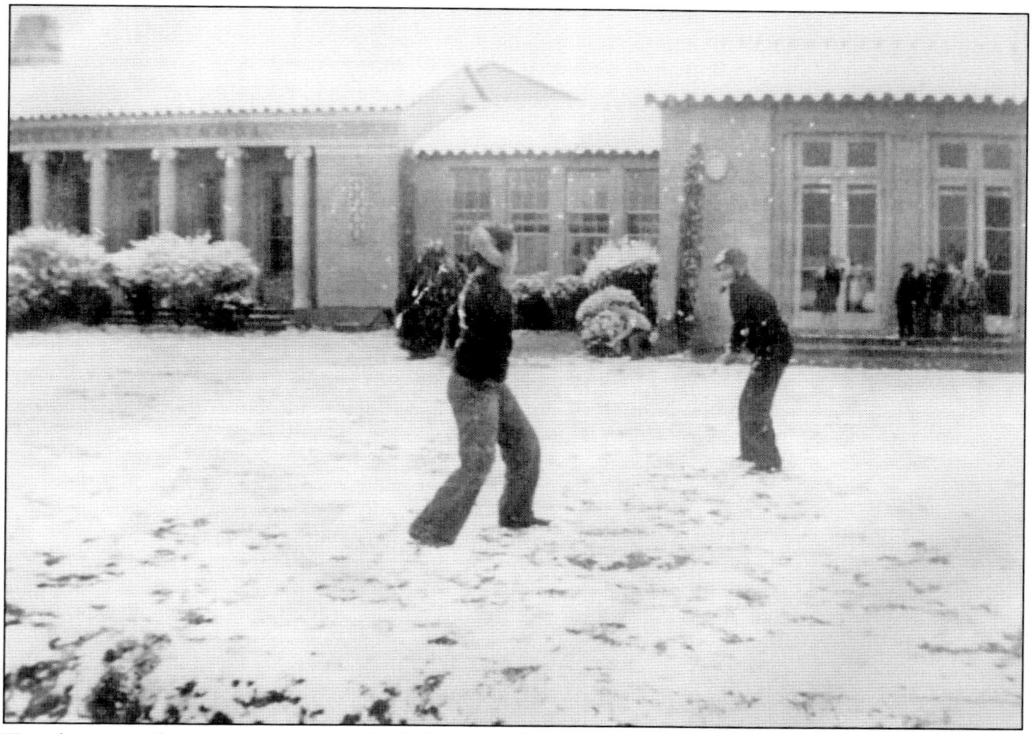

Two boys are having a rare snowball fight in front of South School. When the school was demolished to make way for an apartment complex after it was closed in 1976, many Coolidge residents lamented the demise of what they considered a beautiful building that housed many good memories. (CHM.)

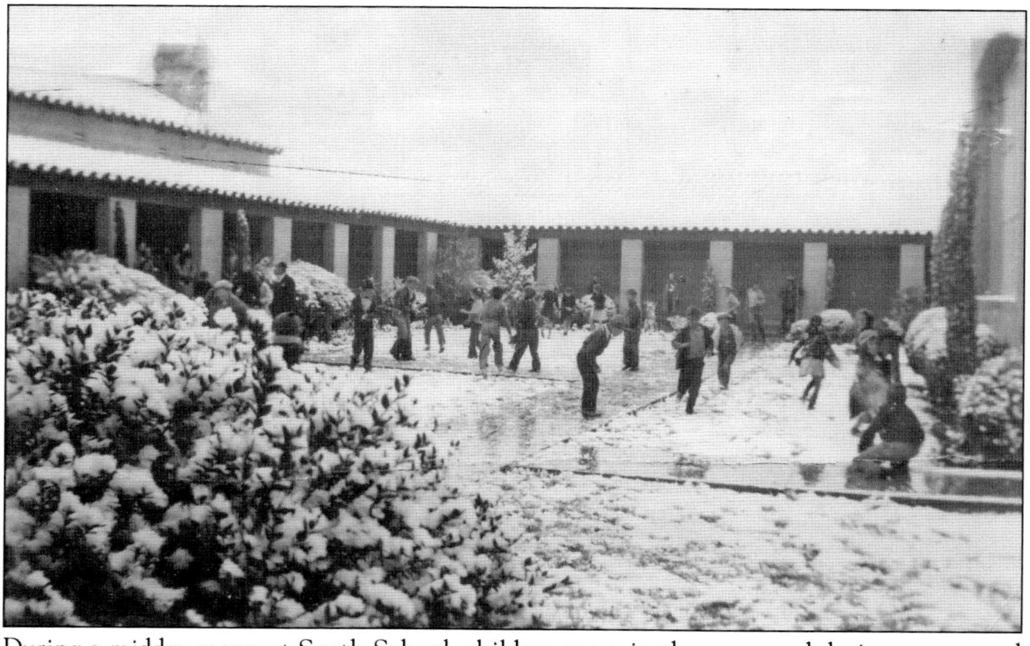

During a midday recess at South School, children romp in the courtyard during an unusual snowfall. Snow is a rarity in the desert in central Arizona and Coolidge in particular. (CHM.)

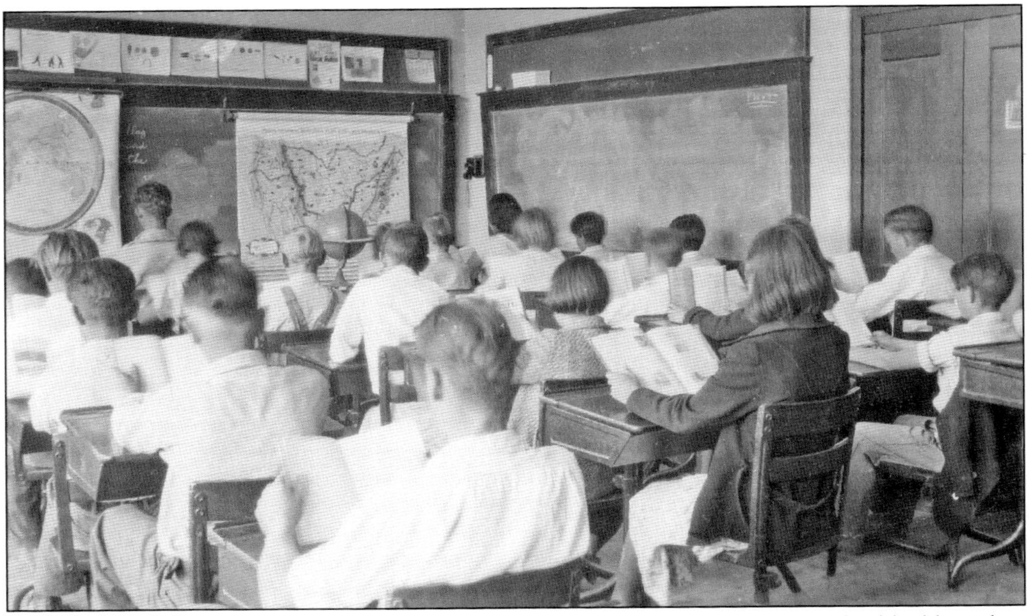

A rare look inside one of the Coolidge schools in 1933 shows posters above the blackboard in front of the class made to encourage eating vegetables that were served in the school cafeteria. A contemporary article published in the Coolidge *Examiner* reported that the world globe in front of the classroom was well used and worn from the many fingers that handled it. (CHM.)

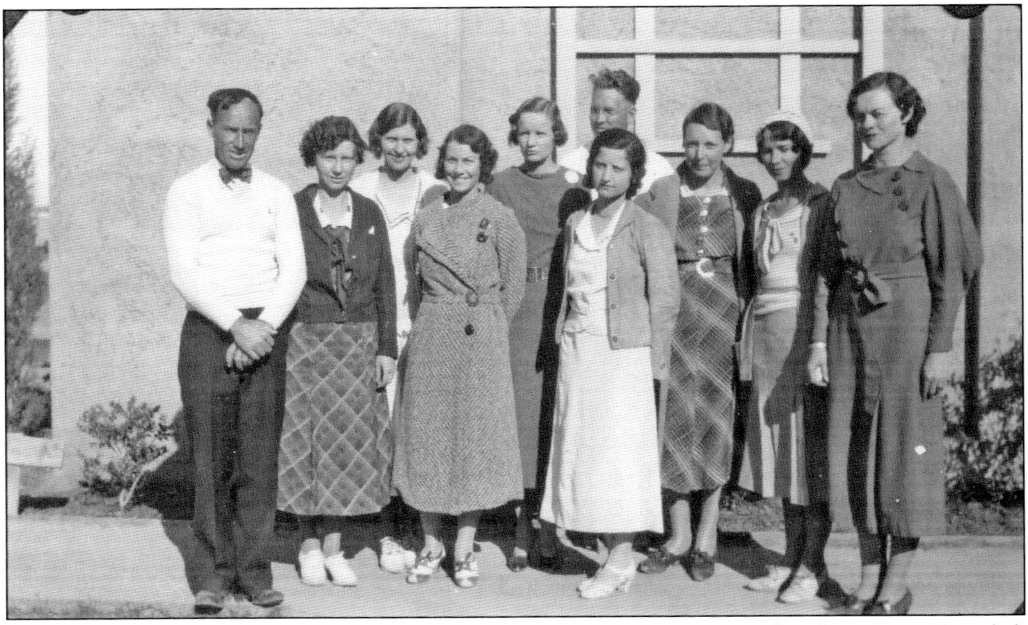

This photograph was likely taken at South School in 1933 of the principal and teachers. From left to right are Mr. Eisenhart (principal), Miss Awrey (fifth grade), Miss Hardwick (art and music), Miss Jones (kindergarten and first grade), Miss Kirkland (second grade), Miss Edwards (third grade), Mr. Smith (eighth grade), Miss Tomlinson (fourth grade), Miss Collins (sixth grade), and Miss Shipley (first grade). The image was snapped by Mr. Culbert, who taught seventh grade. (CHM.)

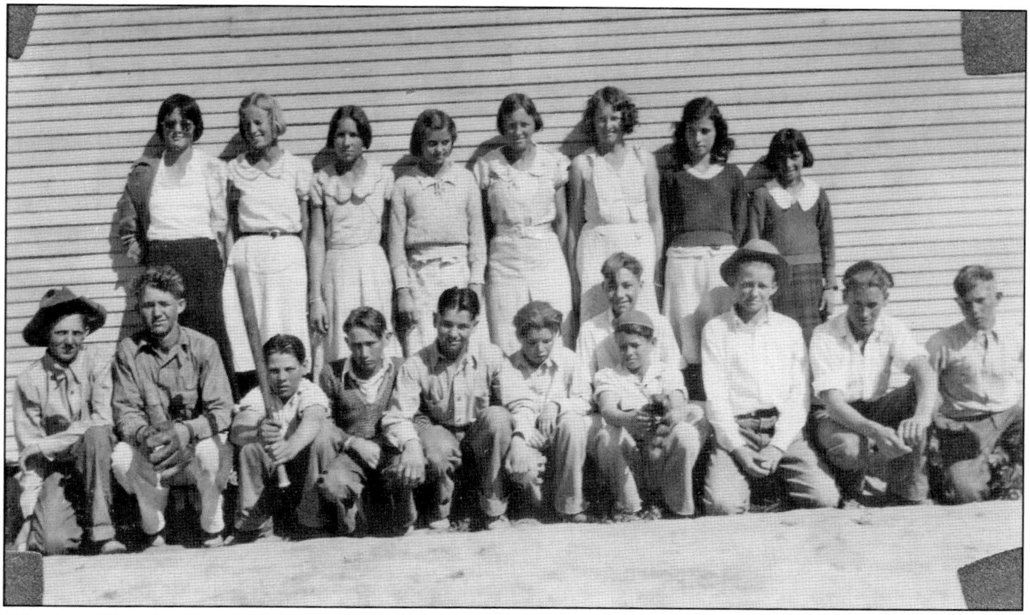

The boys' baseball team for the Coolidge schools in 1933 was undefeated against Kenilworth, Eloy, Casa Grande, and Borree Corner schools. The girls' team won two out of three games against Kenilworth. Pictured here are, from left to right, (first row) Dan Wallace, Joe Dobson, Tim Parker, Louis Johnson, J.C. Rose, Freeman Rose, John DeWitt, Billy Lee, Mershel Homes, Miner Chesley, and Bill ? ; (second row) Marjorie DeWitt, Mable Lee, Doris Wallace, Geraldene Rowe, Bernice Robinson, Norma Sturgeon, Katherine Ridgeway, and Dorothy Ridgeway. (CHM.)

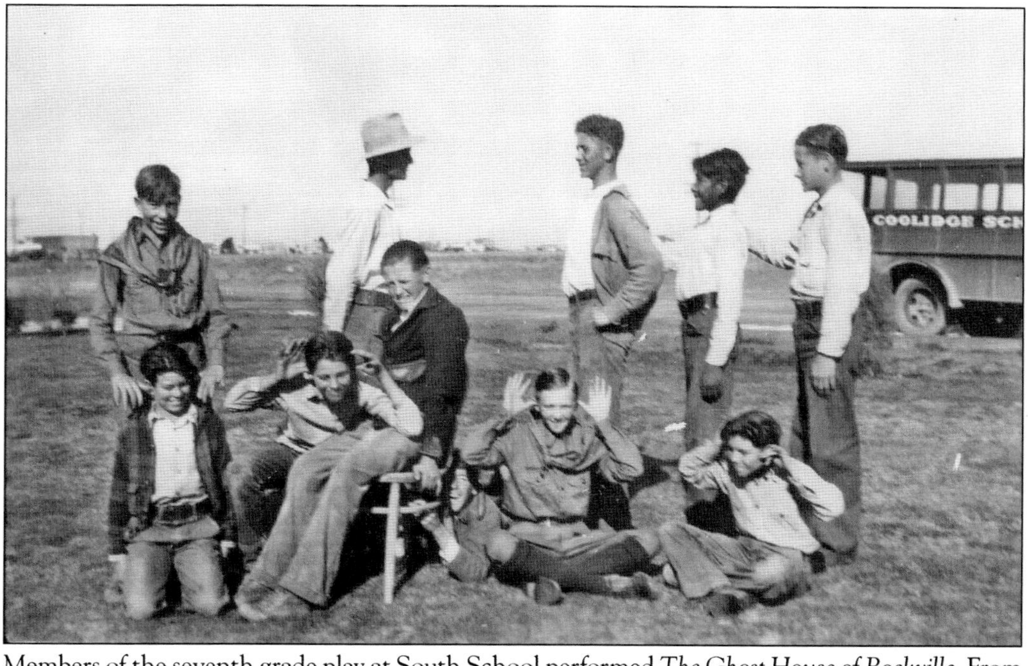

Members of the seventh grade play at South School performed *The Ghost House of Rockville*. From left to right are (first row) Freeman Rose, Miner Chesley, John DeWitt, Ralph Preece, and J.C. Rose; (second row) Jack Collins, Carl Lee, Joe Dobson, Roland Enos, and Billy Lee. (CHM.)

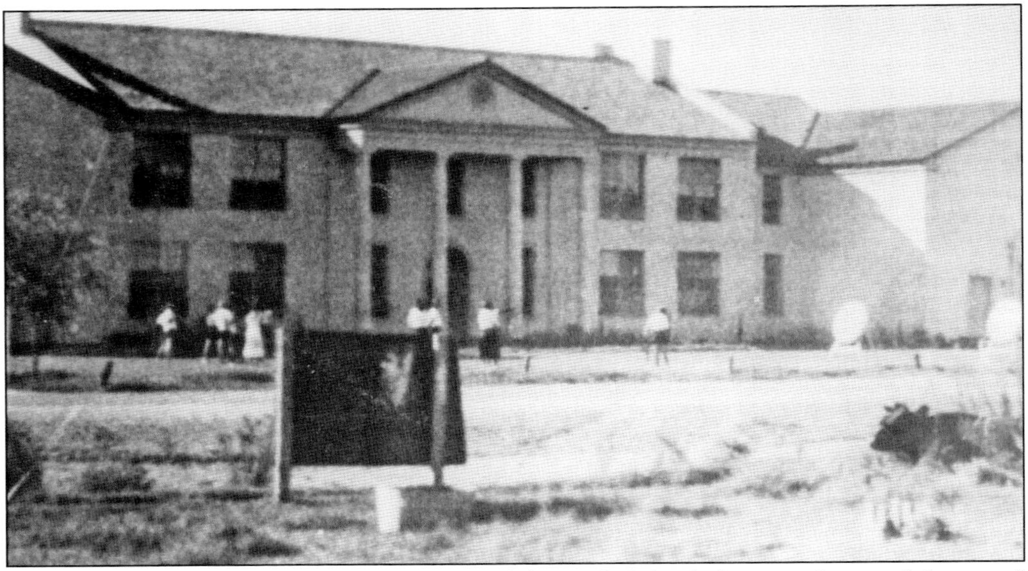

This photograph, taken in 1936 in front of Coolidge High School, shows students with bows and arrows shooting targets on the front lawn, most likely archery practice. In the foreground on the right is a resting cow. Ground-breaking for the new Coolidge Union High School took place on April 6, 1936, and in just five months the school opened with 143 enrollees. When a new high school was built years later, this became McRae Junior High School and today is the administrative office of the Coolidge Unified School District. (CHM.)

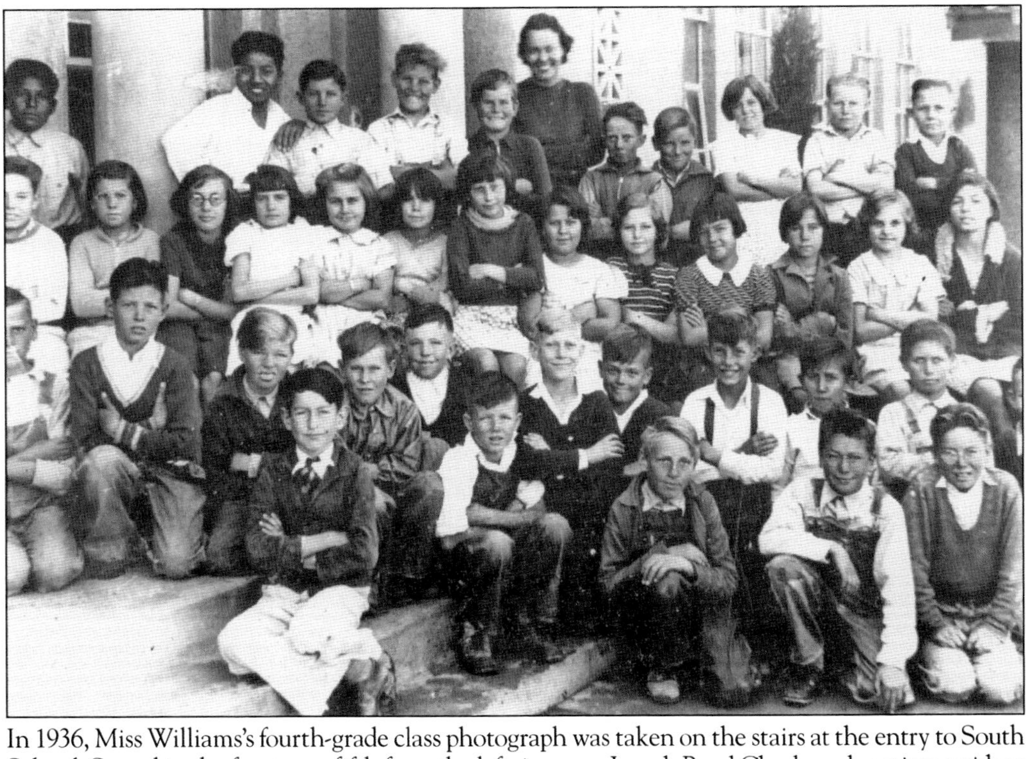

In 1936, Miss Williams's fourth-grade class photograph was taken on the stairs at the entry to South School. Seated in the front row, fifth from the left, is young Joseph Reed Chesley, a longtime resident of Coolidge and now the honorary president-for-life of the Coolidge Historical Society. (CHM.)

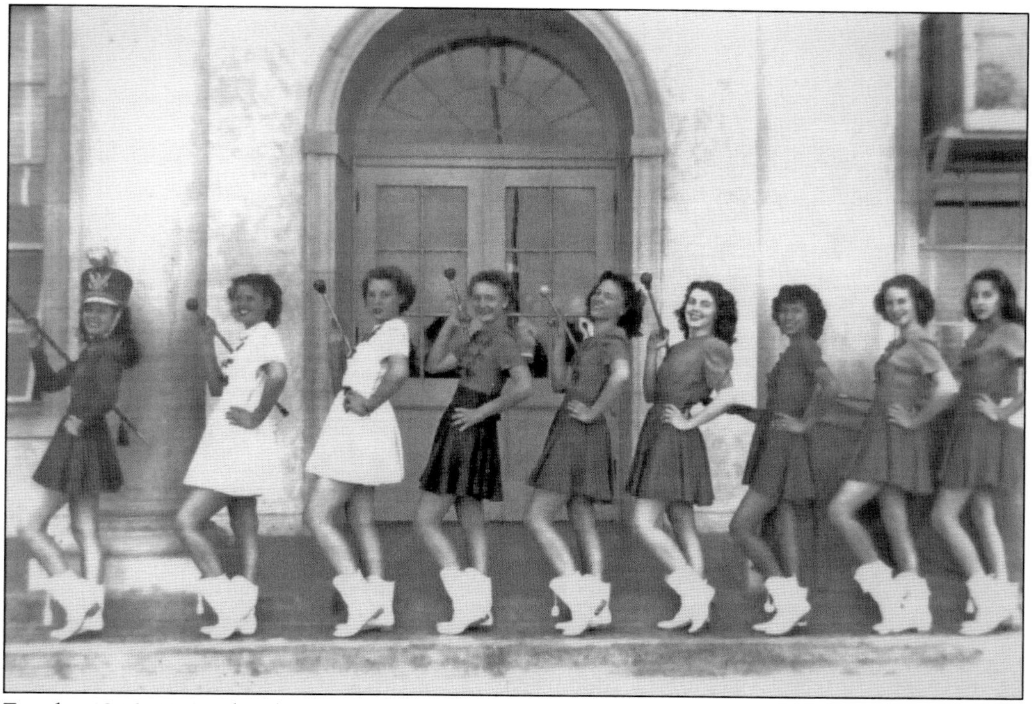

For the 1946–1947 school year at Coolidge Union High School, the official photograph of the majorettes was taken at the entrance. Among those identified here are Bennie Boone, Rosa Lee Horton, Billie McMillan, Bettie Burnside, Donna Letzring, and Rose Mary Davison. In 1936, the first year the school opened, there was a boys' and girls' glee club and a drama club. (CHM.)

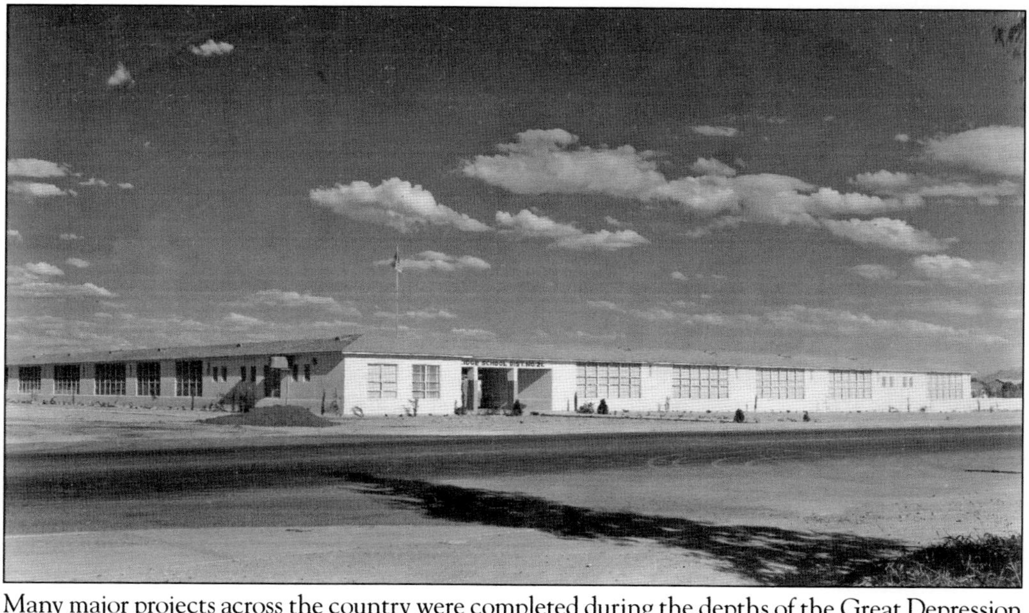

Many major projects across the country were completed during the depths of the Great Depression due to federal New Deal programs. Among them was North Elementary School at 351 North Arizona Boulevard by the Works Progress Administration (WPA) in 1936. In 1954, the school was integrated when the all-black Borree Corner School was closed. North School operated until it was closed in 2009. (CHM.)

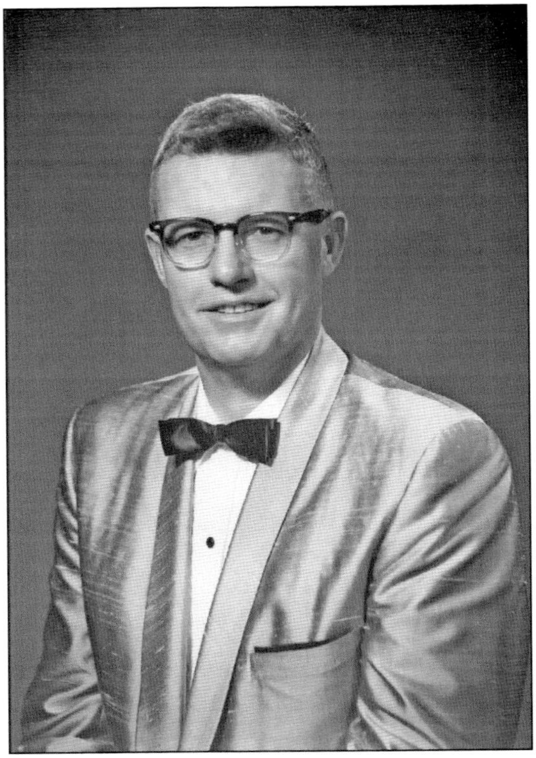

Charles M. Binford moved to Coolidge from Sioux City, Iowa, after a brief stay in Tempe. Binford worked for the Don Mahoney Insurance Agency in Coolidge but enjoyed directing the Coolidge Children's Choir. On May 2, 1964, the Broadmor Theater Group of Tempe presented a benefit performance of *A Night On Broadway* in the high school auditorium under Binford's direction. The multitalented Binford was an accomplished singer and avid golfer. (CHM.)

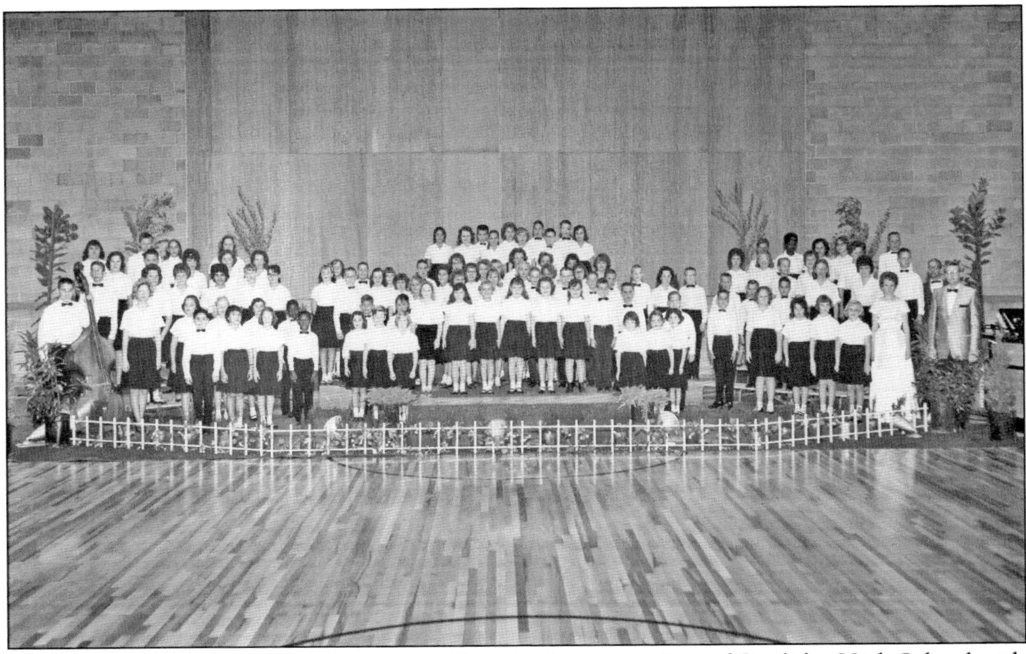

The Coolidge Children's Choir is pictured here in the gymnasium of Coolidge High School with director Charles Binford on the far right and Nita Jo Smith, the choir's piano accompanist, next to him. The choir was organized in 1963 and practiced every Saturday with an average 90-percent attendance record. At one time, there were 113 boys and girls in the choir ranging in age from 8 to 14. (CHM.)

Seven

Places and Spaces

During the years when Coolidge was a much smaller but prosperous town, it boasted three movie theaters, a drive-in theater, a roller rink, three public swimming pools, a country club, and an alligator farm, among other attractions. Longtime resident Elsie Laughlin Reeves recalled when Saturday afternoons were shopping days for area residents who came to Coolidge to purchase their week's supply of household items, parents would drop off their children at one of the movie theaters, where matinee movies cost 10¢ and popcorn was 5¢. Hayduke's Drug Store sold malts for 25¢, and ice cream cones could be had for 5¢ a dip at the soda fountain counter at Hines Drug Store.

Wayne Wuertz recalled arriving in the Coolidge area with his parents, Fred and Eunice, in 1929 and attending the Borree Corner School a few miles west of town on the extension of Coolidge Avenue. Nelson and Josephine Borree operated a grocery store there, as well as stores in Eloy, Florence, and Casa Grande. Henry Appel and his sons Fred and Henry Jr. operated a service station on this rural corner as well. As a rural resident, Wuertz remembered some early landmarks, such as the Valley Church located a mile and a half south of Borree Corner. Pinal County Farm Bureau president Scott Prouty, a native New Englander, built a large stone house on Randolph Road two miles west of Highway 87, and that house still stands today.

Woodruff Road, south of Central Arizona College, was named after a US Army Horse Cavalry officer. His rock-built residence still stands just south of the college entrance as well as the remains of stables where he kept horses for racing on a nearby track. Some of the stables were made of railroad ties and others of rock. Today, the rock-built homes are occupied as private residences.

Just north and west of the railroad overpass on Highway 287 was a large building that housed diesel engines and electricity generators to supplement the hydroelectric power from Coolidge Dam. A small mill existed west of the diesel plant, run by a South Dakota firm that named the plant the Arkota Steel Mill.

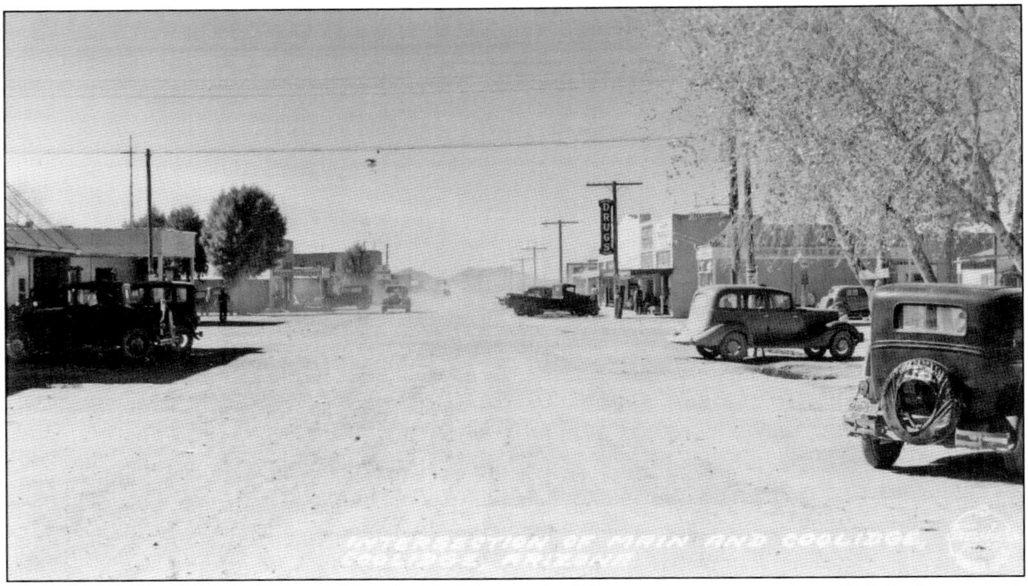

This is a rare postcard photograph taken in the early 1930s at the intersection of Main Street and Coolidge Avenue looking west. This was at a time when the small town began to grow remarkably, as Coolidge became the midpoint stopover for travelers between Tucson and Phoenix. The only north-south route was Highway 87 through town. (Dianna Herrera.)

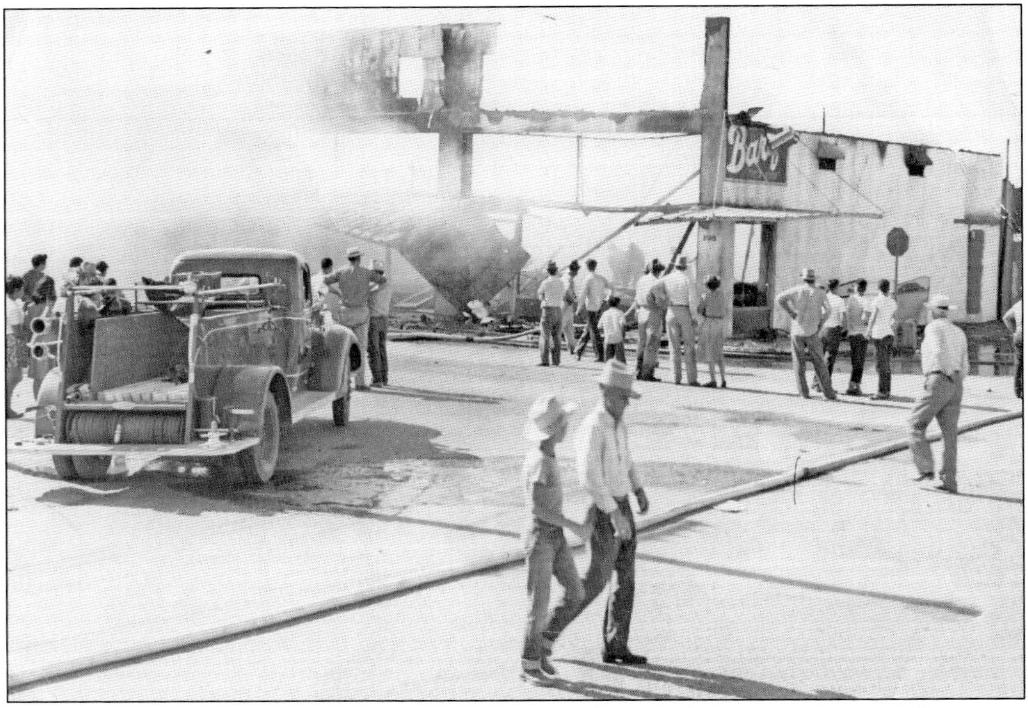

Before the advent of water sprinklers in business establishments, fires were common in downtown stores. In August 1940, Coolidge received its first fire engine, a Seagrave Ford pumper. The following year, a new firehouse was built on the southeast corner of San Carlos Park to house the truck. A more modern firehouse was built years later, and the Coolidge Chamber of Commerce relocated in the former firehouse until vacating in the summer of 2015. (CHM.)

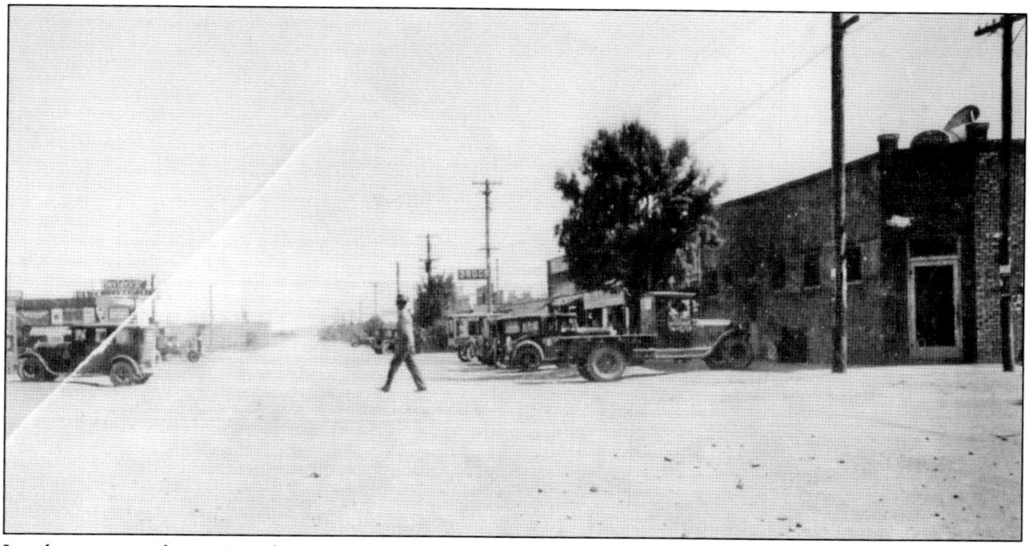

Looking west down Harding Avenue at Main Street shows a typical hot, dry day in Coolidge. The Hayduke Building, constructed in 1938, is on the northwest corner and stands today minus the decorative parapet on the roofline. (CHM.)

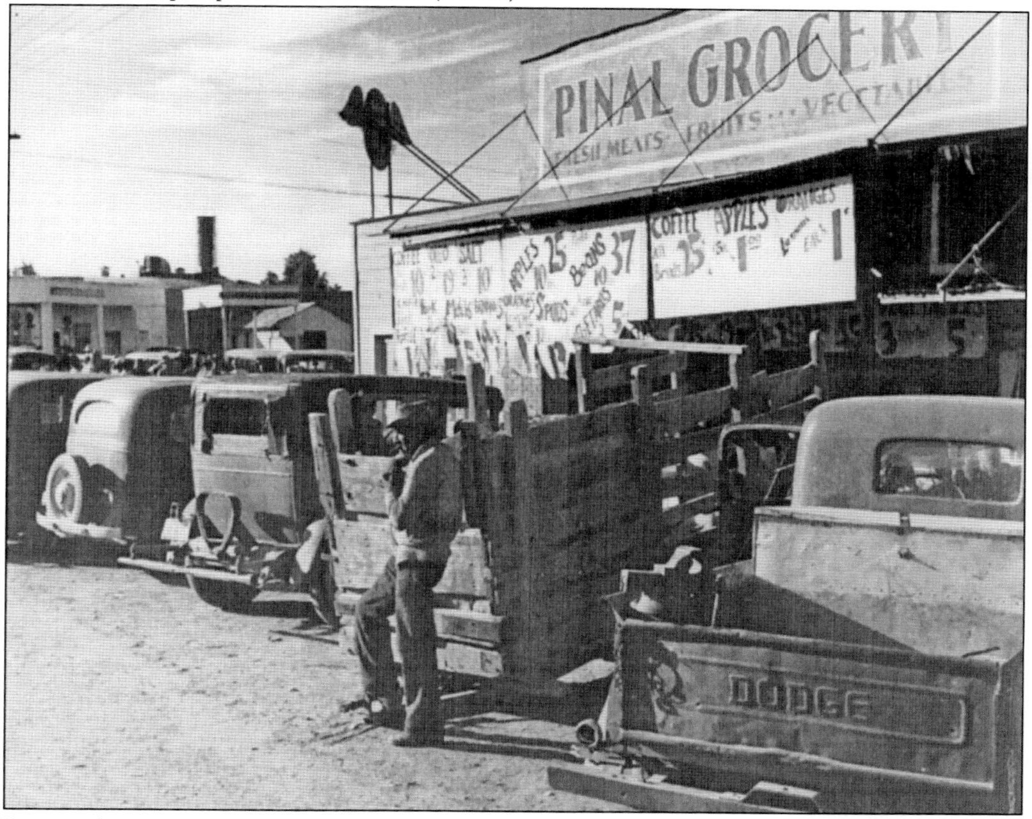

During the 1940s war years, the Pinal Grocery, located off Main Street in downtown Coolidge, was a busy place. The signs indicate oranges and lemons were selling for 1¢ each, apples for $1 a bushel, and coffee for 25¢ a pound. The tall tower in the background appears near the Valley State Bank on Central Avenue. (CHM.)

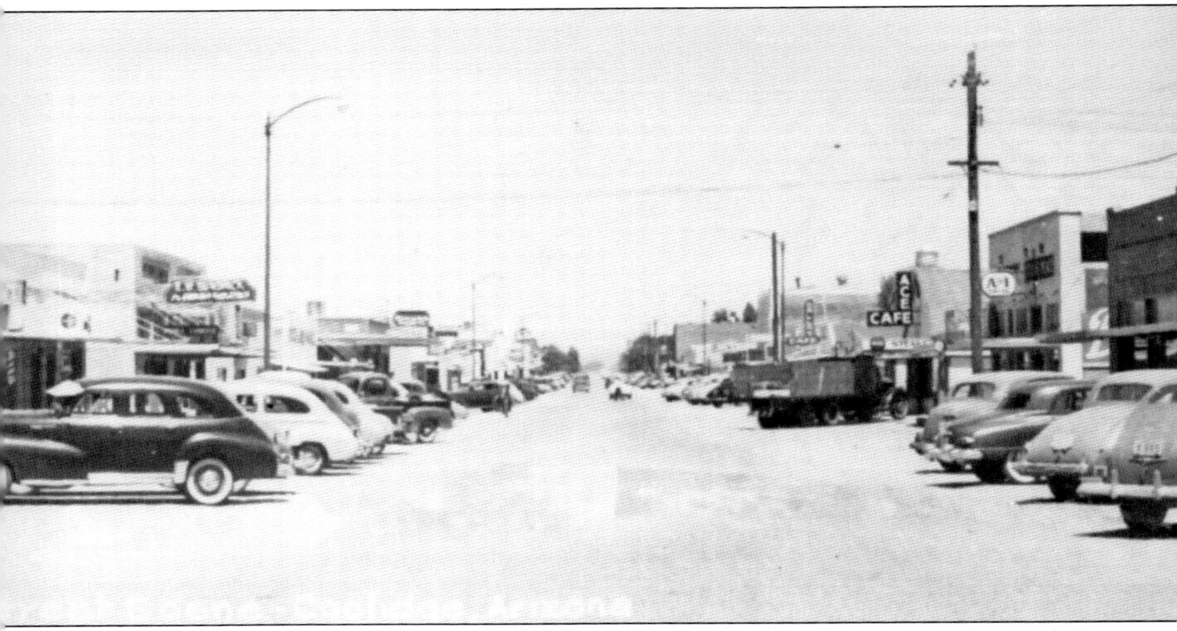

During the 1940s, Main Street in Coolidge was the busiest street downtown and a good place to own a business. This photograph was taken looking north with the top of the water tower visible above the Ace Café. Today, the water tank is still in operation, managed by the Arizona Water Company. Illegal gambling took place in some Coolidge bars even though Mayor Ben Arnold would say publicly that it did not exist in Coolidge. In an article published in the *Arizona Gazette* in the early 1950s, Coolidge was described as a "rip-roarin' boom town where gambling and illegal liquor flourished without any suggestion of interruption by the law." One old-timer recounts that the gambling rooms were unconcealed just off the main barroom, and no secret password was necessary. (CHM.)

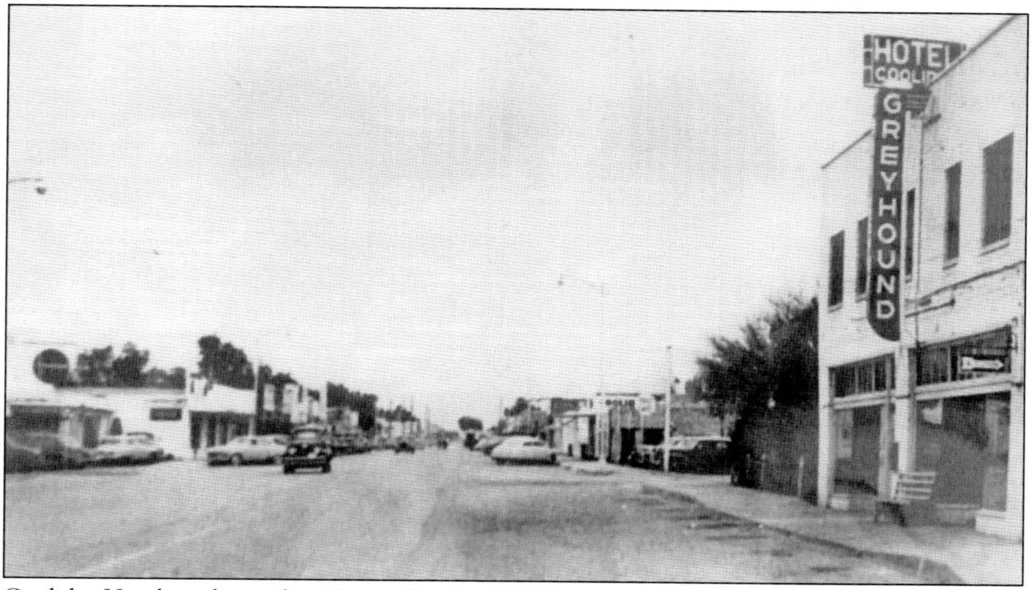

Coolidge Hotel was located on the south side of Coolidge Avenue and three blocks east of Arizona Boulevard. Greyhound bus service began at the hotel in November 1933. If motorists could not afford the hotel, there was an auto court around the corner on Arizona Boulevard operated by Charley Glaubig, which he opened in November 1927. (CHM.)

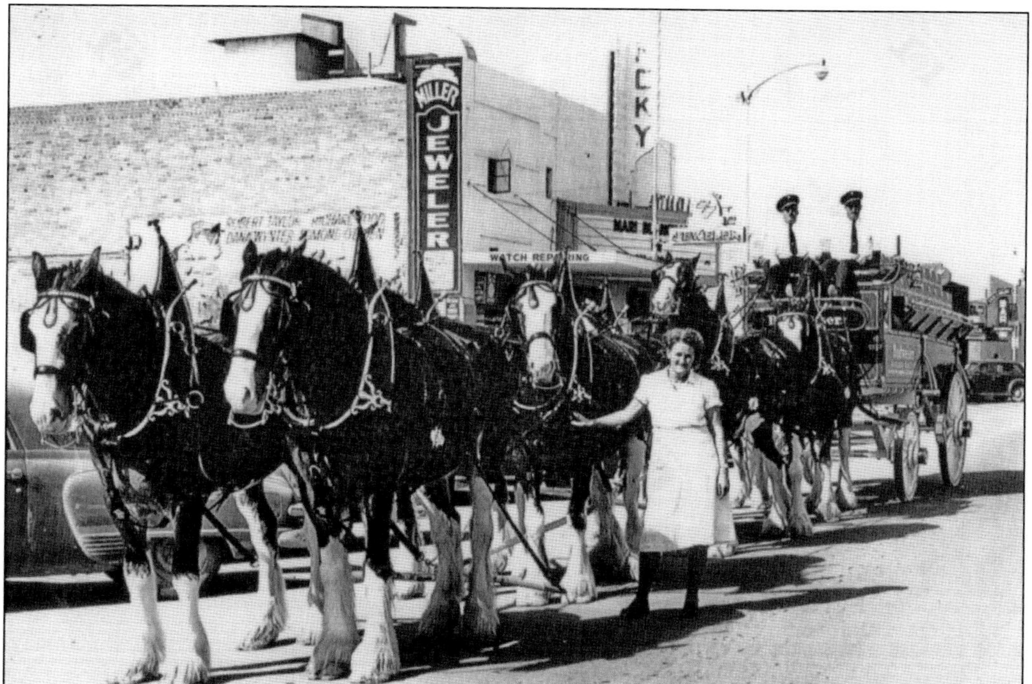

Some time in the 1940s, the Budweiser beer wagon stopped in front of the Studio Theater on the west side of Main Street. The movie poster on the wall of Miller Jewelry indicates a film starring Robert Taylor and Dana Wynter was showing at the time. Above the theater were the radio studios of KCKY, where in the mid-1950s Waylon Jennings and Lee Hazlewood once worked as disc jockeys. (John E. Hill.)

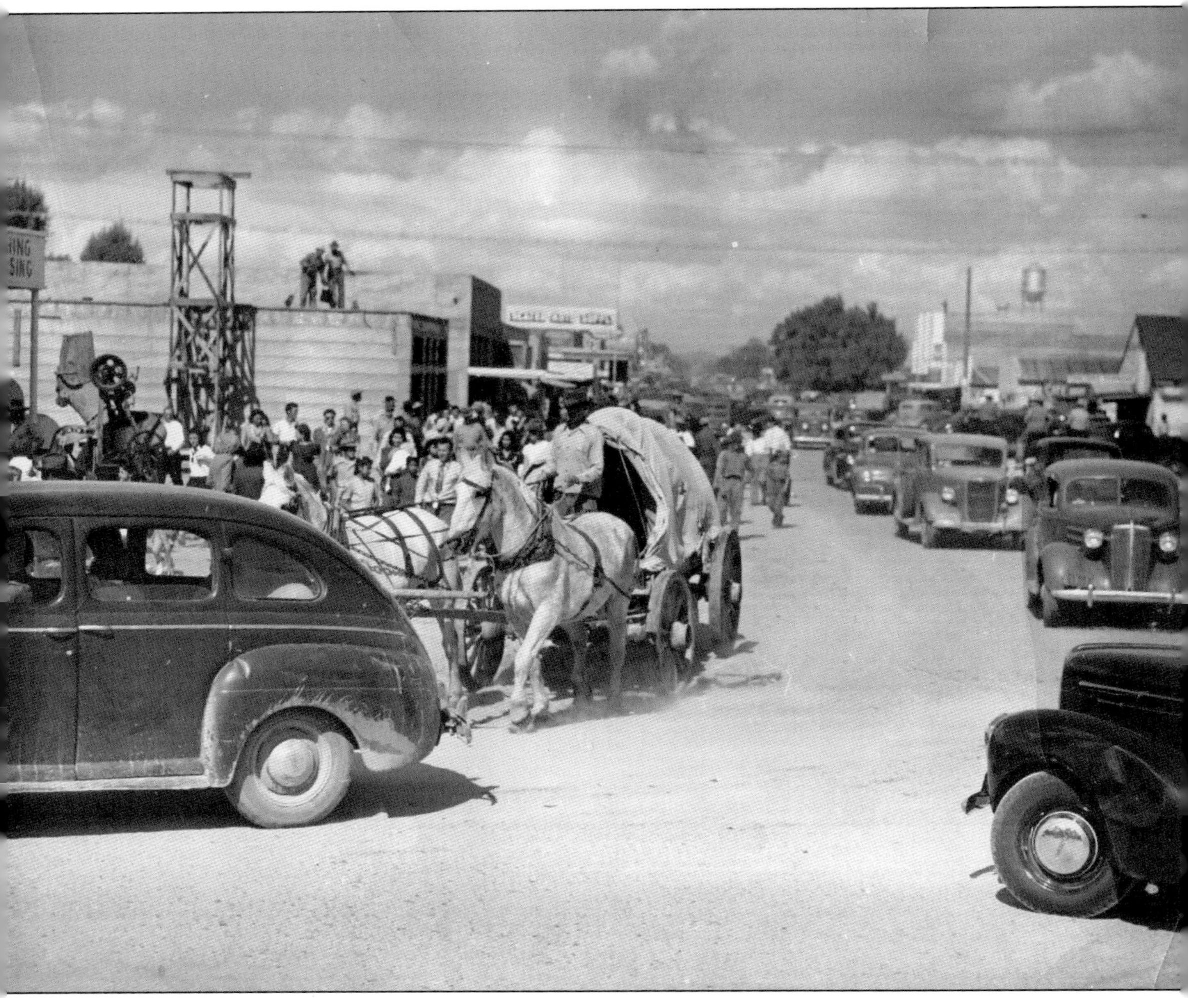

Saturdays were the busiest days in Coolidge, as area residents came to town to do the week's shopping and partake in the many luxuries Coolidge had to offer. This view of Main Street looking north from Coolidge Avenue shows that it was a particularly busy intersection. Several movie theaters were located on Main Street, and parents would drop their children off for the afternoon matinee. Native Americans from the Gila River Indian Reservation at Sacaton would drive their horse-drawn wagons and park them under the tamarack trees in the vicinity of today's Main Street Park. After a day of shopping, families would camp out by their wagons overnight and make the long, dusty trip back to the reservation the next day. (CHM.)

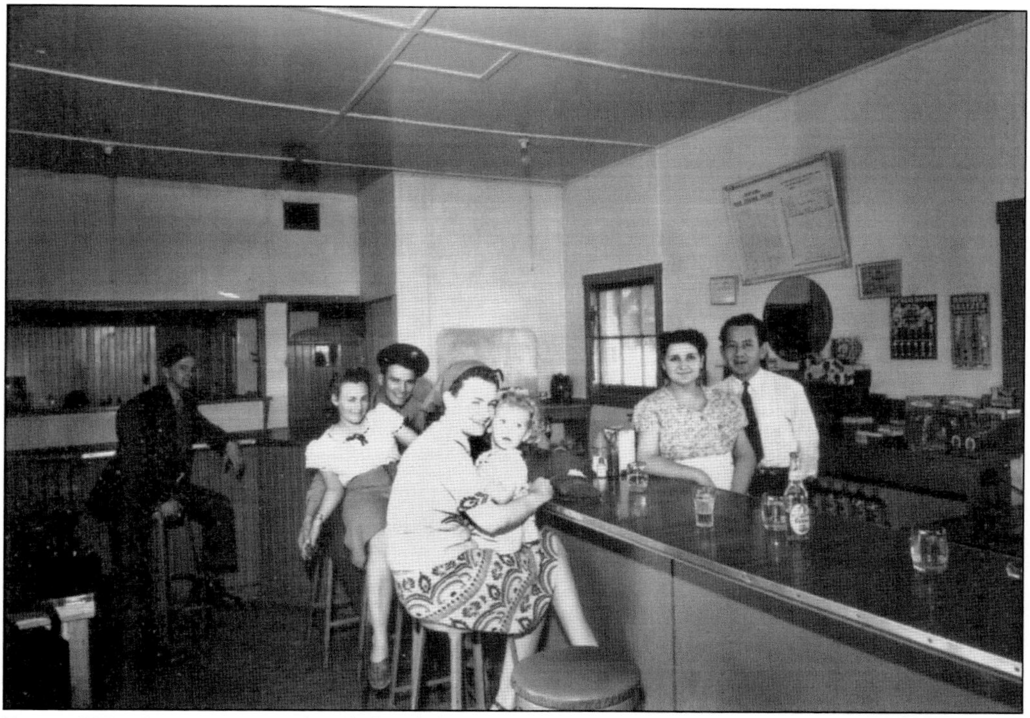

Bea and Tag Guayante, standing behind the counter, opened a business on October 8, 1944, at 112 South Arizona Boulevard. Tag's Taco Stand and Drive In was a popular eatery on the southwest corner of Central Avenue and Arizona Boulevard. (Janice Calvert.)

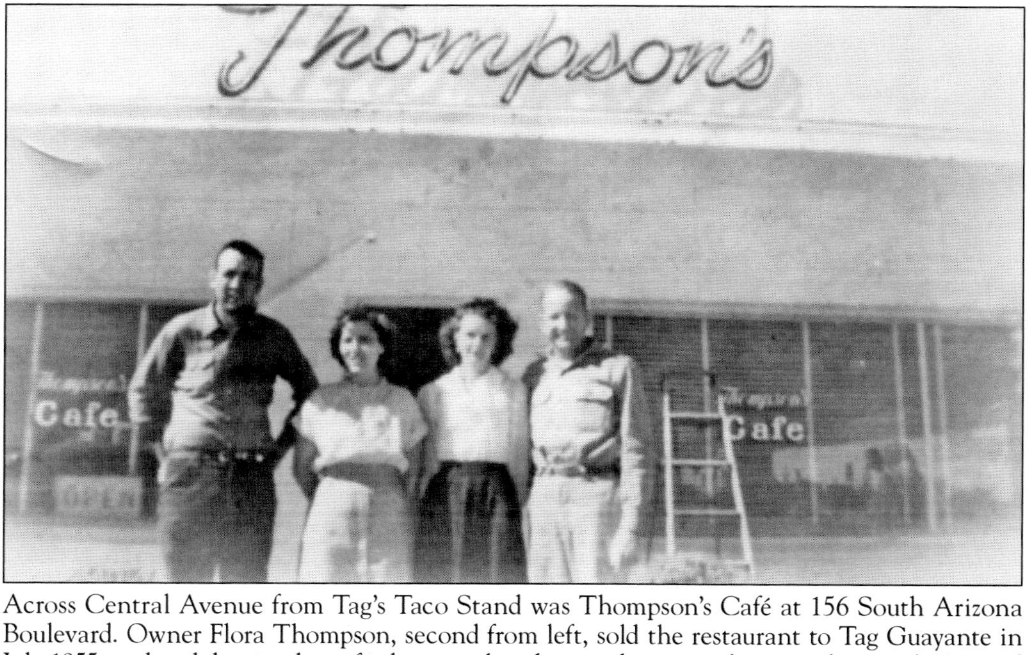

Across Central Avenue from Tag's Taco Stand was Thompson's Café at 156 South Arizona Boulevard. Owner Flora Thompson, second from left, sold the restaurant to Tag Guayante in July 1955, and and despite the café changing hands over the years, the name has stuck. Pat and Dudley Lewis are on the right. (Janice Calvert.)

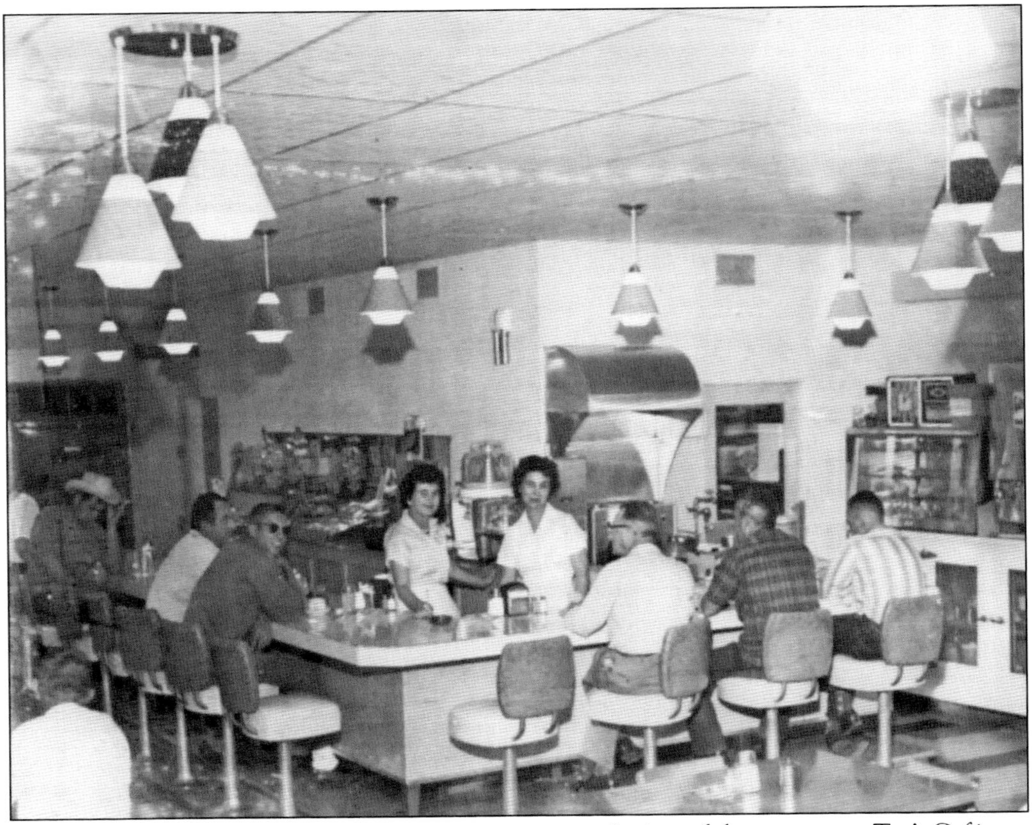

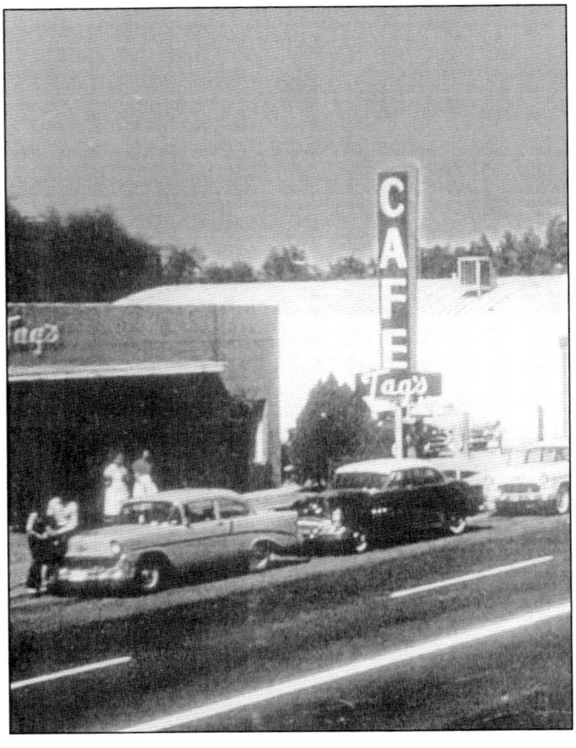

A view of the counter at Tag's Café sometime in the 1950s indicates the interior has changed very little in both décor and customer popularity. Over the years, Tag's has become a popular meeting spot for residents and visitors alike. (CCC.)

Since 2005, Richard Schaar and Janice Calvert have owned Tag's Café on Arizona Boulevard. The menu of American and Mexican fare attracts a regular flow of locals, winter visitors, and motorcycle clubs that make Tag's a favorite stopover point for lunch during bike tours around the central Arizona valley. The large white building on the right is still standing and used by Garrett Motors. (Janice Calvert.)

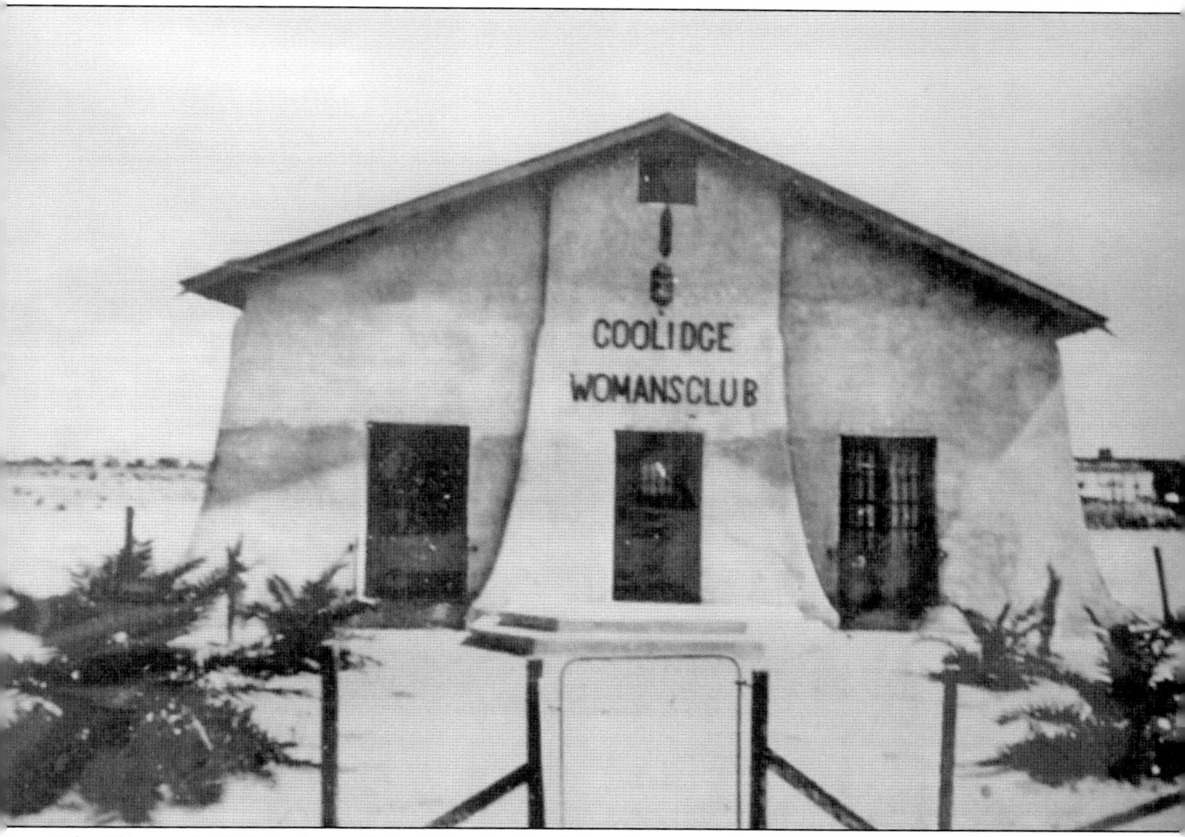

The Women's Club is the only building in Coolidge that is in the National Register of Historic Places. It began on September 7, 1926, when a group of women met at the home of Dora Nutt, the postmistress of Coolidge. Originally called the Coolidge Community Club, the group decided at the second meeting to construct a building for the needs of the community. In February 1928, water pipes were laid, and four palm trees and two pepper trees were planted in front. The building was 32 feet by 66 feet, with adobe brick walls 18 inches thick in a Spanish Colonial design. The total cost of the building was $,2828.49, and a box placed in the cornerstone on the southeast corner contained the honor roll of contributors, the 1928–1929 yearbook, copies of the Coolidge newspaper, and other items. The building contains a kitchen and restrooms. In 1973, a furnace and air-conditioning were added. (CHM.)

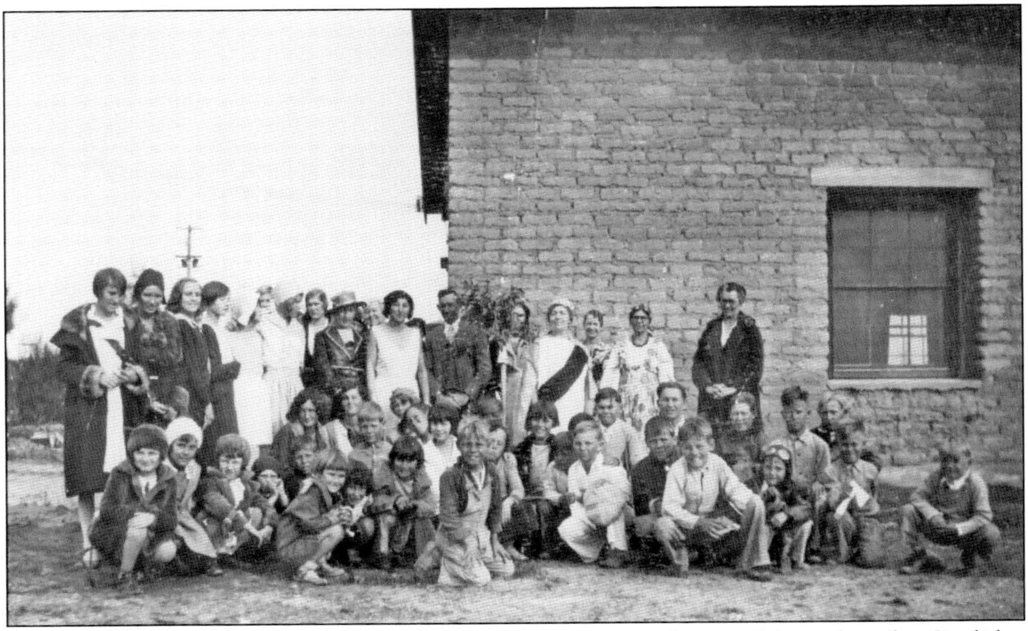

On February 22, 1932, the George Washington bicentennial was celebrated at the Coolidge Women's Club. The adobe bricks were made and laid by George Layman, and Tom Wall did the carpentry. Later, the adobe bricks were covered with stucco. A library was started in the building by the club members with a gift of 12 books. (CCC.)

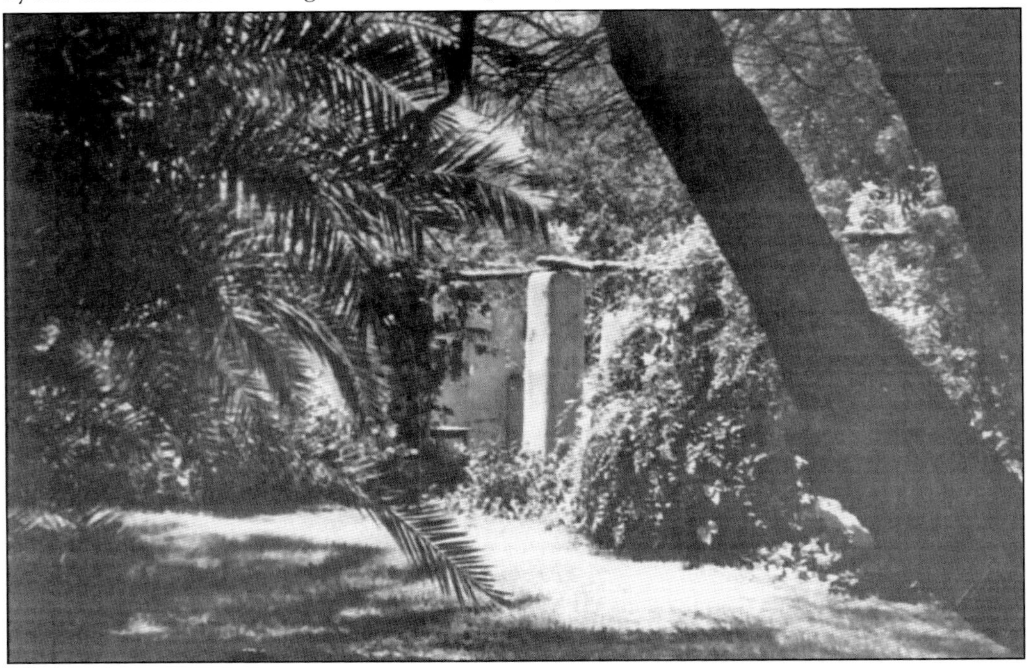

The Vah Ki Inn, a desert inn and guest ranch, had a tearoom and guest lodge that opened in 1930 in the north end of Coolidge and encompassed 40 acres. The inn was built by engineer and architect Walter C. Smith. The grounds provided shaded comfort for the guests and became a well-known rest stop for travelers until it closed in 1940. Water from the San Carlos irrigation canal nearby kept the lawns green most of the year. (CHM.)

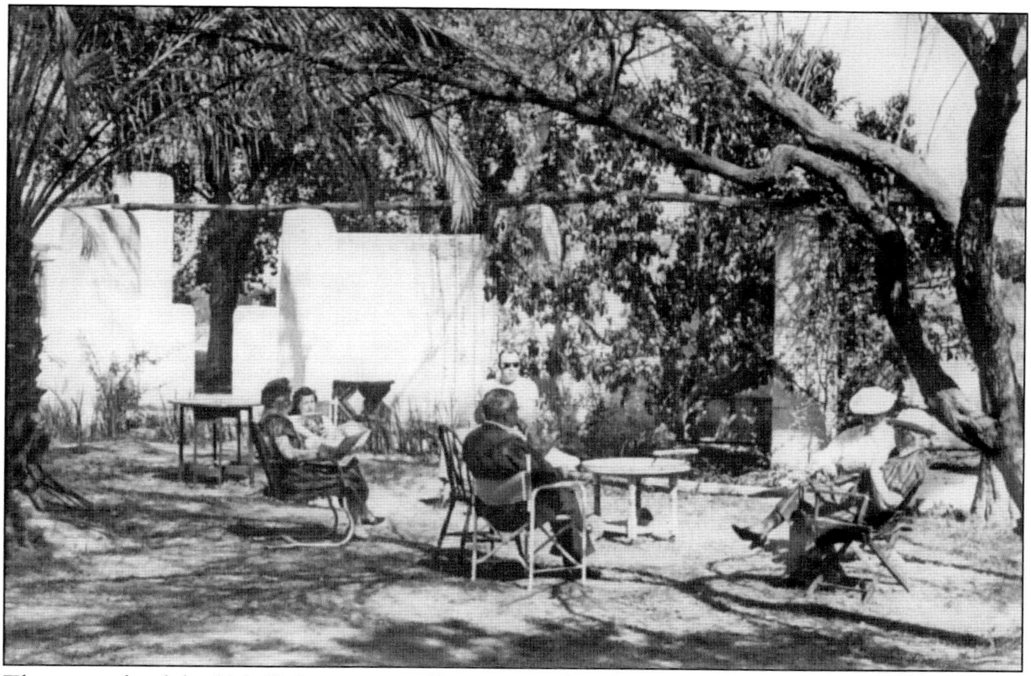

The grounds of the Vah Ki Inn were well maintained with native plants and ample open spaces for the guests to lounge. Many guests living in Phoenix came to escape the bustle and heat of the city. (CHM.)

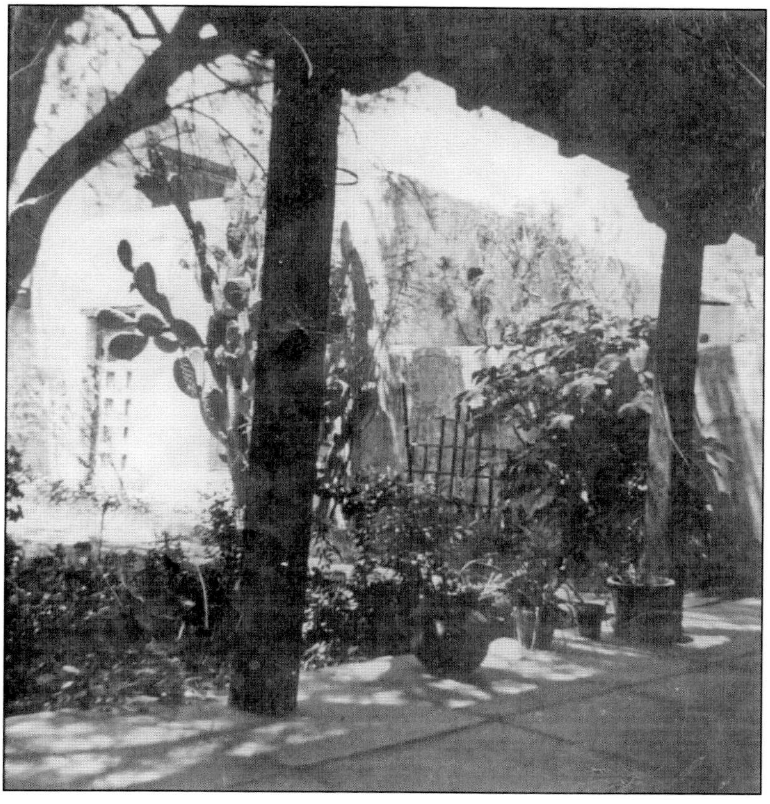

During the years that the Vah Ki Inn was in operation, the grounds were maintained by a skilled staff that took great care to ensure a wide variety of succulents, trees, and shrubs were grown for the pleasure of the guests. (CHM.)

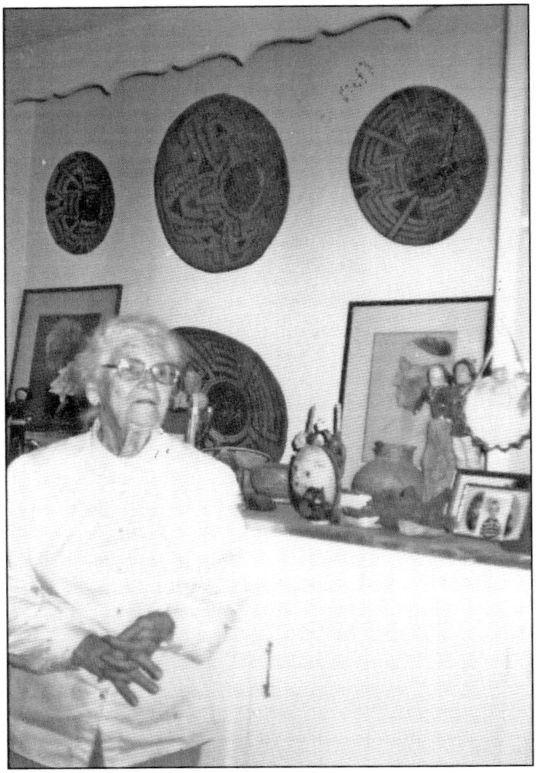

Vertie Smith, the owner of the Vah Ki Inn, took great pride in making sure guests were comfortable and well fed during their stay. While lodged there, guests would visit the Casa Grande Ruins National Monument adjacent to the inn, as well as take motor tours of the surrounding attractions in the Casa Grande Valley. (CHM.)

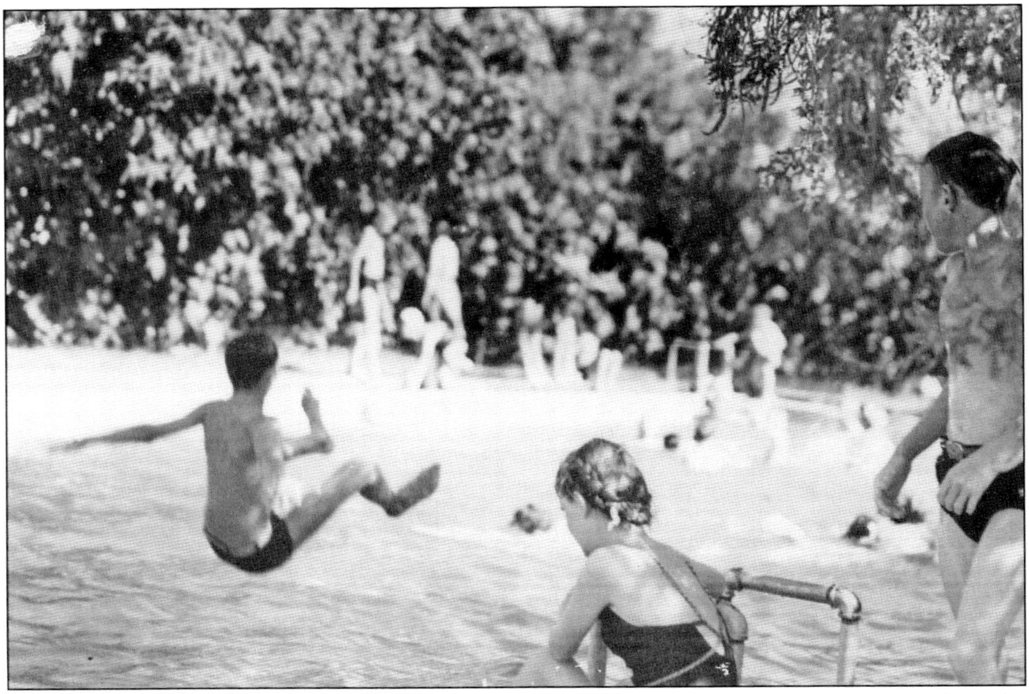

The swimming pool behind the Vah Ki Inn provided welcome relief from the desert heat for guests. Much of the original 40-acre tract of land has been subdivided into residential home sites, but the main building remains today. (CHM.)

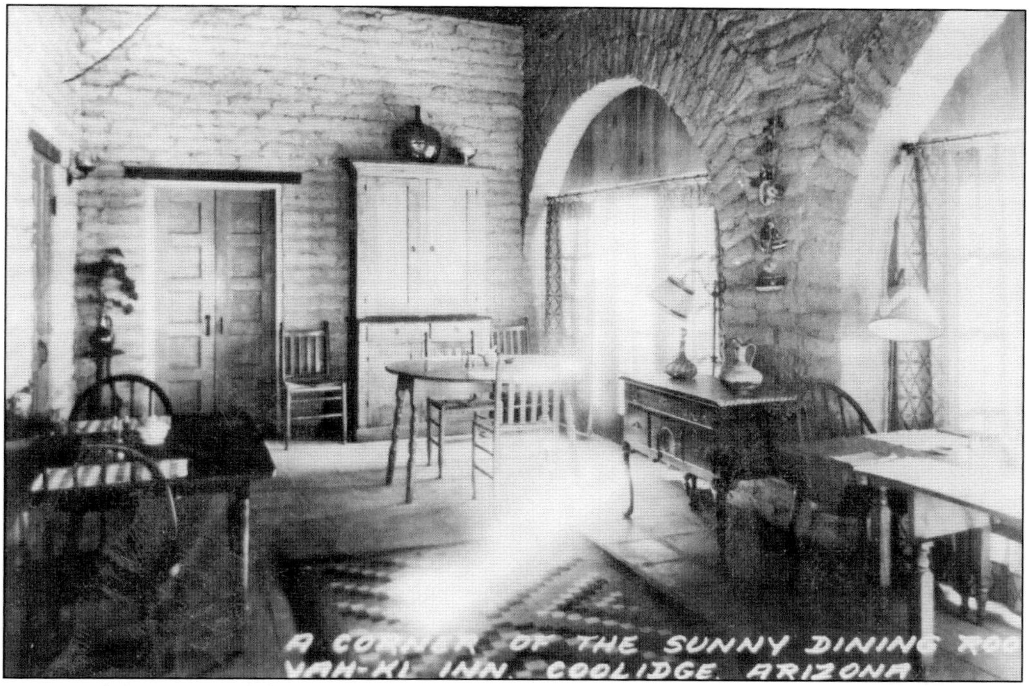

A view of the corner of the dining room of the Vah Ki Inn, taken sometime in the 1940s, shows the unique furnishings and the ample sunlight that the arched windows provided. The inn was once included in food critic Duncan Hines's list of best places to eat in the United States. Hines was the pioneer of national food rating who traveled the country before interstate highways were built and wrote the 1935 best seller titled *Adventures in Good Eating.* (PCHS.)

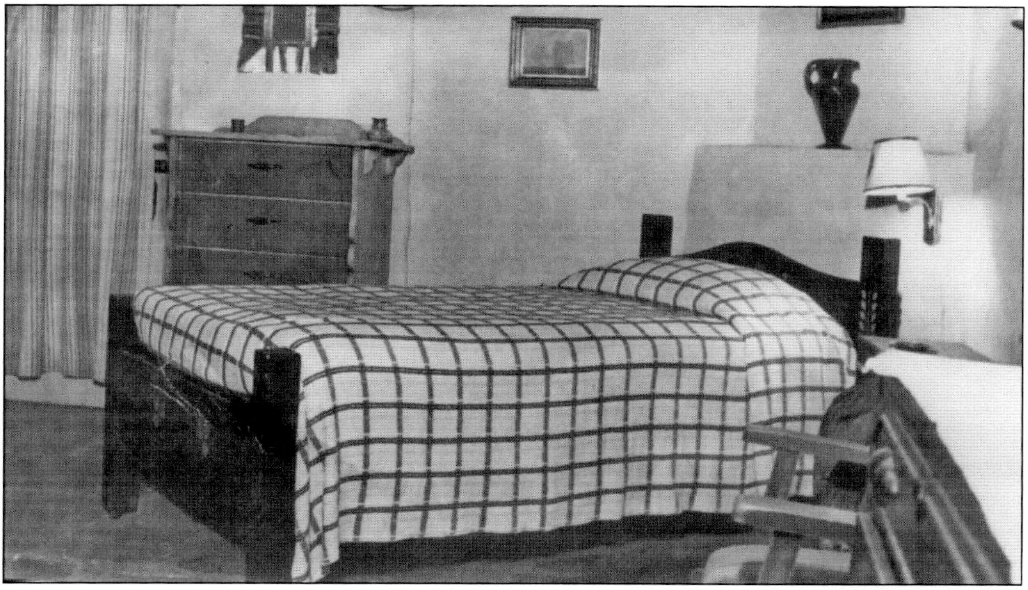

Each of the guest rooms at the Vah Ki Inn were well appointed in the Sonoran Traditional style. Each bedroom had a bath and a fireplace for use during the chilly desert nights. The name of the inn is Pima for "place where our elders dwelt." (CHM.)

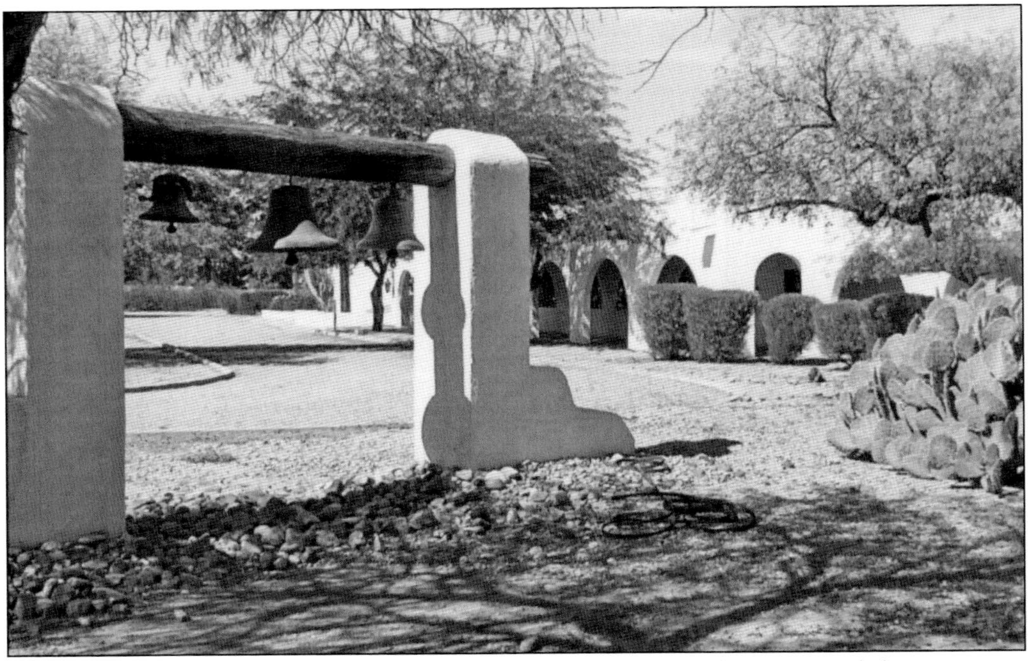

This February 2015 photograph of the Vah Ki Inn shows how well maintained the remaining main structure is thanks to St. Michael's Episcopal Church, which purchased the remaining 3.2-acre site in 1957. In 1963, a fire destroyed the roof and other wooden parts of the building, but repairs were made. In 1980, the church added a large kitchen, dining area, narthex, and sanctuary. (Author's collection.)

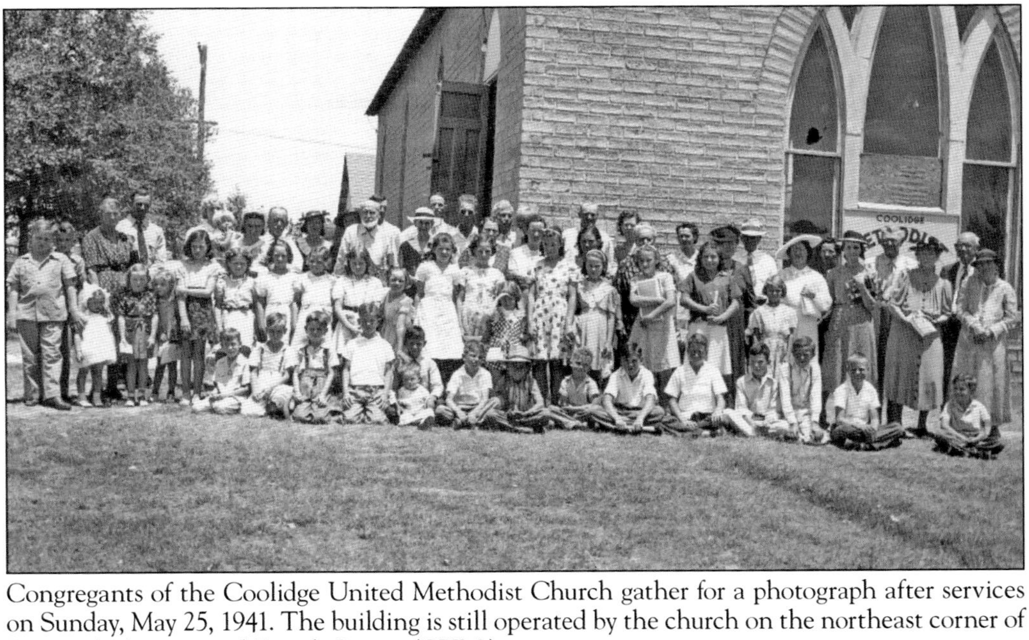

Congregants of the Coolidge United Methodist Church gather for a photograph after services on Sunday, May 25, 1941. The building is still operated by the church on the northeast corner of Roosevelt Avenue and Fourth Street. (CHM.)

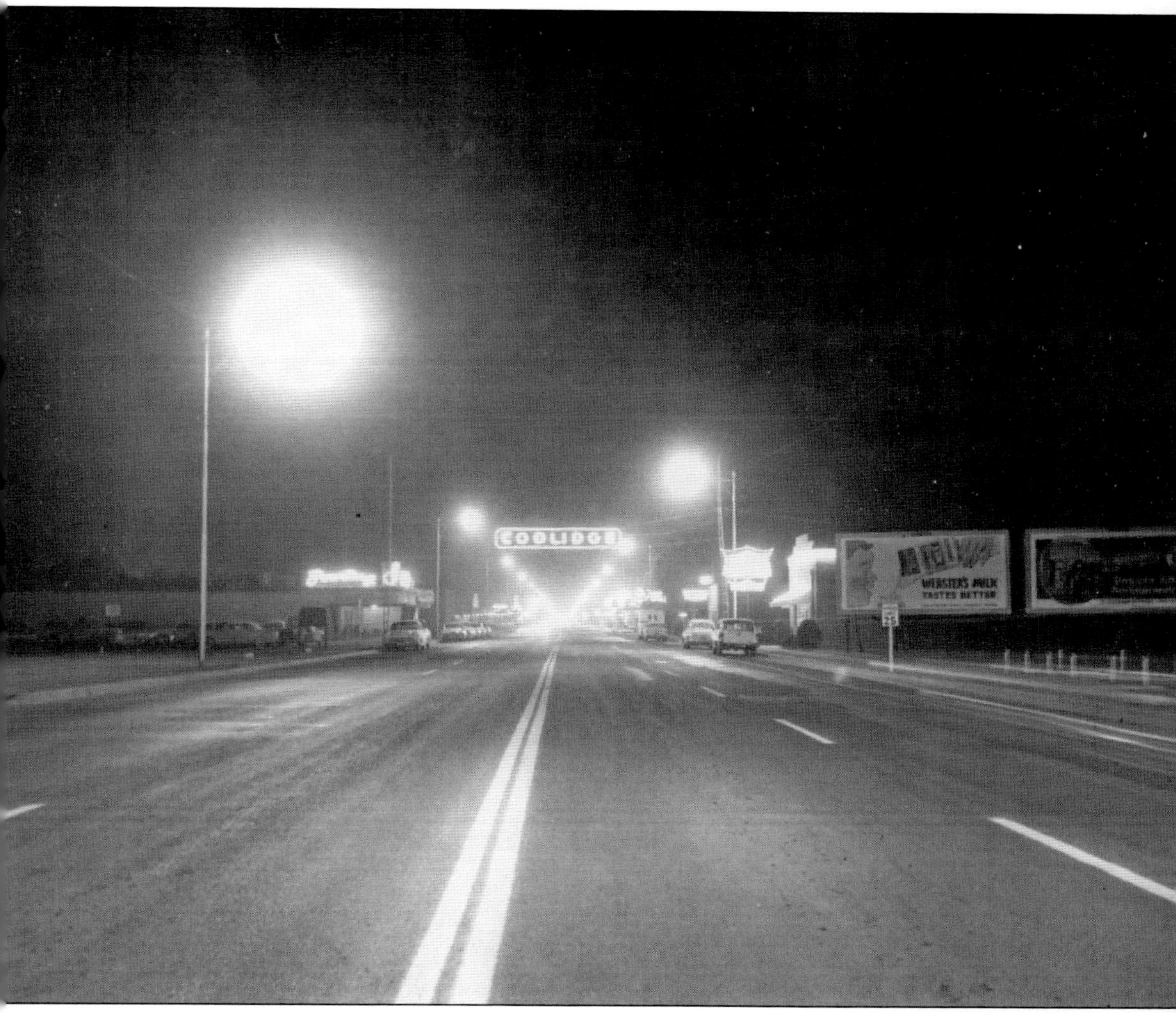

This nighttime photograph looking north down Arizona Boulevard showing the lighted neon sign that identifies the town was taken some time in the 1950s. An unknown photographer took the image near where Coolidge Avenue bisects Arizona Boulevard. A popular sport in the 1950s among the town's teenage drivers was to "drag the Main," a term that signified cruising the loop formed by Arizona Boulevard, Coolidge Avenue, Main Street, and Central Avenue. Those who remember say the method was to drive the loop in one direction and then make a U-turn and drive in the opposite direction. This provided the opportunity for the cruising teens to observe the activities on both sides of the streets and show off their shiny cars. (CCC.)

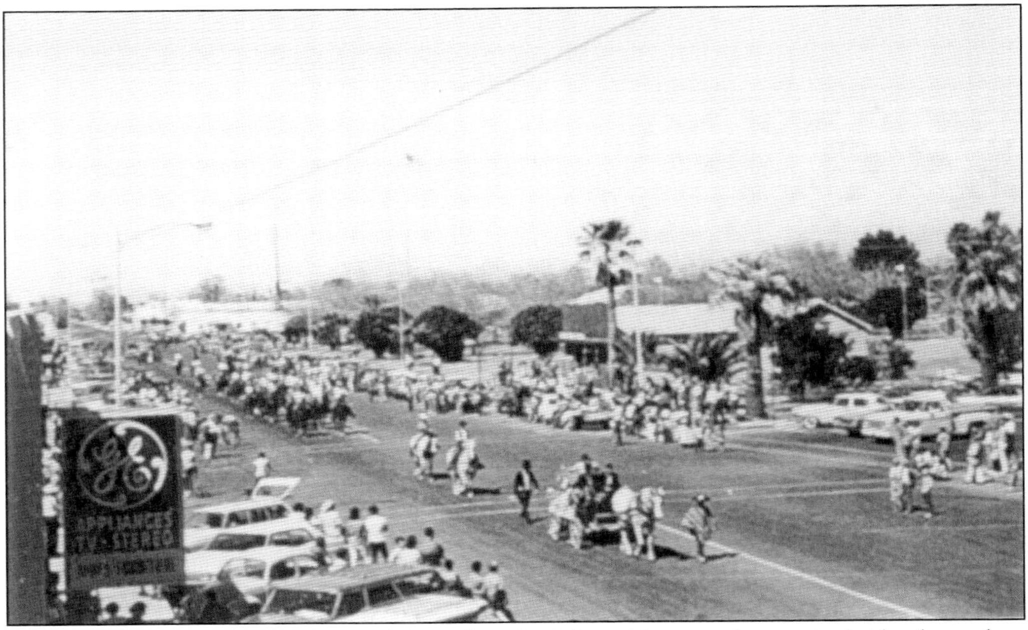

The annual Cotton Days event is celebrated in Coolidge with a parade, carnival rides, horseshoe and cotton bale–rolling contests, and many other family-oriented events over the weekend. This 1960s photograph shows San Carlos Park on Central Avenue. The fire station is the building behind the two palm trees. The public swimming pool was located in the northeast corner of the park behind the fire station. Boys' and girls' softball fields were on the west side of the park. (John E. Hill.)

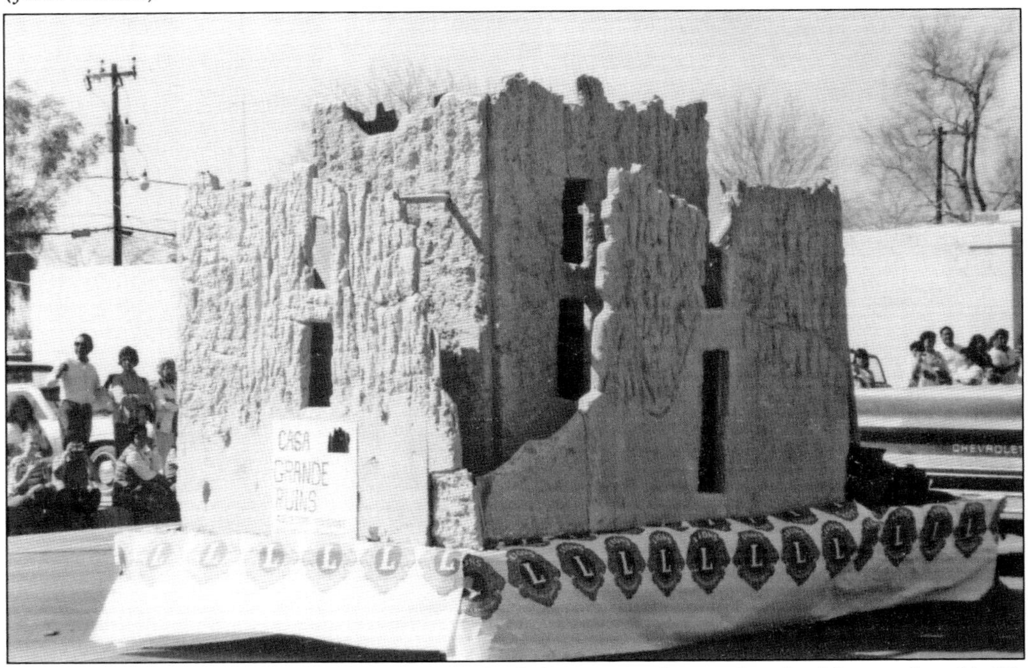

Another annual event is Coolidge Days, which began on the weekend of September 21–23, 1984, as Calvin Coolidge Days. In this photograph, the Coolidge Lions Club and the chamber of commerce sponsored the Casa Grande Ruins float. (CHM.)

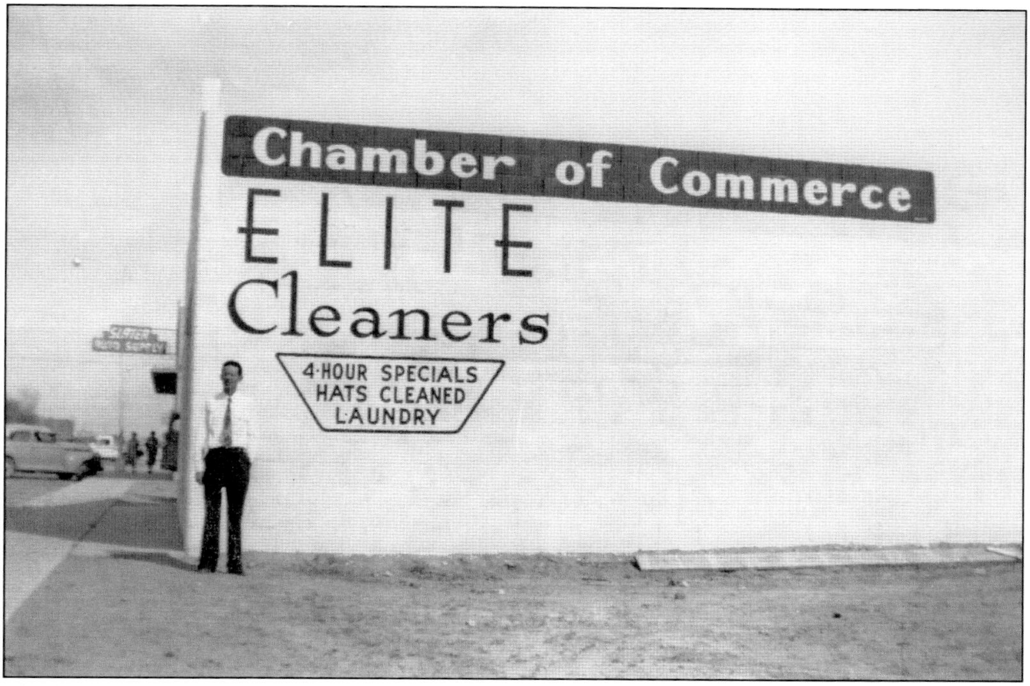

This late-1940s photograph was taken looking east along Central Avenue with Slater's Auto Supply sign visible at mid-block. Fred Slater opened one of the first automobile garages in Coolidge, the Valley Garage. In 1927, Layman's Garage was opened and operated a few years until the Slater and Nofziger Valley Garage took over the business. (CHM.)

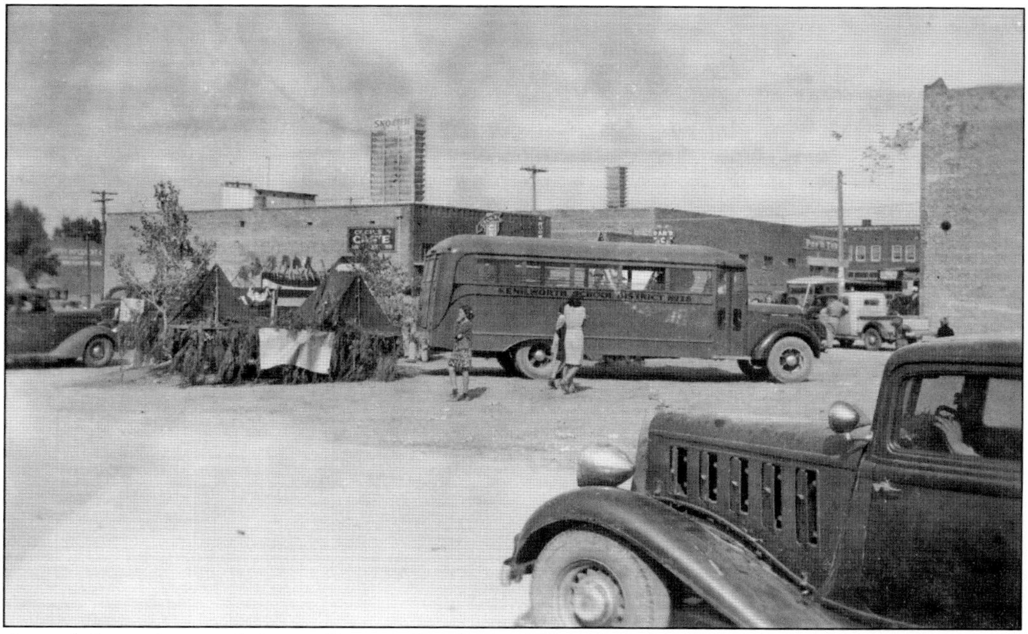

One of the pickup and drop-off points for the Kenilworth School bus was on Main Street in the empty lot next to the Masonic lodge visible on the far right. The Circle Café and Shorty's Bar are directly across the street from the lodge, and the San Carlos Hotel, which was located above Hines Drug store, is visible above the pickup truck. (CHM.)

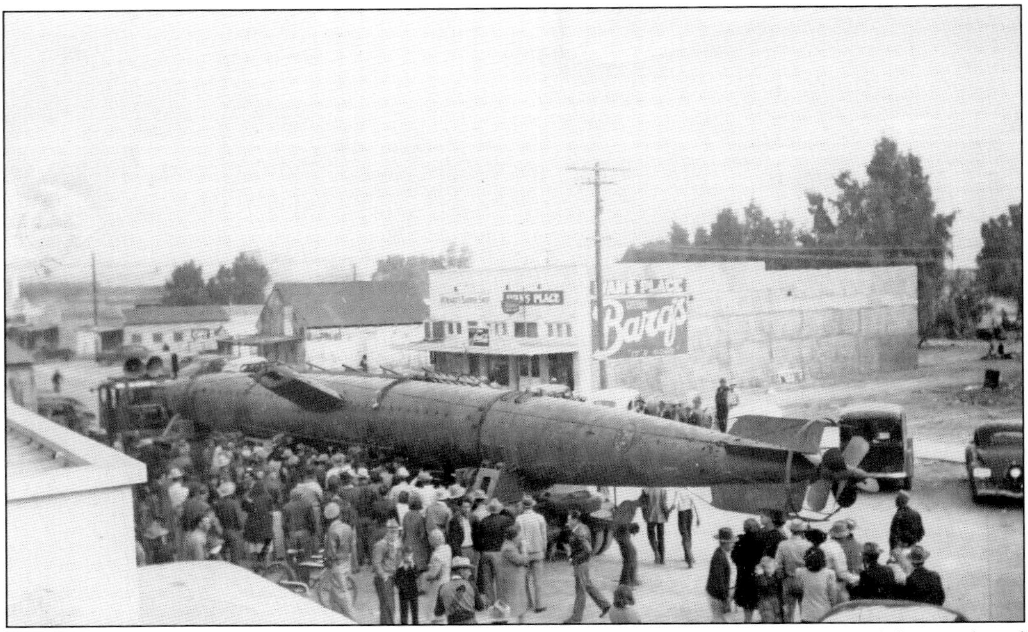

A captured Japanese two-man submarine was brought to Coolidge in 1943 as part of the war-bond drive. This view is looking east on Coolidge Avenue where Wah's Place grocery store, owned and operated by George Wah, was located. Wah was a respected businessman who set up a water hose, horse trough, and bales of hay behind his store for Native Americans from Sacaton who drove their horse-drawn wagons to Coolidge for Saturday shopping excursions. (CHM.)

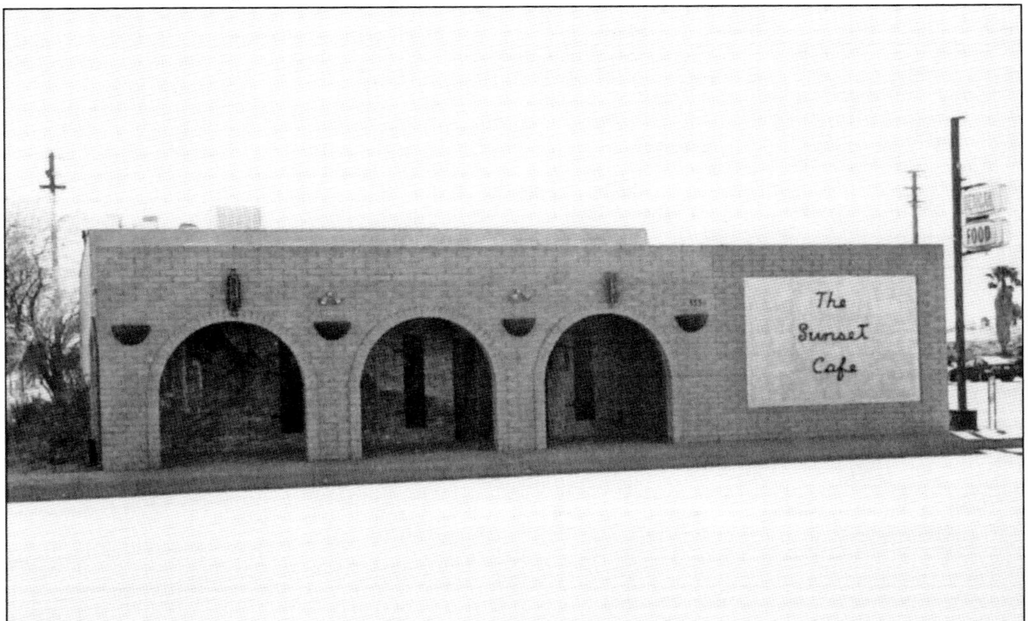

The Sunset Café on Arizona Boulevard was a popular eatery in Coolidge. Just north of the café was the Hub Café, which later became the Trucker's Café on the busy boulevard. The Sunset Café is currently closed, but the building is in relatively good condition. (Author's collection.)

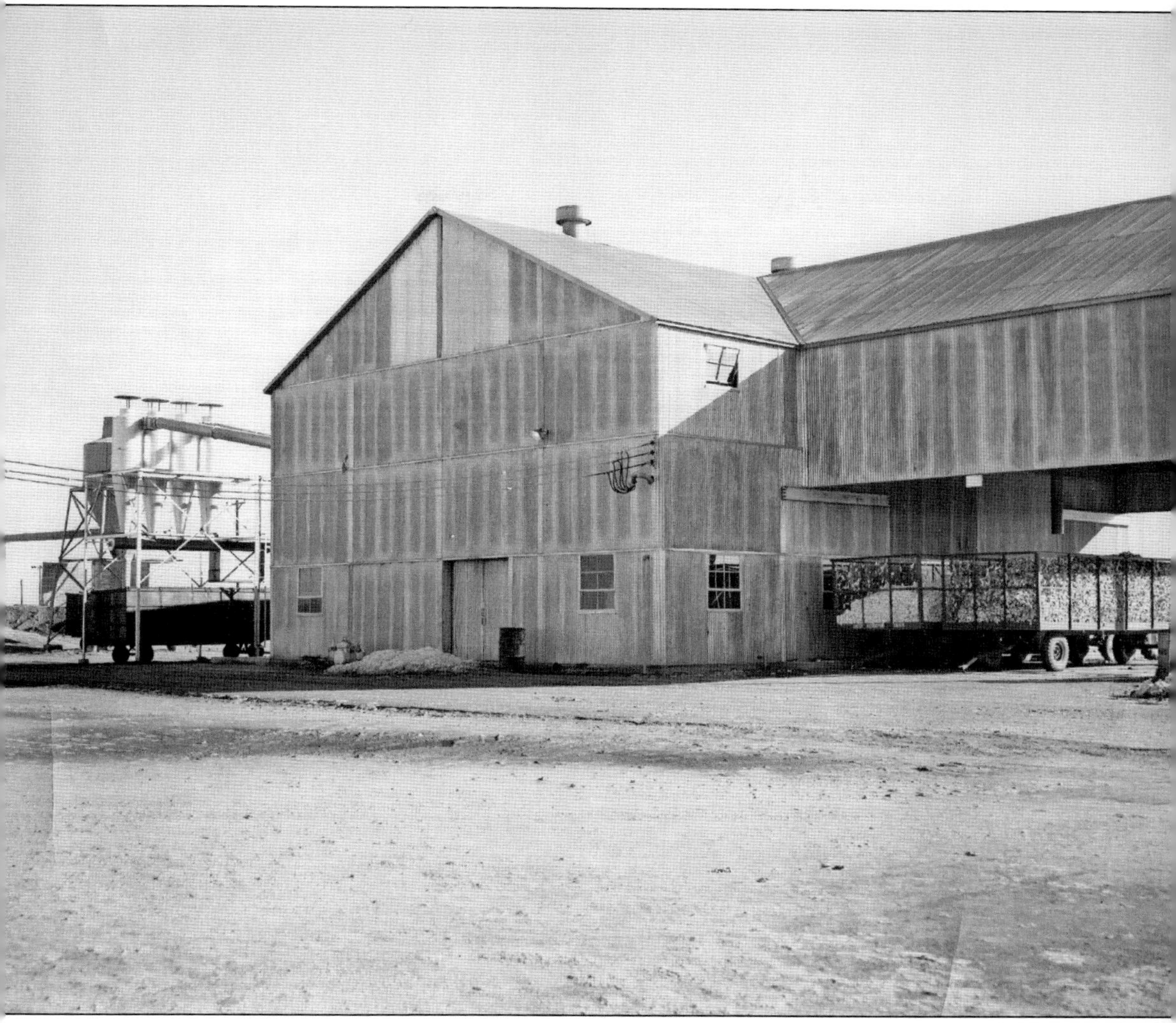

The A.C. Ginning Company was located next to the Southern Pacific Railway tracks on East Coolidge Avenue. Extra long staple (ELS) cotton has been grown in the United States for more than 200 years. An experimental station was established at Sacaton north of Coolidge in 1907, and with the assistance of the University of Arizona College of Agriculture, the US Department of the Interior, and the Gila River Indian Community, a new strain that was called Pima was developed. Pima has become the generic term for all Southwest-grown extra long staple cotton. The rapid demise of handpicked cotton came in the early 1950s with the introduction of the first one-row cotton picker. In the late 1930s, International Harvester had developed a prototype cotton picker, but with the onset of Great Depression, the federal government stopped production of the machinery to prevent further unemployment. Production was further slowed during the war years, but soon after World War II ended the machines went into full-scale production, and the first trainload of one-row cotton pickers arrived by train in Phoenix in 1946, passing through Coolidge. (CHM.)

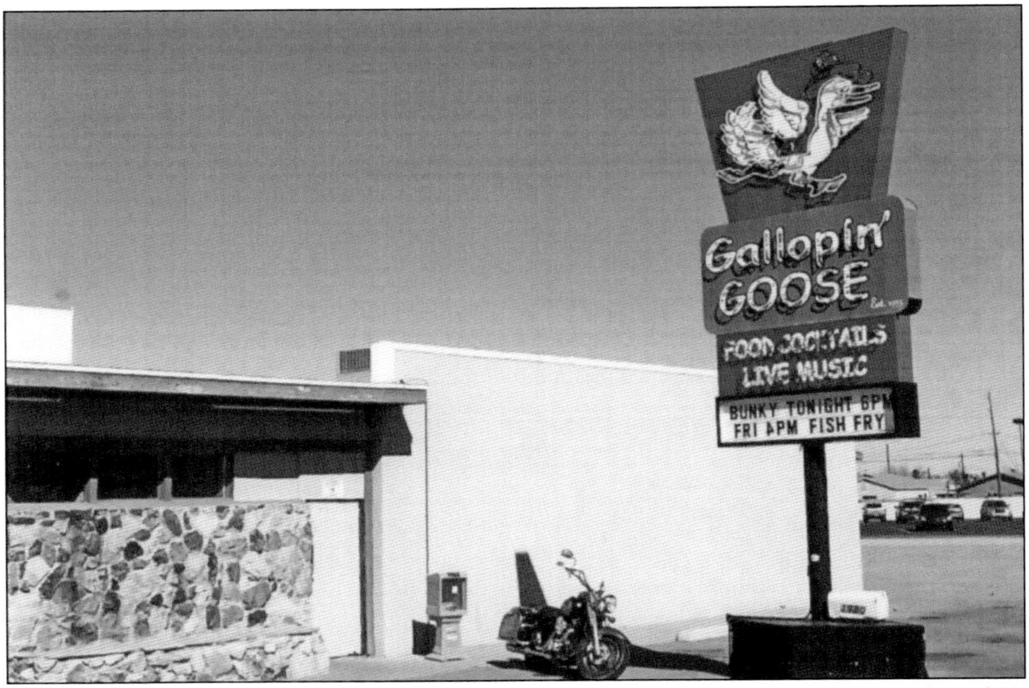

The Gallopin' Goose opened for business in 1935 on Martin Road and Arizona Boulevard. A public swimming pool, the Desert Beach, was located behind the lounge. The Goose was a jumping place in the 1950s and 1960s, when cars would be parked a mile down the road on a busy night. (Author's collection.)

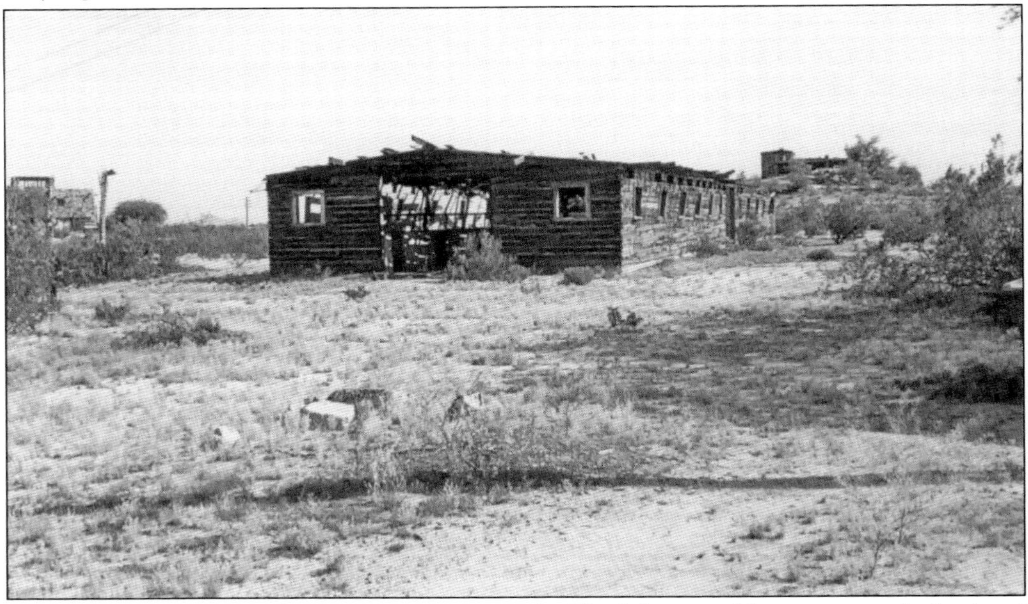

In June 1932, former cavalryman Maj. R.C. Woodruff built horse stables constructed of railroad ties and stone on acreage at the intersection of Woodruff and Overfield Roads at the western edge of the Coolidge city limits. It was opposite the future site of Central Arizona College, where Woodruff managed racing and polo stock. A racetrack was also built at the site, and several of the stone buildings are now private residences. (Author's collection.)

Cedric Downs and Beulah Hess of Coolidge enjoy the Fourth of July at Picacho Lake southwest of Coolidge in 1934. The large reservoir was fed by excess water from the San Carlos Canal, and although the lake has since dried up, the concrete abutments and large spillway are still in place. Picacho was a popular boating, swimming, and fishing spot east of La Palma. (CHM.)

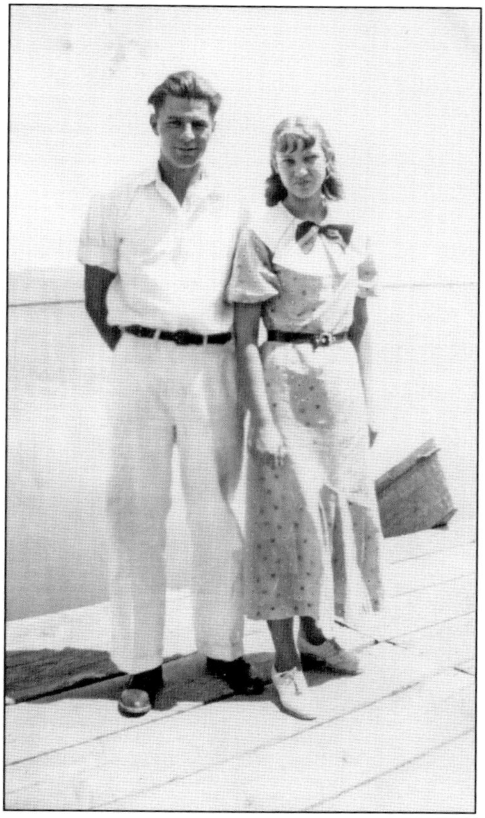

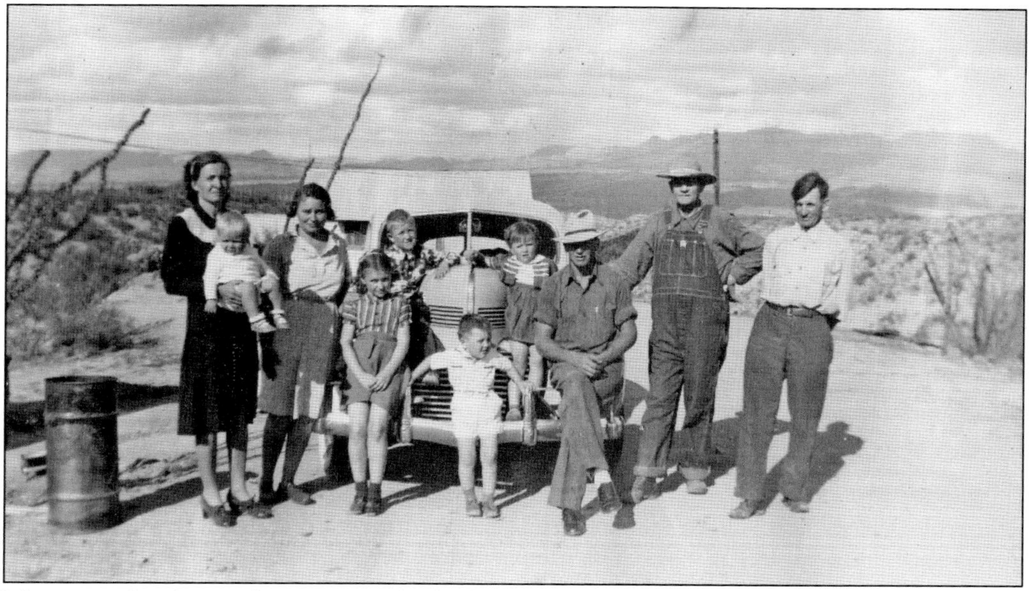

Many area families took outings to the higher desert to escape the heat. Young Gene Carter's family stopped in 1939 along a road east of Coolidge for a group photograph. From left to right are his mother Hattie Bell, sister Nancy, aunt Bessie, sister Chestine, Gene, brother Tony, sister Josephine, father Chester, grandfather Anthony, and uncle Alonzo "Lon" Carter. Chester owned and operated a well-drilling business. (Gene D. Carter.)

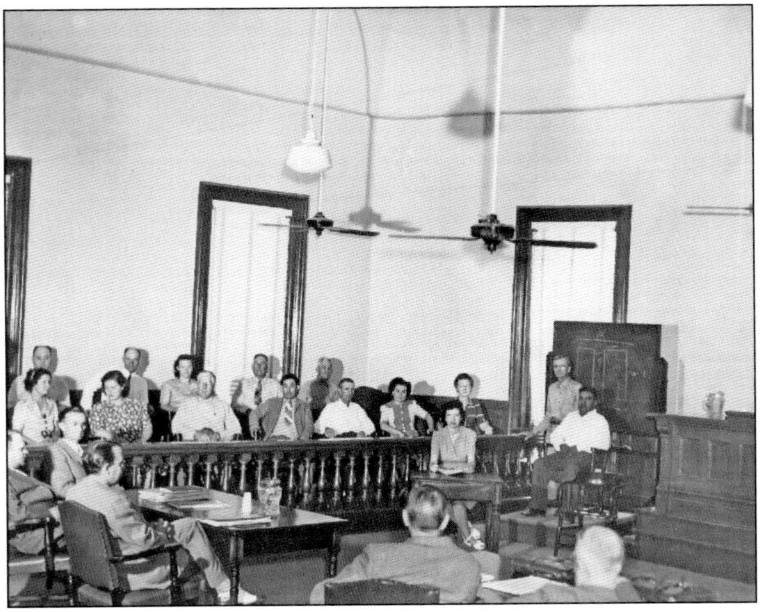

In 1945, the Pinal County Courthouse in nearby Florence sat the first jury that included women. Judge William C. Truman, the former Pinal County attorney, was the presiding judge during this session. Myrna Freeman was the court reporter. Jury members were selected from Coolidge, Florence, and surrounding communities. (CHM.)

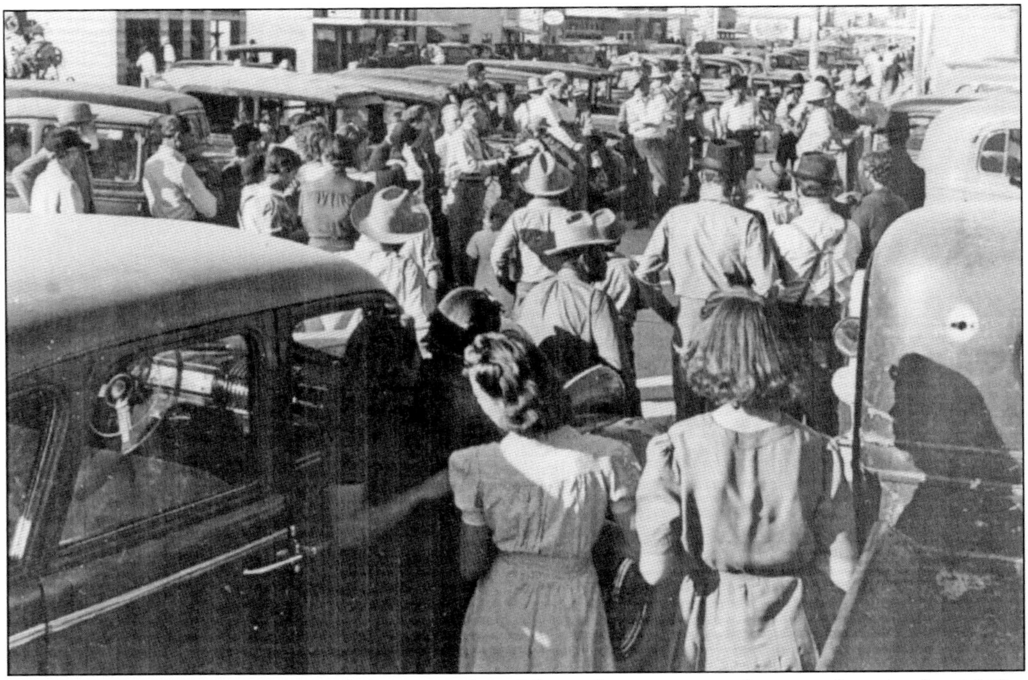

Main Street in downtown Coolidge was a busy place during cotton-harvest days in the 1940s. Impromptu meetings, as well as auctions, were conducted on the street corners and parking lots for a variety of business purposes. (LOC.)

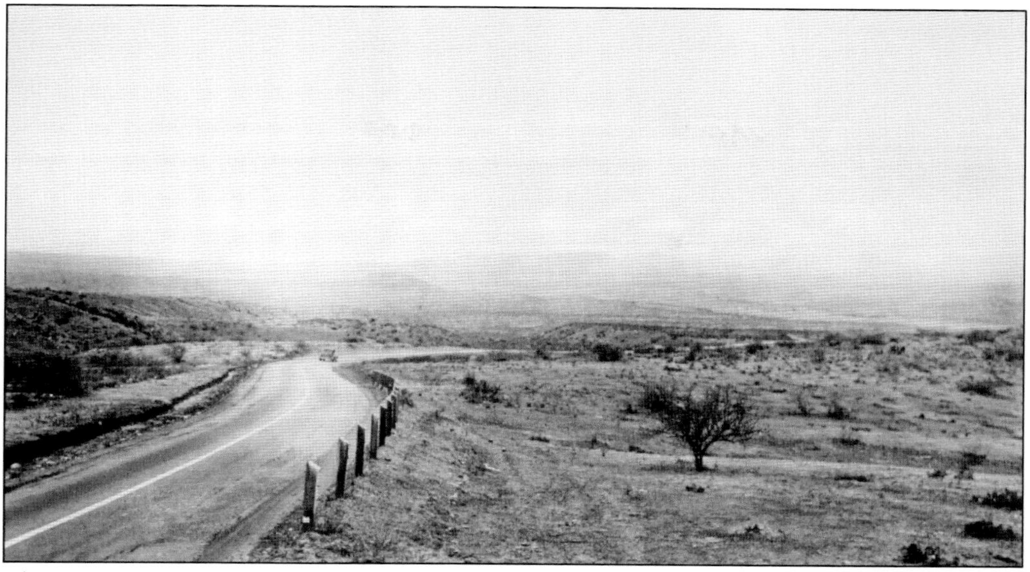

This is a 1939 view of the highway to Superior, 38 miles northeast of Coolidge. At the time the photograph was taken, the road was known as the Coolidge-Globe Highway. Today, the road is designated US 60, and it culminates at Interstate 25 at Socorro, New Mexico. (ASL No. 98-5020.)

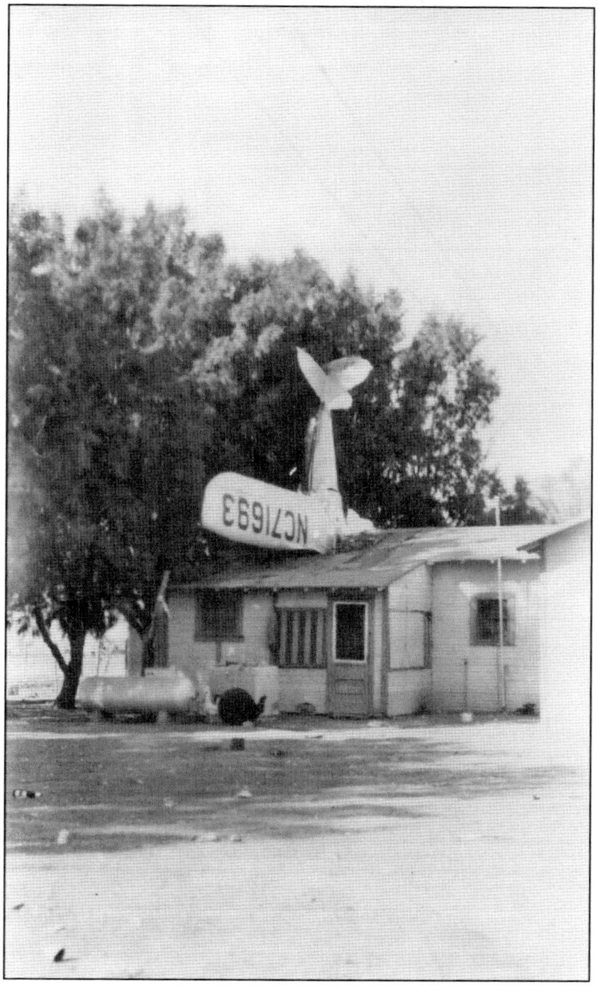

In 1949, a private plane leaving the Coolidge Airport crash-landed on the roof of a house behind the Bell Boy Corner Store a few miles east of Coolidge. The unidentified pilot walked away from the accident, and no one in the store was injured. The Bell Boy Service Station was also located at this rural intersection. (PCHS.)

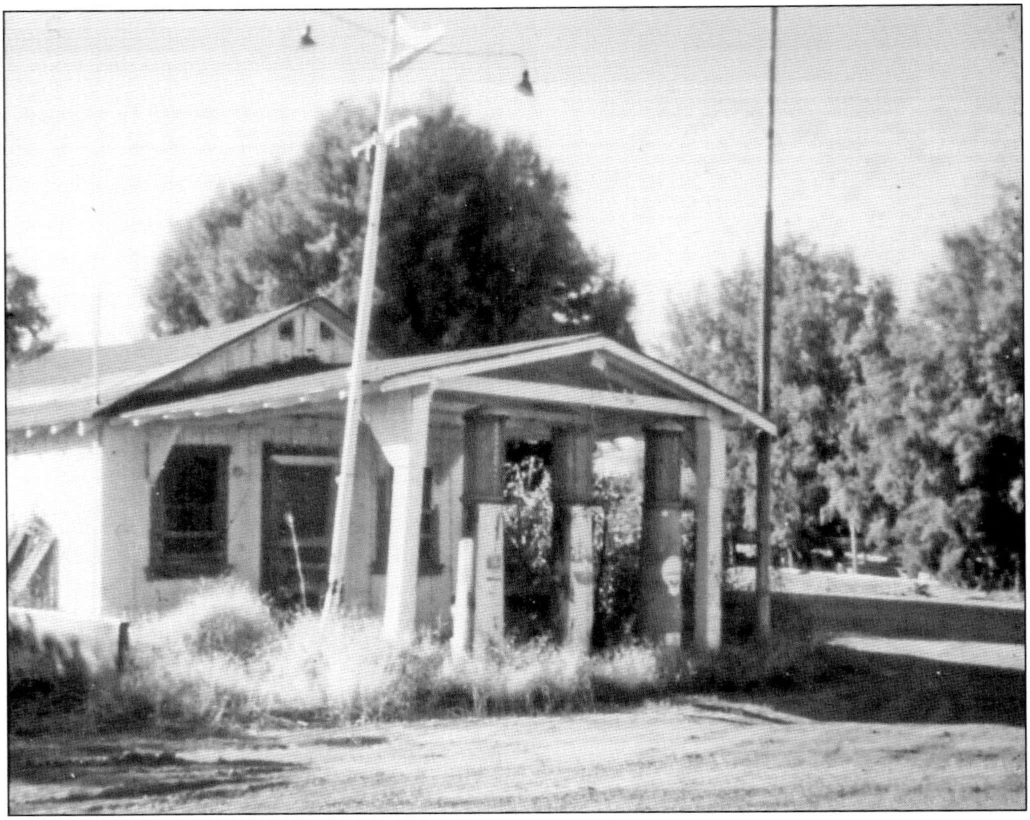

The Bell Boy Service Station, a few miles east of Coolidge, has been torn down. It was a convenient fueling stop for traffic between the town of Coolidge, the Coolidge airport, and Highway 79, which connected Florence to Tucson further to the east. The Bell Boy Corner Store was located nearby. (Tommy Henry.)

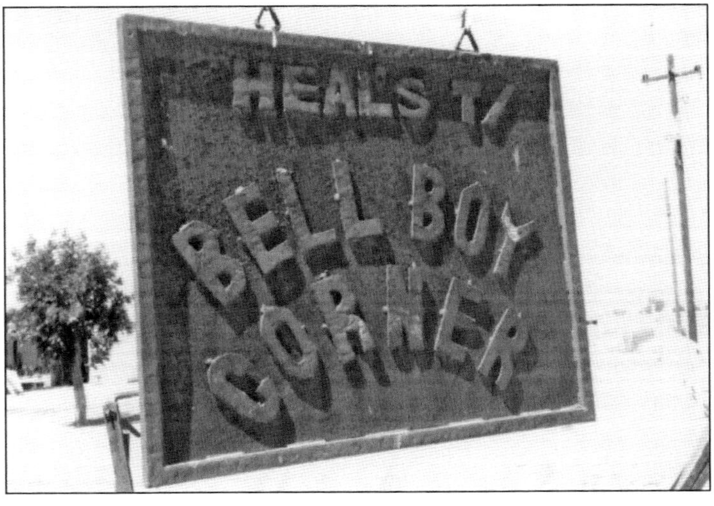

All that remains at the Bell Boy intersection east of Coolidge is this Bell Boy Corner sign on the southwest corner. A house that marked the location of the Bell Boy Corner Store, however, is still occupied. (Author's collection.)

Near the intersection of Highway 79 and Cactus Forest Road east of Coolidge stood a tall, four-story tower on the north side of the road. Atop the tower was a lighted Gulf Oil sign. In this 1948 photograph, Tad B. Lynch can be seen standing beside his fuel-delivery truck. Irma Garcia Salazar, who lives on Cactus Forest Road just east of Highway 79, remembers as a child driving home from Tucson at night and knowing she was getting close to home when she could see the lighted Gulf sign in the distance. (CHM.)

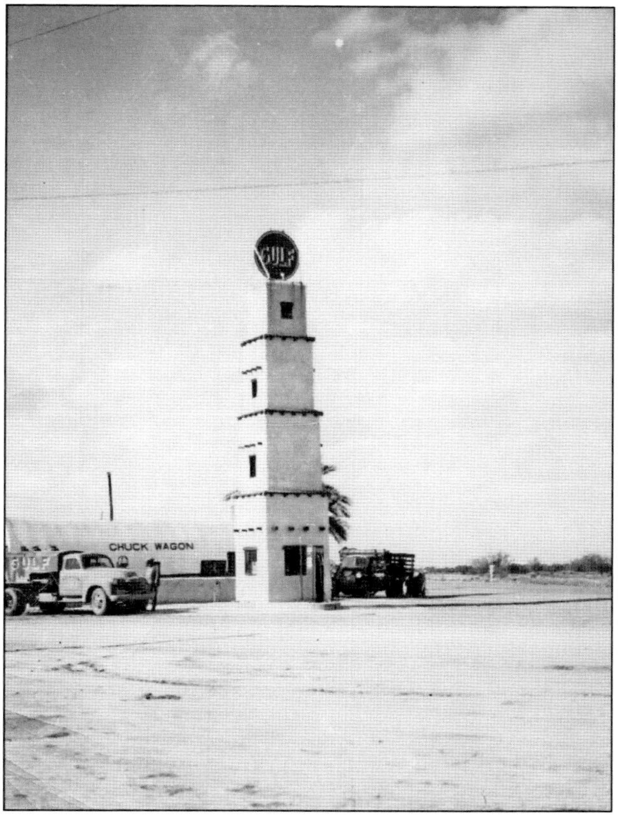

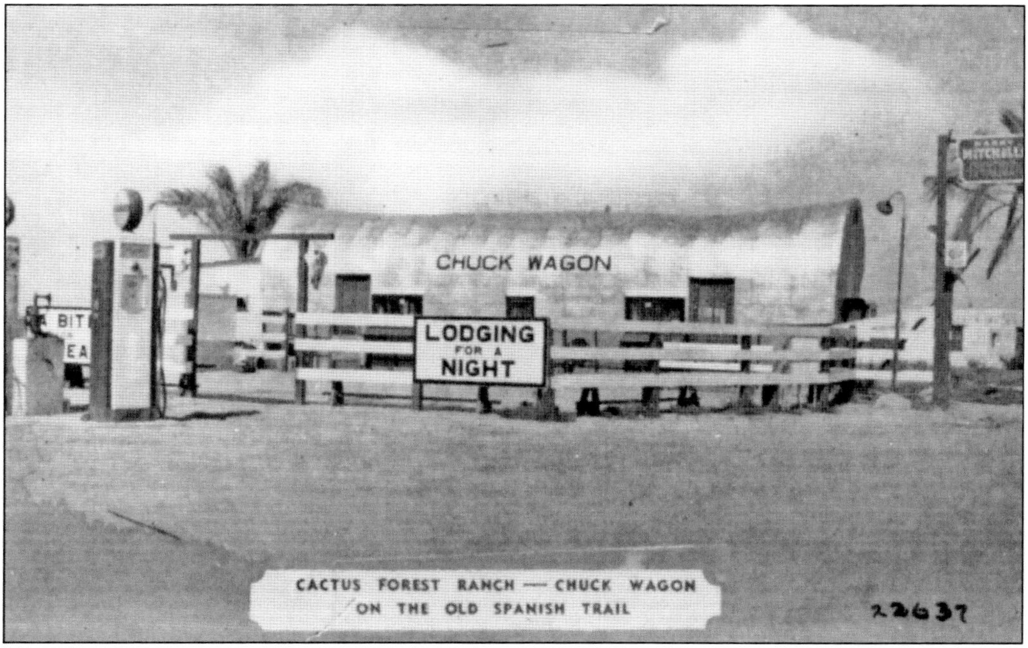

The Chuck Wagon restaurant was a popular eating establishment on Cactus Forest Road, the east extension of Coolidge Avenue. It also provided housekeeping cottages for overnight travelers and Gulf Oil service. This postcard boasted a "desert atmosphere at 1800 foot elevation." (CHM.)

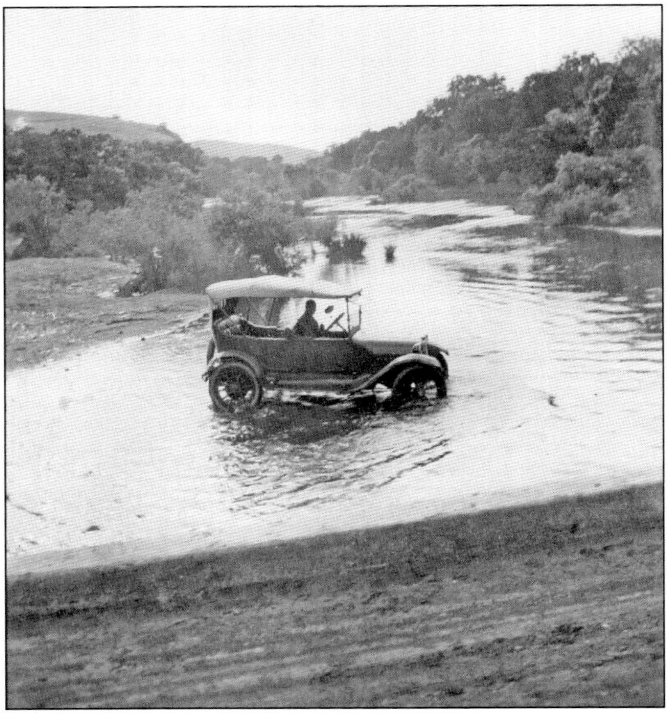

In 1936, the Gila River north of Coolidge on the Gila River Indian Reservation ran year-round. This view is from the Olberg Bridge, and Chester Carter is fording the river in his Model T. Carter and his family operated the first well-drilling service in the Coolidge area. Today, the Gila River is mostly a dry riverbed at this location except during a heavy monsoon. (Gene D. Carter.)

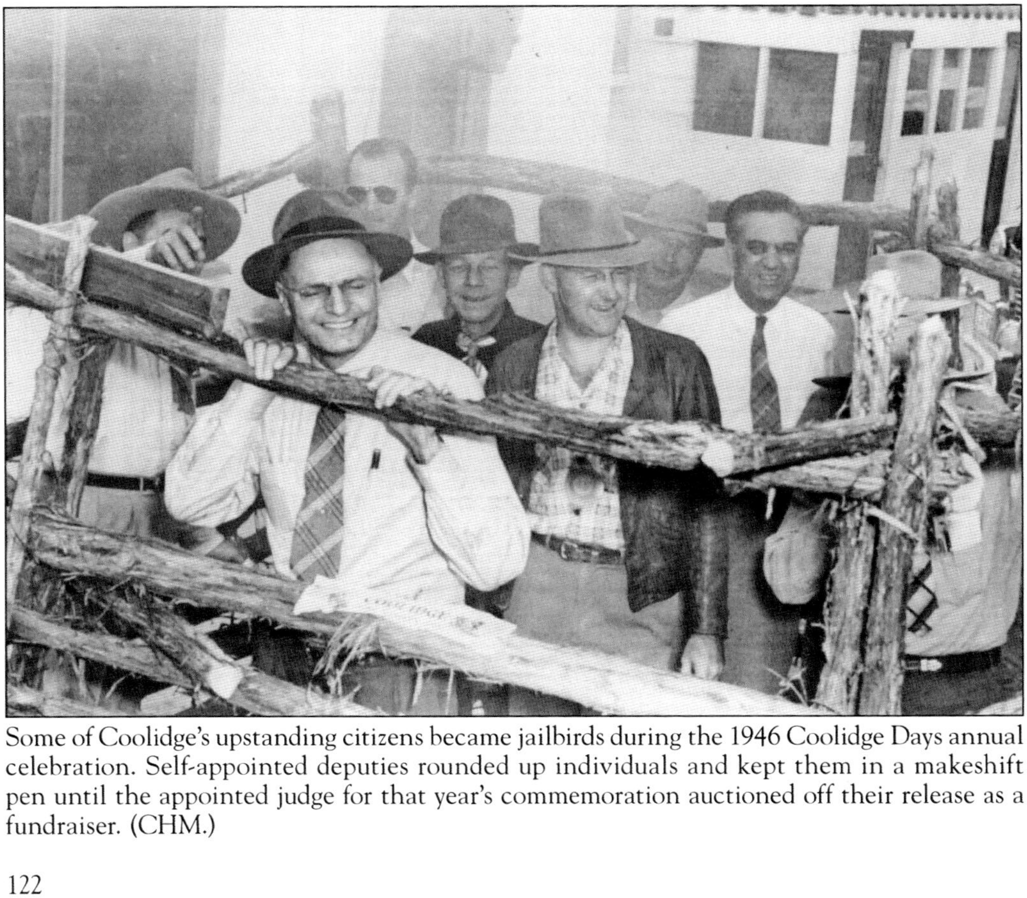

Some of Coolidge's upstanding citizens became jailbirds during the 1946 Coolidge Days annual celebration. Self-appointed deputies rounded up individuals and kept them in a makeshift pen until the appointed judge for that year's commemoration auctioned off their release as a fundraiser. (CHM.)

In 1946, the annual Coolidge Days event included a judge who dispensed injustice by having his henchmen roundup law-abiding citizens and incarcerating them in a makeshift jail. They would be auctioned off to the highest bidder for their release as a fundraiser for the event. (CHM.)

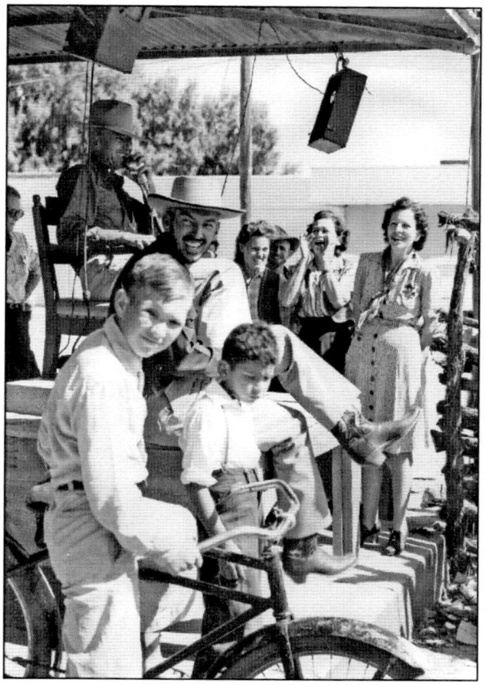

James Newlin (left) and Joseph Reed Chesley observe the mock incarceration from a safe distance at the Coolidge Days event. Chesley delivered the *Arizona Republic* and *Phoenix Gazette* newspaper on the bicycle that he purchased with the $45 he borrowed from Alma Jones, wife of Richard J. Jones, the founder of Coolidge. He paid back the generous lady every cent from money earned by his paper route. (Joseph Reed Chesley.)

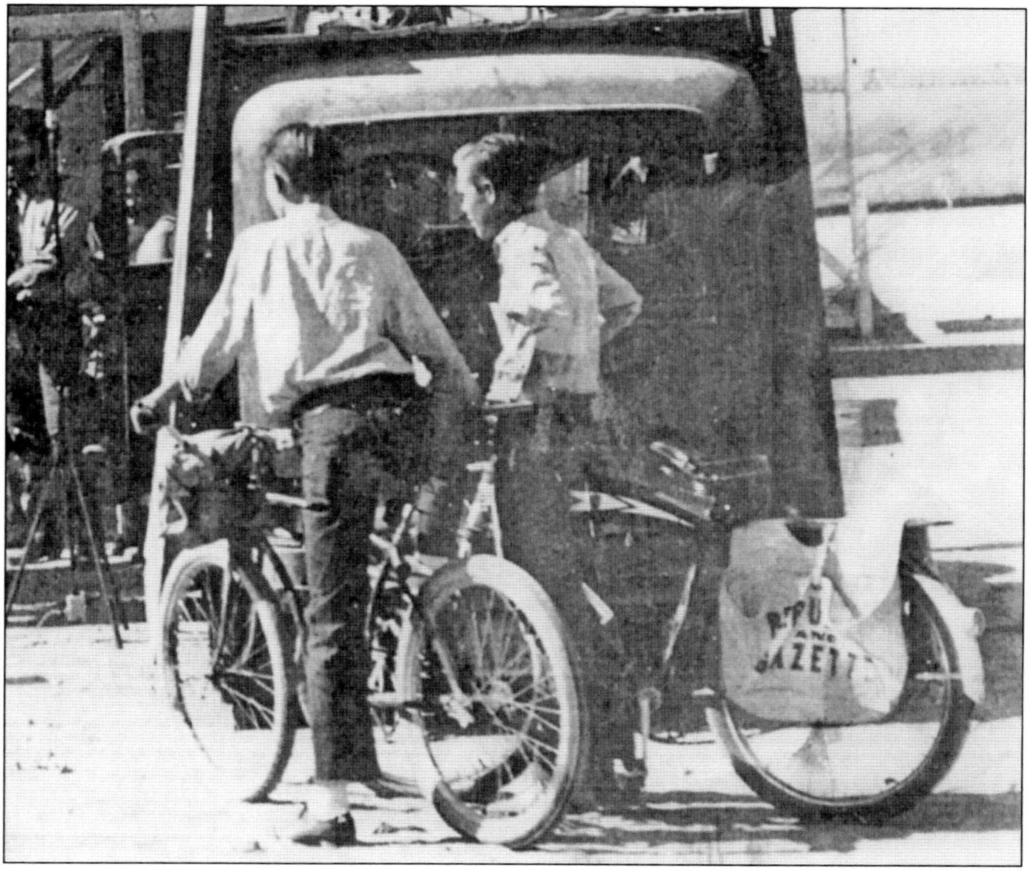

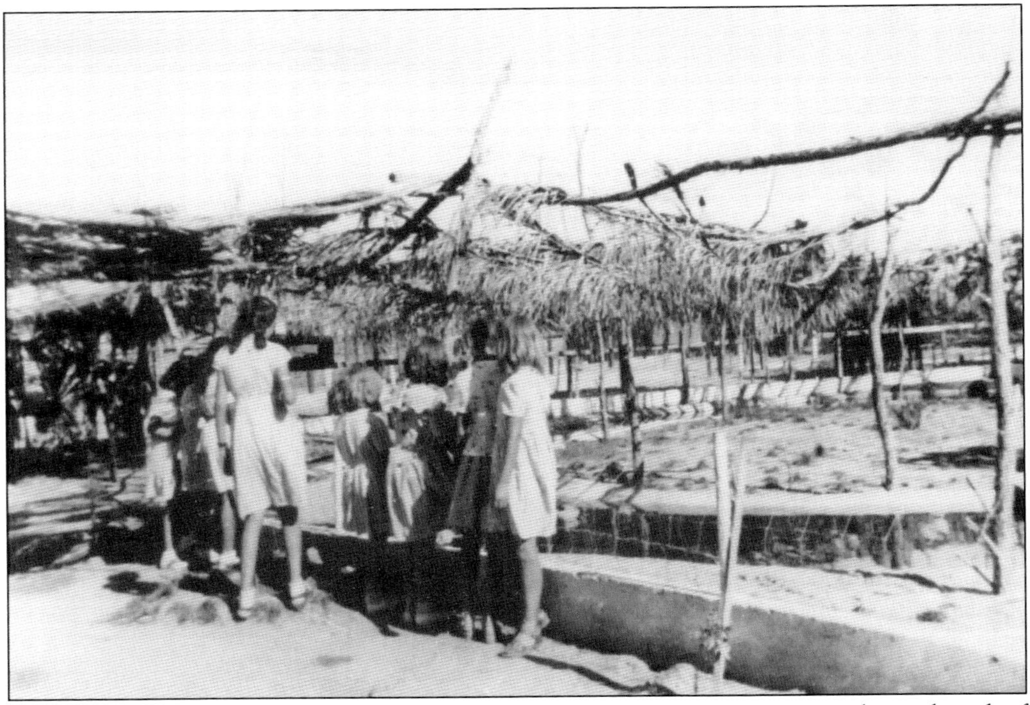

In the mid-1940s, Coolidge boasted an alligator farm. The unusual attraction was located south of town at the Coolidge wye on Fifth Street. Nearby was the Prince Drive-In theater, where today only the large concession stand remains as a private residence. Farther to the north on Martin Road was an open-air roller rink and a public swimming pool called the Desert Beach. (Donna Ovitt.)

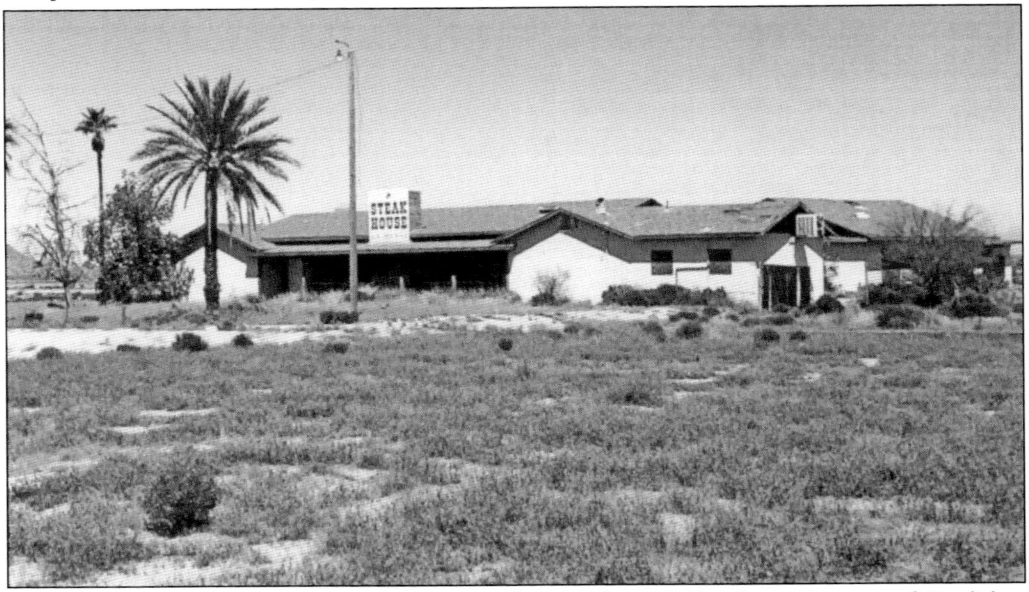

The popular Hohokam Country Club at 8324 East Highway 287, a few miles east of Coolidge, opened in July 1952 and boasted a nine-hole golf course, swimming pool, bar, and restaurant. The land for the par-35 course was donated by E.G. "Guy" Attaway. The two city swimming pools, one at the new high school and the other in San Carlos Park, made the drive to Hohokam inconvenient. (Author's collection.)

Eight

The Coolidge Historical Museum

The new Coolidge Courthouse was completed in February 1935 along with a two-cell jail attached in the back. Judge W.A. Thompson was the presiding justice of the peace with E.E. Stringer as constable and Ace "Asa" Gardner as deputy sheriff. A new jail was needed because the only facility available to house prisoners was a railroad boxcar. Since Coolidge was not incorporated as a municipality until 1945, the Pinal County Board of Supervisors voted to direct the county engineer to supervise the construction of the new courthouse at 161 West Harding Street.

The Coolidge Historical Society was organized as a nonprofit 501(c)(3) entity on May 19, 1986. Early the following year, the museum was opened in the abandoned courthouse and jail. Assistance from the Arizona Historical Society in Tucson, the Maricopa County Historical Society in Phoenix, and the Casa Grande Historical Society in Casa Grande was given to the Coolidge Historical Society and Museum. It was decided that the major artifacts would represent the time period of 1900 to 1950.

The museum is open on a limited basis from October through April, with docents available on an as-needed basis when occasional visitors stop in Coolidge during the hot summer months.

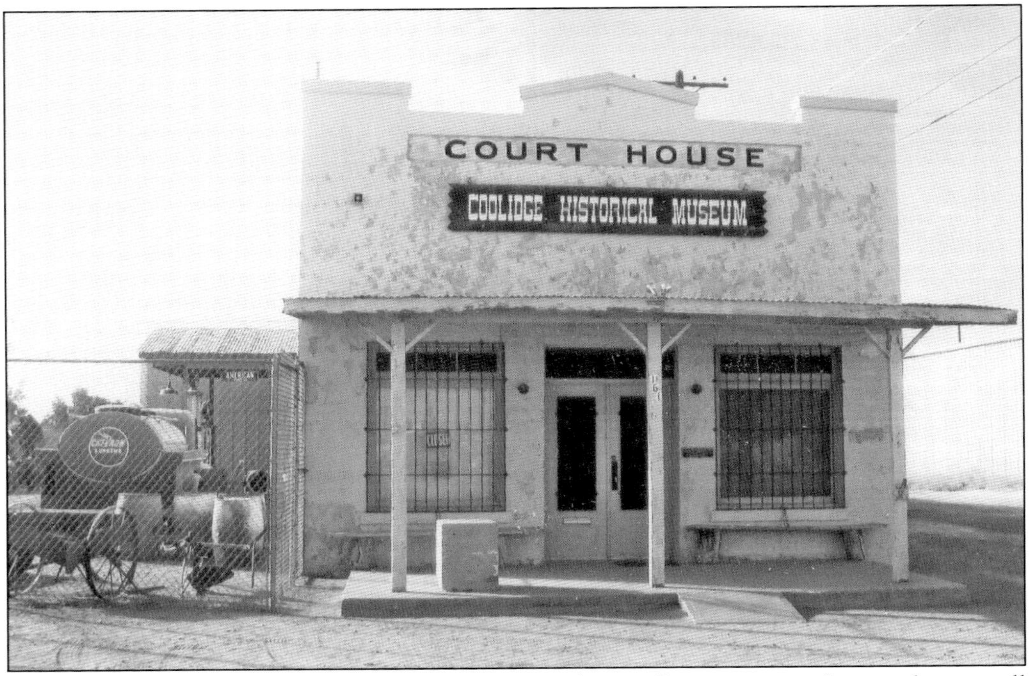

The Coolidge Historical Museum was built in 1935 with a small courtroom in front and a two-cell jail attached. The location includes a large steel, air-conditioned building behind the courthouse where more exhibits are located. The grounds also include a farm-implement display, vintage oil-tanker truck, gasoline pumps, and a completely restored farmhouse. (Author's collection.)

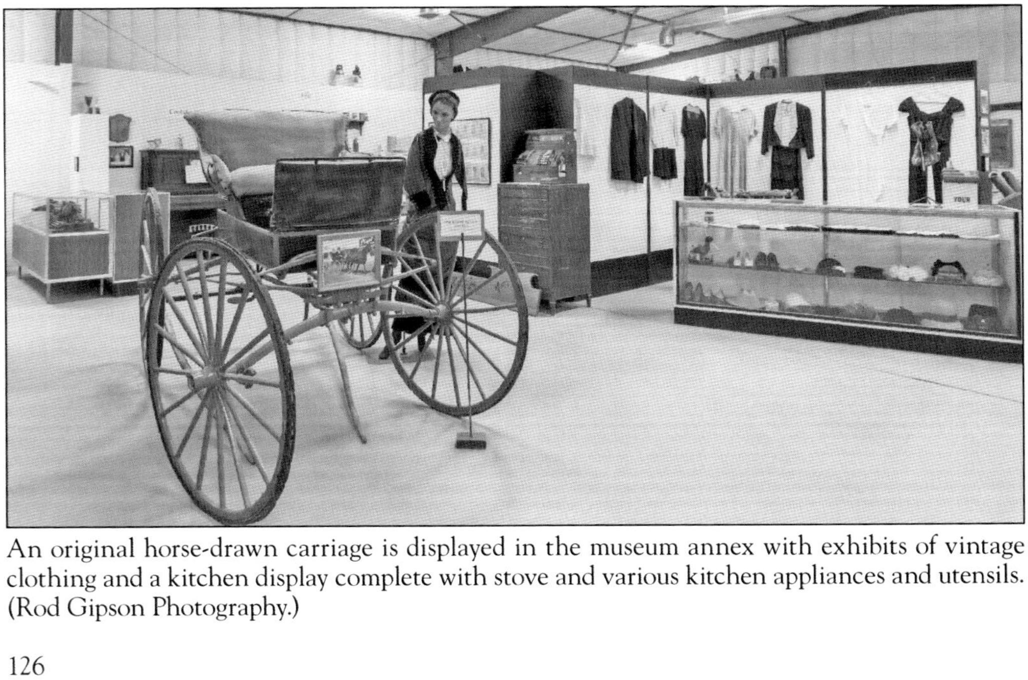

An original horse-drawn carriage is displayed in the museum annex with exhibits of vintage clothing and a kitchen display complete with stove and various kitchen appliances and utensils. (Rod Gipson Photography.)

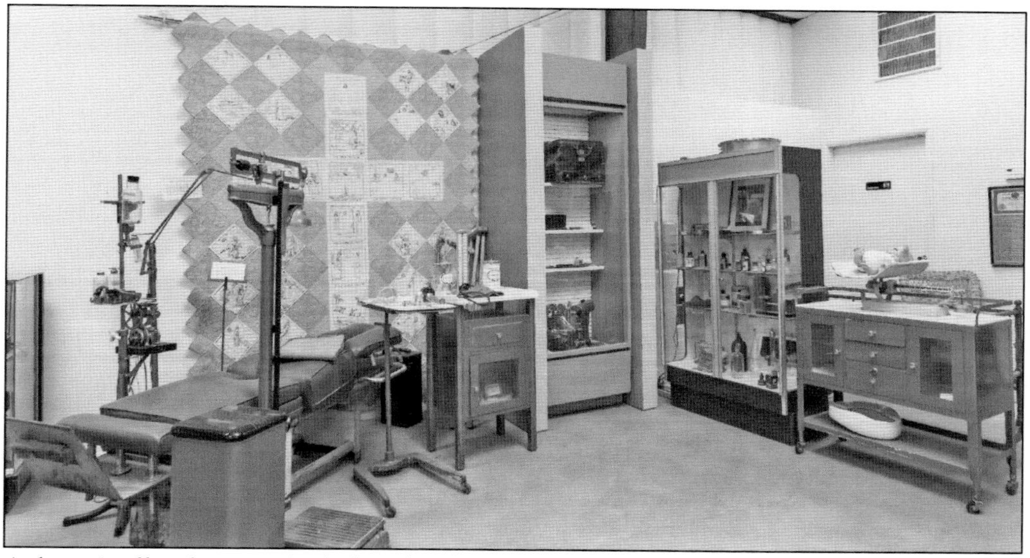

A doctor's office featuring both dental and medical supplies and equipment are displayed in the museum annex. Mannequins reveal the uniforms of the various branches of the military, and a small nook contains school yearbooks from the various Coolidge schools as well as scrapbooks donated over the years by residents. (Rod Gipson Photography.)

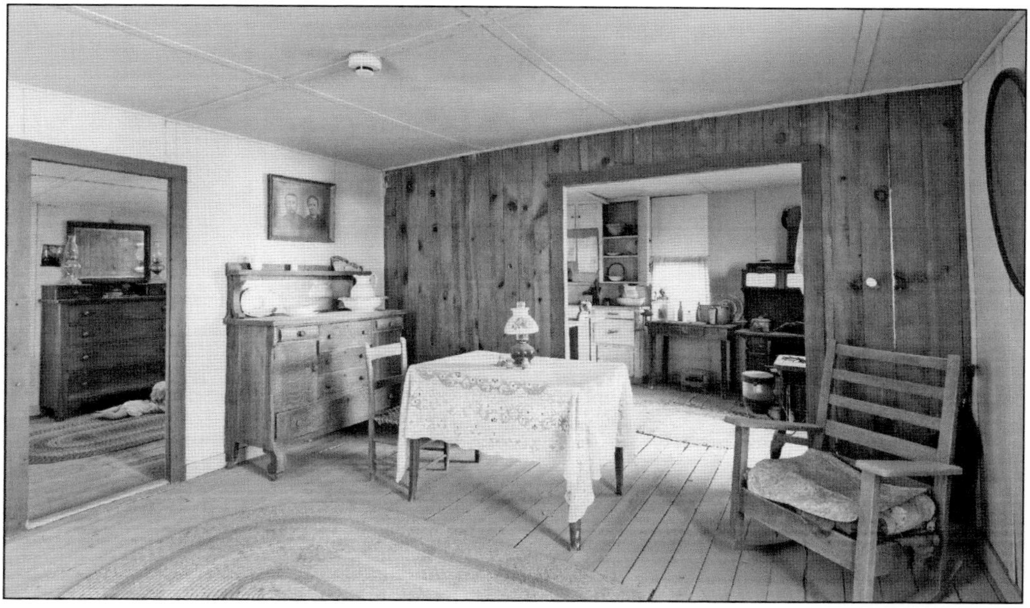

On the grounds of the museum is a farmhouse donated by the Bob Goree family. The two-room house is fully furnished with a living room, bedroom, and period kitchen. Museum visitors and their children enjoy seeing how their forebearers once lived without the luxuries of running water, electricity, or indoor plumbing. (Rod Gipson Photography.)